Contemporary Spanish cinema

Manchester University Press

For John and Oliver
For Margaret, the sunshine girl

Contemporary Spanish cinema

BARRY JORDAN
and RIKKI MORGAN-TAMOSUNAS

MANCHESTER UNIVERSITY PRESS Manchester and New York

Copyright © Barry Jordan and Rikki Morgan-Tamosunas 1998

The right of Barry Jordan and Rikki Morgan-Tamosunas to be identified as the authors of this work has been asserted by them in accordance with the Copyright, Designs and Patents Act 1988.

Published by Manchester University Press
Oxford Road, Manchester M13 9NR, UK
and Room 400, 175 Fifth Avenue, New York, NY 10010, USA
www.manchesteruniversitypress.co.uk

Distributed in the United States exclusively by
Palgrave Macmillan, 175 Fifth Avenue, New York,
NY 10010, USA

Distributed in Canada exclusively by
UBC Press, University of British Columbia, 2029 West Mall,
Vancouver, BC, Canada V6T 1Z2

British Library Cataloguing-in-Publication Data
A catalogue record for this book is available from the British Library

Library of Congress Cataloging-in-Publication Data applied for

ISBN 978 0 7190 4413 7 *paperback*

First published 1998

Reprinted with corrections 2001

14 13 12 11 10 09 08   10 9 8 7 6 5

Printed in Great Britain
by CPI Antony Rowe Ltd, Chippenham

Contents

Illustrations

All stills are reproduced courtesy of BFI Stills, Posters and Designs, except 11 and 23 courtesy of Metro Tartan and 14 courtesy of Rank Film Distributors.

Preface and acknowledgements

This book is intended for students, teachers, general readers and fans of Spanish cinema. It seeks to provide an analysis of some of the main trends and issues which have characterised Spanish cinema during the 1980s and 1990s. We have commented on most of the Spanish films which have had a theatrical or video release in the UK or which are available on video from Spain or the sort of lending library service offered by the Instituto Cervantes. We have also looked at a number of films which will not be readily available to readers of this book in order to provide a reasonably detailed picture of the director, genre, theme, issue or question under discussion.

For those readers whose knowledge of Spanish is slight or non-existent, we have provided as far as possible translations of comments and opinions in Spanish cited in the text, although all film titles are given in the original.

Thanks are due to the staff of the Filmoteca Nacional in Madrid, the Filmoteca de la Generalitat, Barcelona, as well as staff in the Stills Department and Library of the British Film Institute (BFI) who provided valuable help with stills and permissions.

To Thames Valley University for allowing Rikki Morgan-Tamosunas sabbatical leave to work on the manuscript of the book.

To the students of Hispanic Studies at De Montfort University who acted as guinea pigs for some of the material Barry Jordan developed for this book and to sceptical colleagues who thought it would never happen.

To students of Spanish Cinema at Thames Valley University who sampled material being produced for the book.

To Rosa Ferrer and Gloria Casals, plus colleagues and friends in Spain who helped to sort out permissions, library visits and screenings.

To Sally and the Open University for their invaluable support.

To friends and colleagues in the Hispanic Studies field who, wittingly or unwittingly, provided help and support, particularly Peter Evans.

To our editorial assistants Stephanie Sloan and Matthew Frost.

Finally to CiBy Sales Ltd, El Deseo, Electric Pictures, Elías Querejeta Producciones, Iberoamericana/Lola Films, Pedro Costa Productions, Sogepaq International, Sogetel, Tornasol Films and United International Pictures for granting permissions to publish stills.

Introduction

The Spanish film industry in the 1980s and 1990s

In the summer of 1996, following the electoral defeat of Felipe González's Socialist government (in power since 1982) by the right-wing Partido Popular (PP), the newly appointed Under Secretary of State for Culture (at the new 'super' Ministry of Education and Culture) Miguel Ángel Cortés, disdainfully remarked: 'Los últimos 13 años del cine español han sido los peores de la historia' (The last 13 years of Spanish cinema have been the worst in its history) (Fernández Rubio 1996: 4). As the incoming minister and considering that the history of Spanish cinema is a venerable one which dates back to the 1890s, Cortés's comment was highly insensitive. It was made in the context of a wide-ranging speech on cultural matters, full of startling pronouncements, including a critique of the film policy of the previous administration (particularly in relation to public subsidies). Cortés was clearly interested in creating the climate for a major shift in government outlook and policy towards deregulation and its eventual withdrawal from the public support of the film industry. José María Otero, new head of Spain's official Film Institute (Instituto de Cinematografía y de las Artes Audiovisuales *ICAA*) and Cortés's civil servant, attempted to play down the attack, arguing that the minister's words had been 'un malentendido' (misunderstood) and taken out of context. However, the offending remark provoked outrage as well as massive solidarity among film professionals right across the industry. Almodóvar, for example, referred to it as: 'Ridículo, absurdo, grotesco e insultante' (Ridiculous, absurd, grotesque and insulting), adding that in Cortés 'el PP nos ha puesto un verdugo' (PP have sent us an executioner) (Álvarez 1997: 36).

On the surface, quite apart from the obvious anger it provoked, Cortés's remark seems strangely at odds with what we know of the fortunes of Spain's film industry in the 1980s and 1990s. After all, Spain has produced the second-highest grossing foreign-language film in the history of world cinema, Almodóvar's *Mujeres al borde de un ataque de nervios* (1988). It has also enjoyed major international Oscar success with José Luis Garci's *Volver a empezar* (1982) and Fernando Trueba's *Belle Epoque* (1992). Also, more Spanish films than ever are finding their way into foreign markets (including Korea and South East Asia). Overall levels of quality and production values are much improved. The sheer variety and commercial appeal of contemporary Spanish cinema is remarkable (given the size of the industry) and Spanish films and directors are picking up numerous prizes and awards both at national and international film festivals such as Cannes, Venice, Turin, Berlin, Chicago, New York, Tokyo, including recent features by Erice, Miró, Medem, Bigas Luna, Alex de la Iglesia, etc.

Where the minister might well have had a point, however, is in the fact that from the mid-1980s to the early 1990s, levels of film production in Spain were worryingly low and audiences seemed to be deserting the cinema in favour of other forms of media entertainment. Indeed, in 1994, at 6.8 millions, audience figures for Spanish movies were at their lowest for many years, representing only 7 per cent of market share. Moreover, in the same year, Spain's film industry managed to produce a mere 44 feature films, compared to 64 in 1991, 76 in 1985 and a colossal 146 in 1982 (Gubern, *et al.* 1994: 402). These apparently alarming production totals were the end result of a policy, developed under the Socialist government (1982–1996) and inspired by the Miró decrees of the early 1980s.

The Miró legislation (named after Pilar Miró, *Directora General de Cinematografía* 1983–85) was predicated on the production of significantly fewer films, but of higher quality and vastly improved production values. Its central funding mechanism was that of advance credits, which could be used to cover up to 50 per cent of a film's production costs. This gave rise to a large number of often very worthy and well-made features, but government subsidies favoured projects which could best be described as safe, middle-brow, arthouse films, for which the maintenance of certain cultural standards was prioritised alongside a recognition of the importance of commercial viability. Despite this, many of the films made under the aegis of the Miró legislation seriously miscalculated – some would say ignored – the tastes and viewing habits of Spanish audiences. (Not all did, however. Indeed, the Miró formula gave rise to a small number of highly successful films, including *La colmena* (1982) and *Los santos inocentes* (1984), both by Mario Camus). The alarm was sounded in 1988 when the then Minister of Culture, Jorge Semprún, began a process of rationalising the conditions for a publicly-subsidised film industry in order to avoid financial embarrassment. None the less, with very little money returning to ICAA by way of box-office takings from subsidised films, the Government's Film Protection Fund (also funded in part by the sale of dubbing licences to distributors) reached virtual bankruptcy in the early 1990s.

By late 1994, Carmen Alborch, Socialist Minister of Culture, was obliged to radically alter the direction of government policy by scrapping the system of advance credits in favour of a system of automatic subsidies based on box-office receipts. This policy U-turn (for which opposition Partido Popular deputies had been vehemently arguing) signified the virtual dismantling of the Miró reforms. It also meant that advance credits would now depend on the fortunes of the movie in the market place and not, as before, on film projects being designed to please the often whimsical, cultural (and political) outlook of members of adjudicating panels. With film subsidies thus largely decoupled from government committees in favour of market performance, this arguably shifted the balance of power away from directors (who had previously been custodians of government subsidies) to producers, who would now take on the economic risks of film production. According to key Spanish producers, such as Andrés Vicente Gómez, while aware that market pressures might possibly have a negative impact on quality and cultural standards, these changes were necessary and timely in that, they brought Spanish film production back into line with commercial considerations and public tastes and obliged companies to promote their products far more vigorously in home and foreign markets (García 1995: 82).

Though 1994 represented the nadir of film production in Spain, there were nonetheless some positive developments in the industry. Apart from Trueba's Oscar (awarded in March 1994) and the release of a small number of very successful Spanish films, including Juanma Bajo Ulloa's *La madre muerta* (1993) and Manuel Gómez Pereira's *Todos los hombres sois iguales*, the Spanish media conglomerate PRISA (owner of *El País*) created Sogepaq, its film distribution arm, alongside Sogetel, its film production company, and announced plans to invest 6,000 million pesetas in fifteen to sixteen film projects over the following two to three years. Spain's state-run television corporation RTVE (Radio Televisión Española) also announced ambitious plans (funding permitting) to invest up to 8,000 million pesetas into film production and transmission rights over a four- year period (*Fotogramas* November 1994: 116). It was also announced that the regime's old National Film School, the Escuela Oficial de Cine, would be revived in early 1995, run by the Comunidad de Madrid and managed by ex-ICAA director, filmmaker and critic Fernando Méndez-Leite. (The absence of a National Film School, where future directors could learn their craft, had been a major focus of criticism from film professionals, since its closure in 1970/71 after student riots (Gubern, *et al.* 1994: 368). Above all, the then head of ICAA, Enrique Balmaseda, announced a record Film Protection Fund for 1995 of 16,900 million pesetas, demanding for Spanish film a much-increased market share, upwards of 13 per cent (*Fotogramas* 1994: 36). After a disastrous 1994, 1995 could not possibly be any worse.

And so it turned out. Indeed, 1995 became something of an *annus mirabilis* for the Spanish film industry on a number of fronts. Though not meeting Balmaseda's projected total of 60–70, production of full-length film features increased to 56, with an average budget of 247 million pesetas. More significantly, in 1995, audience figures for Spanish films rose dramatically to 9.3 millions, adding 2.5 millions to the total for 1994. This represented between 10 and 11 per cent of market share (*Fotogramas* 1996: 130). In part, this had to do with the major infrastructural changes and programmes of modernisation taking place in relation to Spanish film theatres, which led directly to improvements in conditions for cinema viewing and related leisure facilities. In 1995, the construction of multi- and megaplex entertainment centres continued apace, involving increasing numbers of Spanish and overseas companies (Cinesa, Balañá, Yelmo, Alta as well as Warner, Lusomundo and Sony) linked to projects in Madrid, Barcelona, Zaragoza, La Coruña, etc. (Abad 1997: 127). Above all, 1995 saw a renaissance of attractive and entertaining film production in Spain made by established talents as well as a growing number of new, young directors in films as diverse as Almodóvar's *La flor de mi secreto*, Aranda's *La pasión turca*, Uribe's *Días contados*, Armendáriz's *Historias del Kronen*, Gómez Pereira's *Boca a boca* as well as Alex de la Iglesia's *El día de la bestia*, Agustín Díaz Yanes's *Nadie hablará de nosotras cuando hayamos muerto*, Chus Gutiérrez's *Alma gitana* and Icíar Bollaín's *¡Hola! ¿Estás sola?*.

With the Partido Popular minority electoral victory in March 1996 and the replacement of Alborch by 'Thatcherite' Esperanza Aguirre at the head of Education and Culture, government policy towards the Spanish cinema took a sharp turn to the right. And after some internal confusion regarding their policies towards subsidies in the summer months, PP presented new legislation towards the year end. In specific terms, this included: the retention of automatic subsidies according to box-office takings (introduced by the Socialist government in 1994) and the maintenance of support for new directors and quality projects; changes to the screen quota, allowing exhibitors to screen three American films instead of two for every one Spanish/European film shown; the suppression of selective subsidies and dubbing licences (to be phased out by 1998); the reduction of the minimum percentage of participation in a coproduction for a film to be considered Spanish; the availability of low-cost credits and loans to producers via the *Instituto Oficial de*

Crédito. However, so far, there will be no ticket tax, as previously envisaged (*Fotogramas* 1996: 130). In the wider context, PP is clearly embarked upon a major phase of deregulation in exhibition, distribution and production, with the planned phasing out of film subsidies over the medium to long term.

The above measures, already part of the previous Socialist agenda for deregulation, clearly spell the beginning of the end for a sub-sidised film industry in Spain. If the new PP government has built upon Socialist precedent, it has also acceded far more willingly to the wishes of multinational distributors and exhibitors in their quest for greater market freedoms. Will deregulation kill off the Spanish film industry? Or will it open up new opportunities and perhaps reinvigorate a hitherto publicly-subsidised activity that has for too long been a marginal player in a fast-changing macro-regional and global market place? So far, the signs are far from gloomy. Indeed, over the last two to three years, the Spanish film industry has been undergoing a major transformation which has been generating significant changes at all levels. A striking indication of such changes can be seen in the fact that official government targets for Spanish film production for 1996 were set at approximately eighty full-length features. Final totals, however, exceeded all expectations, with ninety-six features being produced for the year, a stunning increase of forty on 1995 and fifty-five on 1994 (*Fotogramas* 1997: 140).

An industrial renaissance?

Although the multinationals (particularly American conglomerates such as Columbia Tristar, Warner and UIP) continue to exert their stranglehold over distribution and exhibition networks in Spain, Spanish production interests have been strengthened in recent years. As noted earlier, PRISA's Sogetel, as well as Vicente Gómez's Iberoamericana, now lead the field, although Almodóvar's El Deseo is at the forefront of smaller production companies. Indeed, Almodóvar has been instrumental in supporting the projects of several new talents: Alex de la Iglesia (*Acción mutante*, 1992), Mónica Laguna (*Tengo una casa*, 1996) and Daniel Calparsoro (*Pasajes*, 1996). In similar fashion, a number of other smaller production companies, some headed by established directors, have been in the vanguard of encouraging new talents: Fernando Colomo, for example (through his Producciones La Iguana), has supported Icíar Bollaín's *¡Hola! ¿Estás sola?* (1995), Mariano Barroso's *Mi hermano del alma* (1993) and *Extasis* (1996), Azucena Rodríguez's *Entre rojas* (1995) and Daniel Calparsoro's *Salto al vacío* (1995). José Luis Cuerda backed Alejandro Amenábar's *Tesis* (1996) and Fernando Trueba co-produced Juanma Bajo Ulloa's *Alas de mariposa* (1991), Chus Gutiérrez's *Sublet* (1992) and various recent comedies by Emilio Martínez Lázaro such as *Amo tu cama rica* (1991).

However, despite these developments, the vast remaining area of

Spanish film production continues to be fragmented, with 'cottage' production companies springing up, making one film and then disappearing. Such fragmentation does little to strengthen the fragile national industry. Despite the efforts of Sogepaq, nearly 50 per cent of Spanish features are dependent on distribution contracts with the multinationals. This is a mixed blessing for Spanish-produced cinema. On the one hand, it gives the local product access to the powerful marketing machine and key venues controlled by the multinationals. On the other, it places them in competition with other products handled by the same distributor (usually American films, often representing a higher and more guaranteed marketing priority for the distributor), for better release dates, venues and runs. Meanwhile, Spanish television companies – including national channels (public and private), channels in the autonomous regions and pay television – are playing an increasingly crucial role in film production and promotion. Their activity not only involves participation in production funding and commissions, but their purchasing power and guarantees of transmission/repeat contracts are fundamental to the financing of film projects. For example, in 1996, Canal+ showed nearly seventy Spanish films, a clear indication of its importance as a distribution outlet for national production as well as an investor, in conjunction with companies such as Sogetel (PRISA) (Álvarez 1997: 36).

Many of the directors who emerged in the new Spanish cinema of the 1960s are still highly active and developing projects. Saura, for example, after making the thriller *Dispara* (1993), has developed his musical and dance interests with *Flamenco* (1995), returning to the social problem thriller in *Taxi* (1996) and is now embarked on *Tango* and *Pajarico*. Víctor Erice makes his return to filmmaking, after *El sol del membrillo* (1992), with Juan Marsé's *El embrujo de Shanghai*; Mario Camus, after *Adosados* (1996), will make *La ciudad de los prodigios*, based on the novel by Eduardo Mendoza and after an absence from directing of over a decade, José Luis Borau has just finished *Niño nadie*, inspired by a story by Rafael Sánchez Ferlosio. Many established directors, of a slightly younger generation have had considerable success in the 1995–96 period with major film features. These include: Vicente Aranda's *La pasión turca* and *Libertarias*, Fernando Colomo's *El efecto mariposa*, Imanol Uribe's *Días contados* and *Bwana*, José Juan Bigas Luna's *La teta y la luna* and *Bambola*, Pilar Miró's *Tu nombre envenena mis sueños* and *El perro del hortelano*. Also, Pedro Almodóvar's *La flor de mi secreto* and Fernando Trueba's *Two Much*.

New blood
Since the early 1990s, there appears to have been a massive injection of new blood into the industry from virtually all quarters: directors, actors, scriptwriters, producers as well as audiences. For

example, increasing numbers of new, young filmmakers have been able to screen their *ópera prima*. Between 1985 and 1995, Monterde notes approximately 13 new directors per year, responsible for an average of nearly 24 per cent of all films being made (1996: 53). Such numbers should not create false optimism, since of the many new directors, only 17 per cent of their number went on to make a second film and of a total number of 129 newcomers over a decade, only 38 or so managed to establish a career in the movies. Also, from those 129 first films, more than half have never been released. Still, part of the reason for the promising position of Spanish cinema in recent years has to do with the impact of such *directores noveles*. Indeed, in 1996, 7 out of 10 box office hits were from new directors (Álvarez 1997: 34). And since 1991, we have seen not only names with which we are already familiar such as Juanma Bajo Ulloa, Julio Medem and Alex de la Iglesia but also: Agustín Díaz Yanes, Daniel Calparsoro, Alejandro Amenábar, Manuel Huerga, Mariano Barroso, Elio Quiroga, David Trueba, Manuel Gómez Pereira, Santiago Aguilar and Luis Guridi, alias La Cuadrilla. Many new female directors have also been developing their careers in the 1990s, including: Isabel Coixet, Eva Lesmes, Mónica Laguna, Chus Gutiérrez, Icíar Bollaín, Gracia Querejeta, Azucena Rodríguez, etc. Alongside these new directors, the older generation of women filmmakers almost uniquely represented by Pilar Miró and Josefina Molina continue to take their work in new directions.

Also, we find a number of actors who have turned to directing, including established figures such as José Sacristán (*Soldados de plomo*, 1983 and *Cara de acelga*, 1986), Ana Belén (*Cómo ser mujer y no morir en el intento* 1991) and Fernando Fernán Gómez – perhaps the paradigm case of an actor alternating as director and vice versa – as well as Imanol Arias (*Un asunto privado*, 1995) and Icíar Bollaín (*¡Hola¡ ¿Estás sola?*, 1995).

Moreover, we have seen producers such as Gerardo Herrero (*Desvío al paraíso*, 1994 and *Territorio Comanche*, 1999) and young scriptwriters such as Joaquín Oristrell (*¿De qué se ríen las mujeres?* 1996) and David Trueba (*La buena vida*, 1997) winning their stripes as directors. This represents a major sea change in the panorama of Spanish cinema and seems extremely promising.

Virtually all of these newcomers have been well-received by critics and have enjoyed reasonable public responses to their work. In some cases, the reception has been outstanding, thus encouraging their directorial commitment to the business and facilitating the production of a second film in relatively short time. The rejuvenation of the Spanish cinema in the 1990s is perhaps at its most visible in the major injection of new, young acting talents such as: Candela Peña, Silke Klein, Lili Taylor, Cristina Marcos, Mapi Galán, Mónica López, Mercè Pons, Rosanna Pastor, Ruth Gabriel, Nawja Nimri, as well as Juan Diego Botto, Coque Malla, Achero Mañas,

¡*Hola! ¿Estás sola?*, Icíar Bollaín, 1995

Jordi Mollá, Pepón Nieto, Gustavo Salmerón, Toni Cantó, Ernesto Alterio, etc.

Focusing on contemporary Spanish cinema

The ostensibly straightforward title of this book – *Contemporary Spanish cinema* – belies the difficulty of defining what might be understood by each of its elements. Contemporaneity is a relative concept at the best of times, but a whole range of other questions and nuances are introduced when it is applied to a recent Spanish cinema marked by an obsessive focus on the past in narrative and thematics, its retro film styles and prodigious taste for nostalgia. Spain as an entity and Spanish cultural identity are no less difficult to pin down as the concept of the nation state is simultaneously assailed by political, economic and cultural globalisation and the fragmentation of the state by the demands of its autonomous communities. Questions of identity in Spain are further complicated by a history of political manipulation and exploitation of concepts of national and cultural identity. Even cinema itself eludes clear-cut definitions in this age of intertextuality and virtual reality. Film can no longer be regarded as a discrete practice, much less so in a national industry whose production is so dependent on television for much of its funding and exhibition. Despite these difficulties, this book seeks to negotiate the conceptual obstacles and present the reader with a coherent picture of the main narrative, thematic, stylistic and representational trends which have characterised recent cinema produced in Spain.

What is Spanish cinema?

As a broad term, 'Spanish cinema' could be regarded as one taking into account the production, distribution and exhibition of films in Spain, as a broad geographical area. However, we have a problem in that just as films made in Spain are not only shown in Spain, films that are distributed and exhibited in Spain are clearly not just Spanish films. In fact, since the 1930s and before, the majority of films shown in Spanish cinemas have been American. Needless to say, the criteria for classifying what counts as a Spanish film vary considerably, often depending on a film's finance and production circumstances. So, a film largely financed by Spanish producers (including government subsidies, television contracts and possibly bank credits) could presumably be identified as Spanish; a film financed by foreign producers, but made by Spanish personnel might not be seen as Spanish (Trueba's *Two Much?*); one which was only partly financed by Spanish funding would be considered a coproduction. These definitions of the identity of Spanish films tend to rely on economic/financial criteria, which are important from the point of view of Spanish film production, but may not be very helpful when we come to explore the relationships between Spanish film and Spanish culture, which are central to the concerns of this book.

Our study focuses crucially on Spanish cinema as a cultural product and explores the ways in which its representations of class, gender, race, sexuality, regional and national identity both implicitly and explicitly question and revise varying concepts of 'Spanishness'.

The nation; national culture; national cinema

As we begin to explore these representations, it will become apparent that notions of nation, national culture, national identity, etc. are highly problematic in the case of Spain. What do we mean by the 'nation' in relation to Spanish cinema when the nation is in fact made up of four different linguistic identities (Castilian, Catalan, Basque, Galician), three 'historic' nationalisms (Catalonia, the Basque Country, Galicia) and seventeen autonomous communities? The strong decentralising tendencies in Spain over the last two decades have resulted in attempts by all traditional and newly-developed autonomous communities to promote 'national' cultures which are distinct from the traditionally hegemonic, centralist 'Spanish/Castilian' culture, centred on Madrid. And even within Castilian-dominated Spain, for example, different regions (Aragón, Anadalusia, the Canary Islands, etc.) have very different ways of life, different regional, class and ethnic compositions and are anxious to create a clear and separate identity from the political centre and capital of Madrid. And clearly, the existence of indigenous film cultures in Catalonia, the Basque country, Galicia and other regions, makes it more difficult to subsume these areas and cultures within the concept of a 'Spanish ' cinema. So any discussion of Spanish cinema and a national Spanish culture must inevitably acknowledge the existence, claims, products and representations of the many other national identities within the Spanish 'nation state'. All of these different communities cannot be easily integrated into a unitary national identity. Hence, the impossibility of talking of a single national culture in Spain or a uniform national cinema. Any discussion of the Spanish cinema needs to take this heterogeneity into consideration and thus when we look at representations of gender, class, race, sexuality, regional identities, etc., these must be seen as different facets of a heterogeneous national identity.

It may be more helpful therefore to talk of national identities, cultures and cinemas in the plural, since the representations we shall consider will be bound up with questions of national and cultural identity at the micro- as well as the macro-regional level (Kinder 1993: 387–440). The latter will only become meaningful within their particular regional, social and historical contexts. The meanings of films or what they represent are never immanent or already contained in the film. Meaning and representation need to be considered in relation to the specific conditions of production and consumption pertaining to particular historical moments. Our analyses will have to take into account therefore not only when films were made, but when they were set and how they might have been read by different audiences. Each of these facets will have a bearing on how we make sense of the representations in a film. Moreover, we will need to consider comparatively the representation of cultural identity across both fictional and non-fictional, mainstream/commercial and independent films.

If we had to single out one unifying characteristic within the remarkably wide range of films that have been produced during the post-Franco period, it would have to be the preoccupation with questions of identity. This operates in a range of contexts and at a number of levels, but it is largely concerned with the exploration of notions and images of self – both of the individual and groups and communities. In this book, we attempt to trace and interpret the ways in which this broad preoccupation manifests itself in contemporary Spanish cinema, locating it within the context of social, political and cultural developments in Spain and the specific background of Spanish film culture.

This study

Conscious of the different approaches and coverage offered by other survey books in English on the subject (including Besas, Higginbotham, Hopewell, Kinder, etc.), our study aims to complement these as well as update the information and recent developments that have been important, especially since the late 1980s.

In chronological terms, our interest is clearly focused on the cinema produced after the Franco dictatorship, particularly on the period of the 1980s and 1990s, more so the latter. Cinema produced under the regime is referred to in the four main chapters, in as far as it helps to compare and contrast types and styles of cinema in very different political and cultural contexts and to understand what some of those post-Franco trends and styles were reacting against and heading towards. The period which is of most interest to us is a coherent one in that it roughly corresponds to the period of tenure of Spain's Socialist government (1982–1996) and our approach specifically addresses the major changes and developments in the industry, in filmmaking and in the sort of concerns Spanish films have explored over the years and the ways in which these have been represented.

The organisational structure of our main chapters is shaped by a series of factors which we believe are central for an understanding of contemporary Spanish culture. These concern the major changes which Spain has seen since the 1970s in political, historical and economic terms as well as in moral and social structures and mores. We have therefore focused particularly on the all-pervading preoccupation with the past, the search for a kind of cultural continuity and security, the significance of gender and sexuality to the formulation of individual and social identities, and the importance of concepts and images of regional and national identity/identities as a point of reference.

Chapter 1 seeks to explore the obsession of Spanish cinema with the past and its role as part of a wider recuperation industry, and examines the varied forms of historical cinema ranging from literary adaptation and period drama to retro thriller and musical. What we argue is that during the transition period (1976–82), Spanish cinema was seriously concerned with recuperating a historical past and a popular memory that had been denied, distorted or suppressed during the Franco dictatorship. The optimism and hope evoked by the new democratic freedoms and the need for many communities in Spain to reassert their legitimate identities and politics created a 'politicised', sometimes radical cinematic response. Film was directly involved in the process of nation building and the recuperation of a democratic, and in other cases, a nationalist/separatist tradition. However, by the early and mid-1980s, with the waning of the earlier political radicalism and the retreat of politics into committee rooms, a broad cynicism and disillusionment sets in. Socialist government policy gives rise to a filmmaking machine that produces worthy but relatively uncontentious features, politically centrist and aesthetically 'polivalente' (multipurpose) (Gubern, *et al.* 1994: 421). There is also a gradual shift toward a forgetfulness of a problematic past and a reimagining of that past in more convivial ways. By the mid-1980s, radical politics and militancy have given way to films which focus on the past from the point of view of the human story, of the personal, of the effects of historical events and actions on the emotional and psychological outlook of individual characters. In short, the personal becomes the political.

In Chapter 2, we offer an analysis of other main forms of genre cinema which have dominated the commercial industry and the popular imagination in Spain since the 1970s. Dealing with the comedy and its many subgeneric types as well as the thriller, the musical, the fantasy, adventure and horror film, we seek to survey how these areas have developed over the period. We also endeavour to explore the way genre cinema taps into changing contemporary cultural attitudes and how it makes its appeal, what functions it fulfils through its various generic guises and how it acknowledges social change. This can be seen, for example, in the escapist function of retro styles in the face of post-modern uncertainties or in the recasting of female characters in mainstream comedies to reflect, endorse or critique changing perceptions of women in society.

In Chapter 3, we explore constructions of gender and sexuality across a wide range of examples taken from a variety of contemporary movies. We lead into this by looking at relevant filmic representations of gender and sexualities under the Franco regime and how these change in response to democratic freedoms as manifested for example in Madrid's famous *Movida* and the early Almodóvar. We consider the major impact of the recent influx of previously scarce women filmmakers on contemporary Spanish cinema and the significance this might have for the representation of women in film. We then examine images of women in contemporary Spanish cinema as a whole, in relation to their representations of female identity. Constructions and deconstructions of masculinity, both hetero- and homosexual, are also considered, particularly regarding the extent to which images of men in the 1990s reveal a blurring of the previously rigidly-drawn boundaries between the masculine and the feminine.

Finally, in Chapter 4, we focus on cinema in the autonomous communities, mainly Catalonia and the Basque Country. We look at the role of the cinema in the reconstruction of nationalist consciousness and cultural difference in the transition period and beyond, as the autonomies regained their political identities and local powers suppressed under the dictatorship. We examine how the main autonomies rebuild their film industries, the policy choices they make and the consequences of those choices. We then consider the ways in which these industries have diversified in the 1980s and 1990s, and the extent to which commercial imperatives have meant a revision and major redefinition of regional identities in an increasingly macro-regional, global film marketplace.

Going beyond a chronological survey or overview, our book tries to be broad and far-reaching in its analyses. It does not claim to be exhaustive or comprehensive (far from it), though it does focus on the key events, trends and changes which have characterised the Spanish film industry over the last two decades. Informed by recent trends in film and cultural theory, we employ a range of analytical tools to develop our readings of these aspects as well as the relationships between the films and their historical and social contexts, generic and thematic categories, narrative and formal features. Any such study implies an inevitable degree of overlap between generic and thematic considerations. Work by Bigas Luna, for example, demands discussion both within the frame of gender and sexuality as well as reference to its place within genre film or in relation to Catalan cinema. Hence, we adopt a multi-pronged treatment which seeks to elucidate director, film, theme, genre, etc. in relation to the particular concerns of each chapter. We place the primary focus on the films themselves, in the interests of providing an informed and accessible insight into the cultural complexities of contemporary Spanish cinema. We also believe that the main value of our study will be at the level of questioning, through filmic representations, just how we characterise and categorise Spanish cinema in the global communications network and how Spanish movies inflect and reimagine their communities, stereotypes and individual identities.

References

Abad, I. (1997), La fiebre de los multicines en España: ¿Hasta cuándo?, *Fotogramas*, 1840, February, 127.

Álvarez, C. (1997), El cine más cercano, *El País Semanal*, 19 January, 34–6.

Fernández Rubio, A. (1996), El cine planta cara, *El País, Suplemento Domingo*, 4 August, 4.

Fotogramas (1994), Sogepaq Distribución invertirá 6,000 millones en tres años, 1813, November, 116.

Fotogramas (1994), Film Business, 1814, December, 36.

Fotogramas (1996), Decretazo a la vista, 1835, September, 130.

Fotogramas (1997), 1996: Más películas y más baratas, 1841, March, 140.

García, R. (1995), El cine español mira al público, *El País*, 24 December, 81–2.

Gubern R., *et al.* (1994), *Historia del cine español*, Madrid, Cátedra, Signo e Imagen.

Kinder, M. (1993), *Blood Cinema. The Reconstruction of National Identity in Spain*, Berkeley and Los Ángeles, University of California Press, 387–440.

Monterde, J. E. (1996), Un asunto privado. Esforzado debut para una historia insalvable, *Dirigido*, 246, May, 52–4.

Reconstructing the past: historical cinema in post-Franco Spain

1

Introduction

One of the most prominent features of Spanish cinema since the end of the dictatorship in 1975 has been its obsessive concern with the past. This forms part of a wider preoccupation in Spain with recuperating the past. According to Jo Labanyi, 'Recent years have seen something approximating to a "recuperation industry"', with the refurbishing of museums, restoration of municipal theatres, vogue for local history, and reissue of forgotten women writers' (1995: 402). This retrospective trend has been evident in a whole range of cultural products and practices from the 1970s to the 1990s. Popular music has seen the revival of regional musical traditions in the work of such groups as Fuxan Os Ventos and Milladoiro in Galicia in the late 1970s and 1980s, the upsurge of the flamenco-rock hybrid of the 1990s with the popularity of the (ironically French) Gypsy Kings and the revival and reissue of 1930s *canción española* (popular Spanish song) albums by such classic performers as Marifé de Triana. In Spain's designer culture of the late 1980s and early 1990s, retro styles have been a source of inspiration for shops and bars in Madrid and Barcelona (Dent Coad 1995: 377–9) and nostalgic images of the past support endless advertisements and publicity campaigns. In the cinema, this phenomenon has taken various forms ranging from the plethora of glossy adaptations of literary classics and period dramas, to the recycling of retrospective genres such as the noirish thriller and *canción española* musicals. Elements of nostalgia are also prominent in films which are simultaneously showcases for Spain's enthusiastic embrace of modernity (as in Pedro Almodóvar's indulgent recycling of thirties, forties and fifties kitsch and his parodic subversions of classic melodrama and thriller genres).

On the one hand, this cultural trend may be read simply as a local inflection of the widespread nostalgia boom which characterises contemporary society throughout the Western world. As David Lowenthal observes:

Fashions for old films, old clothes, old music, old recipes are ubiquitous, and nostalgia marks every product ... our rampant nostalgia, our obsessive search for our roots [and] our endemic concern with preservation ... show how intensely the past is still felt. Nostalgia fills the popular press, serves as advertising bait, merits sociological study; no term better expresses the modern malaise. (Browne and Ambrosetti 1993: 87).

However, in Spain, such activity also responds to a very culture-specific need to recuperate a past which for forty years had been hijacked and aggressively refashioned by Francoism. The desire to re-examine and represent this past from other perspectives is clearly exemplified by the dominance of the historical film during the transition period (1976–82). Of the nearly three hundred historical films produced since the 1970s, more than half are set during the Second Republic, the Civil War and Francoism.

Historical film, perhaps more than any other generic category, places the question of the relationship between reality, perception and representation firmly in the spotlight. And since historical reality is itself an elusive concept, accessible only through the imperfections of memory and representation, the mediation of that reality (such as it is) inevitably interposes a series of lenses or filters which both facilitate and obfuscate its interpretation. The representation of history in the cinema raises even more complex questions because of the particular qualities of film as the medium most closely able to simulate reality through its moving images and the unique relationship that exists between the spectator and the text.

This chapter initially provides a brief overview of the relationship between history, cinema and the *mitología franquista* (Francoist mythology) during the dictatorship. It then goes on to examine some of the major trends and developments in this very broad grouping of films in post-Franco cinema. It also seeks to identify some of the complex features underlying the relationships between the present and the past in contemporary Spanish culture, their articulation through the medium of film and the interpretative and representational issues these interactions raise.

Since the mid-1970s, two broad periods in Spanish historical cinema can be identified, although the respective cinematic sub-trends inevitably overlap, feed off and merge into one another. From the death of Franco through to the early years of democracy (1975–82), Spanish historical cinema was dominated by an obsessive search for authenticity and historical truth, with various forms of documentary cinema enjoying a brief, but prolific revival alongside dramatised reconstructions of historical events. These gradually gave way in the early 1980s to a less radical and militant, more nostalgic and personalised cinema. There also developed an increasing awareness and acceptance of the inaccessibility of historical truth other than through subjective representation, perhaps offering an explanation for the way in which history and fantasy have become increasingly intertwined. At the same time, throughout the 1980s and 1990s there has been a significant output of both popular movies and less accessible arthouse films which self-consciously reflect on a whole range of relationships between the past and the present, reality and representation, history and memory.

History, cinema and the *mitología franquista*

The ideological agenda of the Franco regime was underpinned by a fundamental appeal to the values of the past. Francoism, if it was an ideology, was one which looked to the remote past in order to create a myth for the present, appropriating its crusading image from Spain's cultural and colonial 'Golden Age'. The appeal to ancient traditions enabled the propagators of the *mitología franquista* to find legitimation in the very weight of that tradition, by constructing a powerful sense of continuity with a certain historical moment which was reimagined as 'utopian' and 'eternal'. The values that Francoism sought to revive in respect of national and religious unity, family morality, paternalistic social and industrial relations, etc., were similarly anachronistic. Their inscription in the cultural products and practices of the time constituted a paradigmatic example of the function and purpose of myth if, as Roland Barthes asserts, 'the very end of myths is to immobilise the world' (1973: 169–70).

And what more appropriate breeding ground for mythology than the cinema – the arch-creator of myths? Although the regime did not exploit its propagandistic possibilities through a systematic programme of propaganda cinema, the political climate and operation of censorship ensured that the myths of the Spanish Dream Factory were those of the regime, myths routinely inscribed in the popular genres of the period. Moreover, complementing the regime's archaic ideology, institutionally approved cinema or *cine oficial* of the early Franco years saw a boom in the production and consumption of retrospective genres. Virginia Higginbotham points out that:

The major genres of Spanish film during the first two post-war decades include the *cine cruzada*, or Civil War films, historical extravaganzas, *cine de sacerdotes*, or religious films, and the folklore musicals. All these film genres presented Spain as it was in the past. They upheld and reinforced the traditional views of Church and Fascist state to which Franco's victory gave the force of law. These genres all had a common goal of reassuring Spaniards that, notwithstanding the devastating Civil War, their country's values and institutions had not changed. (1988: 18)

The effacement of political dialectic and historical accuracy in early Francoist institutional cinema also offered a prime example of Roland Barthes's argument that 'myth deprives the object of which it speaks of all History' (1973: 165). As Higginbotham indicates: 'Imperial attitudes of sacrifice, patriotism, and military glory coincide neatly with the values of Franco's fascism. In them, individual heroism and nationalism predominate, while social history of collective action is almost entirely lacking.' (1988: 22)

Predictably, films about the Civil War celebrated the bravery, honour and righteousness of the Nationalist cause in films such as *Sin novedad en el Alcázar* (made by Italian director Augusto Genina in 1940 – see Gubern, *et al.* 1994: 209). The film celebrated General Moscardó's legendary resistance to the Republican siege of Toledo's military fortress, as well as the sacrifice of his hostage son. Historical epics set in earlier periods rehearsed the same triumphalist rhetoric, glorifying patriotism and militarism in the name of the Catholic faith. Not unexpectedly, the most famous of these, *Alba de América* (Juan de Orduña 1951), sidesteps any problematisation of the issue of colonisation and presents the 'history' of Columbus's expedition as a religious mission, climaxing with the 'conversion' of bewildered native Indians transported to the court of a 'saintly' Isabel la Católica.

The overriding sense of belonging to an unbroken tradition of patriotism, linked to the regime's mythified version of history, is reproduced in the infamous family saga of 'honour' *Raza* (Sáenz de Heredia, 1941), scripted by Franco himself under the pseudonym of Jaime de Andrade. The film traces a personal family history of sacrifice for the sake of the *patria* across three generations. It also conjures up a glorious history of military success for Spain, starting with the conquest of the Americas and ending with the victory parade at the end of the Civil War.

Personal values such as piety and obedience as well as loyalty to God, the monarch and the family were heavily promoted in films focusing on individual responsibility and dedication to the *patria*. Newly imposed definitions of the family and gender roles were legitimised as 'natural' through endless recycling of the same stories. Inevitably, narrative resolutions tended to reinforce the status quo and close off any alternative readings.

The mystifications of this *cine oficial* would become a major point of reference and an irresistible target for an oppositional cinema anxious to find new ways of representing history and contemporary reality. One of the earliest oppositional films to gain a release, Luis García Berlanga's *Bienvenido, Mr Marshall* (1952), used the vehicle of comic realism to mount its attack on Francoist jingoism and the regime's apparent sell-out to the Marshall Plan (US-sponsored programmes for European Reconstruction following World War II). The film parodied a range of institutionalised genres such as the folkloric extravaganza and historical epic (including a skit on *Alba de América*). Berlanga's multi-layered generic satire would show, within the limitations of *cine oficial*, how directors could tackle subjects and develop formal strategies which could turn Francoist rhetoric on its head. Such guile and filmcraft would not be lost on those filmmakers who would produce the New Spanish Cinema of the 1960s and 1970s or on those engaged in 1980s and 1990s pastiche.

During the dictatorship, the impossibility of dealing directly with historical issues or the realities of present-day situations encouraged filmmakers to develop styles based broadly on allusiveness, parable and the use of metaphor and symbol. These forms of 'indirection' became the dominant ways in which the more problematic aspects of life under Francoism were made amenable to exploration. Filmmakers also constructed their narratives around such foci as the family, young children, hunting, etc., subjects which acted as microcosms and correlatives for real political events, institutions and situations. Of course, audiences were sensitised to this language of allusion and cross-reference; indeed, they were already prepared for it, whether a film hinted at its intended transpositions or not. In other words, under dictatorship conditions, film audiences were already primed to 'overread' filmic signs and inevitably they over-interpreted their meanings; in a filmic nutshell, less nearly always meant more. And even when the censor worked hard to obfuscate more obvious meanings or decontextualise political and historical references, particularly those relating to the Civil War, historical settings were one of a number of strategies filmmakers adopted to create a critical space for commentary on the present. The practice of making oblique reference to the present by reference to the past continued well into the transition period, not only because of the delay in the abolition of censorship in November 1977, but also because of its well-established effectiveness.

Reconstructing the past

Documentary revival in the transition period

The Francoist *Noticarios y Documentales Españoles (No-Do)* newsreels had monopolised filmed reportage from 1943 until 1976–77 and the end of censorship. Their disappearance created the critical space for a brief, but enthusiastic resurgence of the documentary film which tackled questions of historical reality and its representation head on. Many films sought to overturn Francoist documentary practices in both subject matter and form and eagerly seized the opportunity to present demystificatory reports on subjects previously banned. They also rejected the rhetorical style of the *No-Do*, where voice-over commentaries had subordinated competing or conflicting points of view to a dominant, official outlook and where reportage was reduced to something 'entre el desfile militar y la foto de familia' (between the military parade and the family photo) (Tranche and Biosca 1993: 40). The salient features of this new documentary trend were its reintroduction of previously excluded points of view and its appeal to authenticity.

Historical interrogations of the Civil War, for example, typically incorporate interviews with key political figures of the time and contemporary archive film footage. Though a commercial failure, one of the most incisive analyses of the period was Jaime Camino's *La vieja memoria* (1977). The piece combines footage from the time of the Second Republic and the Civil War with commentaries by major figures such as La Pasionaria and Gil Robles on events leading to the demise of the Republic and the root causes of the war. *¿Por qué perdimos la guerra?* (Diego Abad de Santillán 1978) also includes interviews with political figures of the period in an attempt to analyse the reasons for the tragic outcome of the conflict, particularly regarding the problematic role of the Communist Party. Given the uncertainty of the political climate during the transition and the proximity of the period under examination, films examining the dictatorship were, not surprisingly, more tentative, frequently adopting an ironic, indirect approach. Some of the more sinister idiosyncrasies of Francoism are examined in Basilio M. Patino's *Queridísimos verdugos* (1973–76). The film considers the extraordinary method of execution by garrotte which so notoriously symbolised the macabre violence and judicial anachronism of late Francoism. It features the gruesome reminiscences of two inebriated ex-executioners against a background of flamenco dancers and folk song (Hopewell 1986: 127). In similar vein, Jaime Chávarri's *El desencanto* (1976) examines the 'sicología patológica de la familia franquista' (the pathological psychology of the Francoist family) (Gubern, *et al.* 1994: 359) in conversations with wacky members of the family of defunct Francoist poet Leopoldo Panero.

Recognising the way in which film form had served the triumphalist rhetoric of the regime, a number of films drew attention to their formal break with the past or made the practices of Francoist cinema the focus of their examination. Self-consciously aware of the manipulative effects of editing and camerawork, some of these documentaries made a point of emphasising the mediating effects of camera angles, framing and *mise-en-scène*. John Hopewell cites the use of Pere Portabella's pointed exaggeration in *Informe general* (1977) of 'the visual rhetoric of the political interview by placing the aged, pear-shaped Gil Robles in an armchair to match his patrician status but siting Communist intellectual Tamames in a university office to confirm ... his "theoretical context"' (1986: 172).

A widespread and recurrent formal feature of many of these documentary films juxtaposes images of mystification with contrasting images of the 'real' in order to signal the distortions to which history and contemporary reality had been subjected during the regime. The role of the cinema in constructing the mythology of Francoism was the explicit focus of Basilio M. Patino's *Canciones para después de una guerra* (completed in 1971 but not approved for release until 1976). The film deconstructs the way in which Francoism appropriated popular cultural forms and images to obscure the daily realities of postwar Spain. The film is a montage which juxtaposes recordings of popular songs and film clips of historical epics, comedies, folkloric musicals and melodrama with contemporary archive images of hunger, poverty, devastation, rationing, tendentious education and militaristic propaganda. Perhaps the most entertaining example of this deconstruction of Francoist mythology is Gonzalo Herralde's *Raza, el espíritu de Franco* (1977) which similarly addresses the relationship between image and myth. Extracts from *Raza* (Sáenz de Heredia's notorious 1941 apologia) are combined with interviews with Franco's sister and Alfredo Mayo who played the hero in the film. The film demonstrates a mimetic relationship between the José Churruca character and the fictional bases of Franco's own self-image.

Historical Reconstruction

During the dictatorship, the boundaries between documentary and fiction had become seriously blurred. Whilst the form and content of official Francoist documentaries severely exceeded the boundaries of the most liberal definitions of testimonial realism, the effects of censorship destabilised the parameters of fiction. In the absence of a free press, many oppositional writers and filmmakers promoted the testimonial function of literary and film fiction, introducing forms of neo- or social realism in a bid to represent contemporary and recent historical reality as accurately as possible through fictional characters and narratives. Novelists frequently adopted cinematic techniques of juxtaposition in order to emphasise social inequity and injustice, while minimising the role of an omniscient authorial voice and allowing the textual 'evidence' to speak for itself as in Fernández Santos's *Los bravos* (1954), Sánchez Ferlosio's *El Jarama* (1956) or Juan Goytisolo's *Campos de Níjar* (1960) (Jordan 1990: 129–71). In the cinema, Spanish articulations of this neorealist tradition began with Nieves Conde's *Surcos* (1951) and Bardem's *Muerte de un ciclista* (1955) and performed a similar 'objectivist' function in films such as *El pisito* (Ferreri 1958), *Plácido* (Berlanga 1961) and *La caza* (Saura 1965). In the censor-free context of the transition, the testimonial function of fiction-film formats was no longer limited to allusive comedies or metaphorical dramas. The dramatic possibilities of fictional narratives were placed at the service of reconstructing those histories which had been distorted or suppressed under the regime and could now be told from an oppositional perspective.

The documentary thriller

In 1977, Susan Sontag remarked on the ironic fact that the cinema had become a cultural point of reference for events which had become so dramatic, they 'seemed like a movie' (1977: 354–5). The dramatic character of a number of events during the final years of the dictatorship clearly lent themselves to filmic treatment through the vehicle of the historical reconstruction. This generic hybrid offered audiences the dual satisfaction of witnessing 'real-life drama' packaged within classic, popular narrative forms. The structural and stylistic features of the thriller genre, for example, captured both the dramatic impact of events as well as the excitement of bringing politics to the screen after years of repression.

One of the first films to broach recent political events in Spain, Juan Antonio Bardem's *Siete días de enero* (1978), presents itself as a chronicle of the tragic events which occurred in Madrid in January 1977. These involved the right-wing terrorist assassination of five labour lawyers (four of them Communist) in the Atocha district of the capital. The killings seriously threatened Spain's embryonic pre-democracy and required a television appeal for calm by the then Prime Minister Adolfo Suárez. Bardem's film opens with a factual and formal authentication of the events to follow via snippets of archive film overlaid with teleprinted news flashes, summarising the sequence of events. The deaths of two students in demonstrations, the kidnapping of a military official and the assassinations of the five lawyers are placed within the context of the negotiations between government and opposition representatives which resulted in the legalisation of Spain's Communist Party, the first democratic elections in Spain since 1936 and the Pactos de la Moncloa in October 1977 between government and trade unions. Other formal strategies, however, work against this testimonial flavour in order to maximise drama and suspense. These arise, for example, in the repetitions of the assassination sequence, initially withholding shots of the victims and later imaging them in slow motion. This is also the case with the dramatic use of non-diegetic music in the funeral sequence (Hopewell 1986: 108–9). Whilst the film adheres to the factual evidence of the events themselves, in the manner of a documentary reconstruction, the thriller framework relocates those events within a fictional conspiracy involving imaginary characters, attempting to precipitate an armed coup through the destabilisation of the political situation (Hopewell 1986: 108–9). Caparrós Lera points out, however, that the latter clearly resemble members of the ultra right-wing *Fuerza Nueva* (New Force) and *Guerrilleros de Cristo Rey* (Guerrillas of Christ the King) (Caparrós Lera 1992: 176).

Following his documentary examination of the infamous trial of ETA suspects in Burgos in 1970 in *El proceso de Burgos* (1979), which reunited the sixteen now-amnestied men to discuss their experiences, Imanol Uribe adopted the adventure-thriller mode for his next feature in *La fuga de Segovia* (1981). The film reconstructs the 1976 prison break-out by a group of ETA members, one of whom, Ángel Amigo, was the author of the book on which the film is based. This textual source, Amigo's collaboration on the script and the participation of eight of the men involved in the escape as actors gave the film a crucially important profile of authenticity. At the same time, both films were particularly controversial because of their sympathetic representation of ETA militancy, which some critics regarded as tantamount to a glorification of terrorism (Besas 1985: 207; Hopewell 1986: 233).

Following the end of censorship in 1977, there developed something of a boom period for the political film, in which all manner of controversial subjects could be tackled. However, the importance of testimonial detail was gradually eclipsed by a more pronounced concern with its narrative packaging within popular fiction film formats. This can be seen in Gillo Pontecorvo's *Operación Ogro* (1980). Dealing with the assassination in 1973 by ETA of Admiral Luis Carrero Blanco, Franco's right-hand man and the embodiment of Francoist *continuismo*, the film had an almost ready-made script and cast for a high-octane action movie. The historical importance and controversy surrounding its subject matter and its thriller/special mission framework ensured the film's commercial success. However, while its relatively sober, 'respectful' narrative treatment of the subject was generally welcomed, its underlying endorsement of ETA terror was criticised and its historical and contextual accuracy widely questioned (Caparrós Lera 1992: 189–90) (see chapter 4: Basque cinema).

The biopic
From the mid-1980s onwards, the historical film is characterised by a more personalised approach to history. This is typified by the proliferation and popularity of historical reconstructions in the form of the biopic.

Reconstructing the *Caudillo*
The figure of Franco was inevitably a major focus of interest for biographers and historians during the transition period. Films such as Patino's *Caudillo* (1976) had already offered a documentary assessment of Franco based on interviews with a range of people that knew him. Like Herralde's *Raza, el espíritu de Franco* (1977) as well as García Sánchez's and Linares's monographic study of 'La Pasionaria' in *Dolores (1980)*, *Caudillo* offered another film contribution to the boom in documentary biographies of key political figures. In the world of print, such investigations were complemented by a rush of (previously rare) autobiographical memoirs of former Francoist politicians during the transition (Labanyi 1995: 402).

However, by the turn of the decade, the practice of documentary montage and the full-length documentary feature virtually disappeared from Spanish screens (Monterde 1993: 155). Spanish audiences were demanding something different (Besas 1985: 196). The boundaries between fact and fiction became even more blurred as filmmakers increasingly sought to package their historical reconstructions in more varied and complex fictional formats.

Dragon Rapide (1986) is one of the few films to have attempted a factual reconstruction of any part of the Spanish Civil War in the two decades since the death of Franco. Jaime Camino's film is ostensibly a historical reconstruction of the days leading up to the Nationalist uprising. A framework of investigative journalism establishes the hermeneutics of the thriller and once again the ambiguities of this genre are apparent in the tension between the dramatic narrative structure and other strategies seeking to present the film as objective history. The décor is broadly simple and unobtrusive, minimising nostalgic indulgence in period iconography. The sensationalist exploitation of dramatic events is avoided – the murder of Calvo Sotelo, for example, is not shown. At the same time, periodic departures from the central plot focus on the authenticating strand of an orchestra rehearsal led by Pau Casals for a performance which was curtailed by the news of the uprising. *Dragon Rapide*'s dominant agenda, however, is biographical, privileging the personal and psychological profile of Franco over political and ideological analysis of the conspiracy, and giving the film a strong biopic dimension.

Through a series of carefully observed military, conspiratorial and especially domestic sequences, the film constructs an ironic representation of the Caudillo (Juan Diego). He is portrayed as the embodiment of physical, emotional and psychological repression through the self-control, detachment and obsessive fastidiousness which characterise his professional conduct and family relations, daily routine, posture and mannerisms. Both acting style and framing (frequent long shots which isolate Franco within his surroundings) emphasise the artificiality and restraint of this unusual figure.

More recent films appropriate the cardboard cutout version of Franco to reconstruct the Caudillo as caricature according to popular mythology. Antonio Mercero's *Espérame en el cielo* (1987) adopts a comic fictional format eschewing any pretence of documentary realism and became one of the most successful Spanish films in 1988, ranking third at the box office (Alberich 1991: 129). The film's narrative structure rests upon the supposition that Franco had been substituted at all key official functions by Paulino Alonso (played by popular comic actor José Soriano), a lookalike who was kept prisoner in the El Pardo palace. The situation lends itself to a series of comic scenes as Paulino is trained to imitate Franco by adopting his voice, gait, mannerisms and habits – for example, walking up and down with his arm attached to a pulley which periodically raises it in a characteristic salute to the public. The film also touches tangentially on characteristic practices of the period, such as the provision of copious packed lunches to encourage crowds to attend the dictator's public appearances. The representation of Franco thus recuperates a range of popular conceptions of the personal idiosyncrasies of the Caudillo to create a biting satire.

Reinventions of the Caudillo continue to be a source of fascination in the 1990s as Vázquez Montalbán demonstrated in his *Autobiografía del general Franco* (1993), which mixes fiction and documentary sources within the printed biographical genre. Francisco Regueiro's *Madregilda* (1993) makes further incursions into the realms of fantasy and collective myth to produce a highly personal – some might argue over-exuberant and self-indulgent – film. Although the dialogue is based on the dictator's actual words taken from *No-Do* newsreels, *Madregilda*'s psychological portrait of Franco is neither biographical nor historical. The film is set in a cold, mid-1940s winter in a Madrid which Regueiro has described as Dickensian, alluding to the atmosphere of fear and secrecy which characterises its various underworld locations. The two key pivots of the film are the cinema release of the notorious film *Gilda* (Charles Vidor 1946) and Franco's regular meetings with three friends from the Africa campaign in a Madrid bar to play a card game of *mus* every first Friday of the month. The film focuses on fictional events leading up to the repeated idea of Franco's replacement by a lookalike following his supposed assassination in 1950. When Miguel, the son of one of the *mus*-players (Captain Longinos) sees the figure of *Gilda*, he thinks he recognises his supposedly dead mother in the form of Rita Hayworth. The Hayworth character then subsequently steps out of the screen as Ángeles to walk the streets of Madrid and to organise Franco's assassination. However, it is finally Captain Longinos (Gilda/Ángeles's husband) who pulls the trigger on discovering that it was Franco that gave the order to rape his wife during the war.

By using cinema as the focus of this dark tale, the film draws attention to its own status as historical fantasy and places iconographic figures centre stage in the shape of the two principal mythical characters, Franco and Gilda (Rita Hayworth), which are both demystified and remystified (Fontenla 1993: 23). At the extremes of this baroque fantasy world, however, the film clearly connects with another plane of reality in which, according to Juan Luis Galiardo, it captures 'nuestro propio *esperpento*. Es un cine de identidad nacional' (our own esperpento. It's a film about national identity) (Galiardo cited in Montero 1993: 21). Franco is reduced to a caricature, a ridiculously childlike despot who cheats at cards, sits in the loo swapping pictures of Snow White with Longinos or cries over a tin of condensed milk in 'la más corrosiva y demoledora visión del dictador en la intimidad – y también del franquismo cotidiano – que jamás haya dado el cine español' (Spanish cinema's most corrosive and devastating vision of the private life of the dictator and of everyday Francoism) (Torreiro 1993: 34). However, the film's abandonment of traditional narrative structure and its mix of reality and dream-fiction make for a complexity of story and style which are compounded by a consistent refusal to privilege audience identification with any one character. A powerful, suggestive film, despite enthusiastic critical responses, *Madregilda* performed disappointingly at the box office.

Popular myths

As noted above, recent sardonic reinventions of the Caudillo contrast significantly with the triumphalist images of Franco in classic treatments such as *Raza* (1941). The latter type of film, which dominated the early postwar official cinema, focused on symbolic or mythical individual 'heroes' embodying the nation's imperial aspirations and 'eternal values'. This subgenre has been reappropriated and redirected in a number of highly popular biopics, focusing on figures whose marginalisation and persecution under Francoism elevated them to the status of popular heroes and mythical figures.

For example, Carlos Saura's *Llanto por un bandido* (1963) is an ambitious, if arguably flawed pre-democratic precursor of the subgenre. His film, set in 1820s Andalusia amid the chaos arising from the tensions between the oppressive regime of Fernando VII and his liberal opponents, featured the legendary bandit, 'el Tempranillo', José María Hinojosa. The film yielded a number of contemporary parallels, most tellingly between 'el Tempranillo' and Franco himself, thus perversely casting the dictator as a kind of 'glorified bandit' (D'Lugo 1991: 47–8). Its most challenging aspect, however, is its deconstructive examination of historical representation and the manipulation of the popular image of the idealised heroic individual, used to serve the interests of a privileged social and political class (D'Lugo 1991: 49–53).

Vicente Aranda also takes a deconstructive approach to the manipulation of popular myth in his extremely popular two-part biopic *El Lute: camina o revienta* (1987) and *El Lute II: Mañana seré libre* (1988), the first of which became the highest grossing Spanish film in 1987 (Alberich 1991: 101). The films concern the legendary *quinqui* (delinquent) Eleuterio Sánchez who became the focus of an obsessive pursuit by the Francoist authorities and the object of massive popular interest in the 1960s. Aranda's hybrid combination of period drama, thriller and social realism reveals how the criminal career and media profile of this petty thief were manipulated and exploited by the authorities as a diversionary tactic at a time of political unrest.

Set in the underworld of 1960s delinquency, and drawing on El

Contemporary Spanish cinema

Lute's own memoirs, the films trace his progress from early petty crime and domestic affairs to his elevation as folk hero. The always conflictive relationship between gypsy culture and the authorities, particularly the Civil Guard, is introduced in the early stages of the first film when the hero's shanty house or *chabola* is bulldozed to the ground as a result of his refusal to pay protection monies to police-snout Colorín. The contextualisation of his involvement in more serious crime (the robbery of a jeweller's shop in which a man is shot by one of his friends) and his subsequent arrest (and death sentence, later commuted) clearly position El Lute as a victim of social and political circumstances. The causal relationship between his criminal activities and his social and economic position at the bottom of the social ladder is emphasised by a series of emotive sequences showing the demolition of his home, unsuccessful attempts with his heavily pregnant wife to make a living through the sale of tin pots and pans and his arrest for stealing chickens. Maximum coverage of the jewellery robbery becomes a diversionary strategy to distract attention from contemporary student strikes, and the violence, torture and humiliation to which Lute is subjected in police custody present a clearly critical image of a corrupt and abusive police and judicial system. Compared to the strongly realist and political tone of the first instalment, the second took a more fictionalised, folkloric approach, adopting a more pronounced thriller profile. Although the film included, as Caparrós Lera disapprovingly remarks, 'numerosas concesiones eróticas y violentas' (numerous concessions to violence and eroticism), it delivered a resounding critique of the Franco regime and its brutal treatment of the Spanish gypsy population (Caparrós Lera 1992: 317).

Juan Antonio Bardem's film *Lorca, muerte de un poeta* (1987), made for television, brought Spain's leading modern poet Federico García Lorca to the screen. Well-established as a major literary figure in the 1930s, Lorca had been particularly associated with the collection and re-evaluation of traditional popular cultural forms of music and verse and their incorporation into his own dramatic and poetic work. His interest in making both contemporary and classical theatre available to the population at large was also well-known through his involvement in the travelling theatre group *La Barraca*. Lorca's notorious assassination at the hands of Falangist extremists at the beginning of the Civil War as a result of his Republican sympathies and homosexual orientation transformed him into a cultural icon for liberal, popular and intellectual classes alike throughout the world.

The appeal of *Lorca, muerte de un poeta* (1987) centres on the combination of the careful reconstruction of the events and circumstances surrounding Lorca's execution in 1936, (drawing on Ian Gibson's investigative study), with the hermeneutics of a politically-loaded thriller. The collaboration on the production of both

Gibson and Mario Camus no doubt contributed to the film's ability to combine a strong sense of historical accuracy with the visual allure of the period look. This was evoked in an effective reconstruction of pre-1930s middle-class bohemia as well as Madrid's Residencia de Estudiantes, in which the creative energies of Lorca, Dalí and Buñuel first began to coalesce (Caparrós Lera 1992: 305–6). Despite its slightly hagiographic tone, Bardem's balanced, well-structured and sympathetic film makes an important contribution to the post-Franco project of retrieving a dispersed cultural heritage and reappraising those leading literary and artistic figures suppressed by Francoism.

Cultural retrieval: Carlos Saura and the reinscription of cultural identity

The recuperation of Spain's cultural heritage partially responds to the need to retrieve a literary, artistic and historical past manipulated and misappropriated by Francoism in order to reinstate and reinterpret its significance. It also importantly indicates the coexistence of a strong desire for cultural continuity alongside the rhetoric of breaking with the past, which characterised the transition period.

In the very different cultural and political context of democratic Spain, directors whose names had been closely linked with an oppositional cinema during the dictatorship faced the challenge of finding new approaches to their work. For some (such as Bardem and Saura) the project of cultural recuperation provided one of a number of foci for their work in the post-Franco period. Some critics have seen this thematic and aesthetic shift as evidence of the depoliticisation and commercialisation of previously committed *auteurs* and such accusations have been levelled at Carlos Saura's work of the post-Franco period (Gubern, *et al.* 1994: 425–6 & 441). Others have recognised the continuation of a characteristically critical discursive activity within the very different generic frameworks of Saura's films of the 1980s and 1990s (D'Lugo 1991: 192–224).

The release of a trilogy of films exploring Saura's long-standing interest in flamenco dance appeared to signal a radical *volte face*. Far from his neorealist exposés of the sixties and his complex metaphorical examinations of the repressive Francoist family of his seventies films, Saura seemed to have opted for the middlebrow mainstream. *Bodas de sangre* (1981), *Carmen* (1983) and *El amor brujo* (1986) turned to literary and musical classics for narrative frameworks within which flamenco, dance and musical forms are recuperated from the cultural ghetto of the *españolada* film and the tourist *tablao*. Their elevation to an art form has been reaffirmed in his subsequent *Sevillanas* (1992) and *Flamenco* (1995). The 1980s dance trilogy, however, goes beyond this exercise in cultural retrieval to address a range of issues relating to identity and representation. Like flamenco, the three classics on which these films are based – García

Lorca's play, Manuel de Falla's ballet and Bizet's opera (following Mérimée's novel) – have all been institutionalised in one way or another as representations of Spanishness, which Saura now reappropriates and reinterprets.

As well as reappraising and recasting the flamenco tradition itself, his focus on performance and his reinterpretation of the classic originals demonstrate the separation between cultural production and cultural identity and the susceptibility of the both to reinvention. Again, drawing on the performance framework, the films engage critically with such issues as the operation of rigid social structures (*Bodas de sangre*) and the destructive attitudes and behaviour prompted by Spanish *machismo* and traditional constructions of male pride, jealousy, honour, etc. (*Carmen*). Saura's later musical-comedy-drama hybrid *¡Ay, Carmela!* (1990) also touches on flamenco – this time with its *canción española* offshoot, epitomised in the title song, which was one of the emblematic popular songs of the Republic during the Civil War. Here the film's dramatic climax has the effect of retrieving the *canción* from its reactionary, escapist expression in classic folkloric musicals. By deliberately subverting this traditional nostalgia mode, Saura reinstates the popular song as a symbol of resistance and a reaffirmation of solidarity and integrity. Following his controversial flamenco dance trilogy, in the late 1980s and early 1990s, Saura produced two films within the biopic genre. The first of these constitutes a rare and expensive incursion into the historical epic.

Historical epics in the style of *Novecento (1900)* (Bertolucci 1976) are a rarity in European cinema as a whole, mainly because of the high costs associated with large-scale historical productions. The Second Republic, Civil War and Francoism, which one might have expected to inspire film projects of similar type, were largely addressed within smaller-budget films like *Dragon Rapide*, which focused on very well-defined events or offered monographic studies of individual figures. Otherwise these events were covered by television serialisations which permitted lengthier, in-depth examinations of the period. When filmmakers did attempt such big-budget projects in the Spanish context, the results were usually disappointing. For example, amidst chaos and confusion in other aspects of the celebrations (Hooper 1995: 68–9), the 1992 fifth centenary of Columbus's voyage to America, failed to produce any successful historical reconstructions of the 'encuentro con las Américas' (the encounter with America). This was despite major injections of Spanish taxpayers' money into film projects. Ridley Scott's co-produced *1492: La conquista del paraíso* (1992), for example, received a highly controversial 200 million peseta investment from the Spanish Ministry of Culture (about a fifth of its budget); the project backed by the Salkind brothers, *Christopher Columbus: The discovery* (1992), was also supported by the *Quincentenario* fund. Spanish-made films set in the period stuck to more familiar comedic territory. Despite a lengthy opening historical orientation in voiceover, José Luis Cuerda's *La marrana* (1992), which also received *Quincentenario* funding, resembles a road movie set in the fifteenth century. It draws freely on the Spanish picaresque tradition and, though starring well-known comic actors Alfredo Landa and Antonio Resines, it remains little more than a flimsy scatological comedy.

In terms of Spanish filmmaking, then, the epic dimensions of Carlos Saura's *El Dorado* (1988) are a rarity and clearly demonstrate the risks attaching to such projects. In 1989, John Hopewell observed that Hollywood's domination of the cinema in Spain had americanised the tastes of Spanish cinema audiences and raised expectations of a comparable level of spectacle in domestic films, an observation endorsed by producer Andrés Vicente Gómez's view that European cinema depends on the combination of 'espectáculo más cine de autor' (spectacle plus *auteur* cinema) (Hopewell 1989: 419). *El Dorado* is a clear example of this formula. Directed by Spain's foremost living *auteur*, and with a budget of 1,050 million pesetas, which permitted exotic locations, a huge cast and detailed period accuracy in sets and décor, the film became Spanish cinema's most expensive production to date. *El Dorado* constituted one of the few attempts to debunk some of the mystifications surrounding the colonisation of the Americas, which were so consistently promoted and reaffirmed under Francoism. Inspired by the Werner Herzog film of 1972, *Aguirre, der Zorn Gottes/Aguirre, la cólera de Dios* and Ramón Sender's novel, *La aventura equinoccial de Lope de Aguirre*, Saura's epic represents history in biographical mode and traces Lope de Aguirre's 1560 expedition to search for El Dorado in Peru. The film focuses on the conquistador's rise, through a succession of plots, counter-plots and brutal killings, to Príncipe de Perú/Chile (Caparrós Lera 1992: 318). Although the film was quite well received by the critics, its Cannes profile as 'académica y shakesperiana' (academic and Shakespearian) gained it no awards at the Festival and failed to inspire much public interest. And when compared to Herzog's less grandiose though more evocative and magical version, Saura's rendition appeared rather detached and pedestrian and though beautifully photographed, lacking in dramatic focus and energy. Although it came second to the massively successful *Mujeres al borde de un ataque de nervios* (Almodóvar 1988), *El Dorado* performed disappointingly at the box-office, taking less than a fifth of its budget (177.114.412 pesetas) in its first year and becoming yet another example of the much-criticised film-funding policy of the Socialist Ministry of Culture (Alberich 1991: 129).

Saura followed *El Dorado*, perhaps surprisingly, with another excursion into the historical biopic with *La noche oscura* (1988). A much more intimate, smaller-scale production (though still costly), the film attempts to recreate the life and work of sixteenth century

El Dorado, Carlos Saura, 1988   **2**

mystic poet San Juan de la Cruz. It focuses mainly on his nine-month imprisonment in a convent in Toledo as a result of his reformist activities, where he is subjected to extremes of deprivation as well as mental and physical abuse. The spectator accesses the subject via a form of interior monologue in which the poet enters into a dialogue with his own darkest fears and temptations, fore-grounding both the sensuality and the spirituality of his work. Sadly, though perhaps not surprisingly, given its subject, theatrical *mise-en-scène* and 'intellectual' tone, the film did not do well. Indeed, as Saura himself admits: 'Fue un desastre del cual estoy orgul-losísimo.' (It was a disaster of which I'm immensely proud) (Castro 1996: 65). After the even larger scale disaster of *El Dorado* and now this, Saura appeared to be entering a downward spiral of critical and financial flops. He managed to retrieve the situation, however, and indeed make money at the box-office by returning to his musical territory with the much more successful and engaging *!Ay, Carmela!* (1990).

Reimag(in)ing the past

The majority of post-Franco historical films concern fictional characters and events set against the background of a particular historical moment or period, most prominently the Republic, Civil War and particularly the first postwar decade of Francoism. Although the use of fiction film does not preclude the fulfilment of a historical realist function (as Italian neorealism demonstrated in its mediation of postwar Italy or the British New Wave cinema in the UK), the extent to which these films engage with their historical context varies tremendously. In 'historical' or 'period' cinema the relationship between the spectator and history is mediated by a hierarchy of narrative and stylistic filters which in themselves present a series of representational problems and contradictions. These filtering or mediating devices in Spanish period cinema of the 1980s and 1990s are considered in the following sections which include discussion of the representational effects of the literary adaptation, the personalisation of historical memory, nostalgia and the revival of retrospective genres, the role of the rural genre, and the symbiotic relationship between the past and the present.

Literary adaptations: Socialist film policy and a *cine polivalente* (multipurpose cinema)

The 1983 Miró film legislation envisaged a Europeanisation of the Spanish cinema, which would simultaneously reaffirm Spanish cultural identity and promote a combination of high-quality films which showed commercial potential. This strategy clearly recognised the changing characteristics of Spanish cinema audiences in the 1980s. As Francesc Llinás observes, by the time of the transition, the traditionally large popular cinema audiences for low quality sex films and comedies were being drawn to television and home video. Increasingly, the new cinema-going public saw itself as middle-class, educated and liberal (Llinás 1986: 3). The cultural revival of the 1980s continued to appeal to these middle-class audiences beyond the boom in political film of the late seventies. An important part of this recuperative exercise was directed at the retrieval of Spain's cultural roots, embodied in the historical and artistic production of the past.

The new PSOE (Partido Socialista Obrero Español) legislation also emphasised the development of close links between television and the film industry, thus generating funding for film productions ultimately destined for the small screen. Dramatised monographic studies of particular cultural figures and periods were particularly suitable for such treatments. Bardem's *Lorca, muerte de un poeta* (1987), for example, made with funding from several European television channels, was produced as a six-hour television serial with a final section destined for cinema release. Literary adaptations, of course, also constituted one of the tried-and-tested formulae for both film and television productions and became the bedrock on which the government's policy of film subsidies in the 1980s rested.

The strategies introduced by Pilar Miró and continued by her successor at ICAA, Fernando Méndez-Leite, undeniably gave a much-needed boost to the Spanish film industry. However, numerous critics have remarked on the fact that the values enshrined within PSOE film policy produced a certain homogenisation of Spanish cinema in the 1980s and 1990s, both in terms of its 'look' and its middlebrow liberalism. Esteve Riambau has called it a 'cine polivalente' (multipurpose cinema), designed to fulfil a range of different market functions by adopting a standard formula usually consisting of ' (cine de autor + géneros + adaptación literaria + *star system* + *look* formal) en diversas proporciones pero con idéntica voluntad de polivalencia' ((auteur cinema + genre + literary adaptation + star system + formal look) in varying proportions but with the same multipurpose aim in mind) (Gubern, *et al.* 1994: 421). Riambau cites *El rey pasmado* (Imanol Uribe 1991) as a prime example of this formula (Gubern, *et al.* 1994: 419–21). The film is an adaptation of *Crónica del rey pasmado* (1989), by well-known historical novelist Gonzalo Torrente Ballester, whose work has been the subject of numerous television adaptations; Imanol Uribe is a recognised director with a reputation established on the basis of his very different earlier political films. The film's period setting looks back to a key historical and cultural moment which has acquired a mythical status in the formation of traditional Spanish cultural identity. On the one hand, the seventeenth century embodies the contradictions of the power and decadence of Spain's age of imperialism and the excesses of militant Catholicism in the shape of the infamous Inquisition. On the other, in cultural terms, the setting represents a Golden Age of Spanish literary and artistic production. The period has been repeatedly invoked as a benchmark for Spain's subsequent historical and cultural 'decline'. As regards the cast, *El rey pasmado* also reflects an essential concern with combining notions of quality, tradition and popular appeal. Alongside younger actors, such as Gabino Diego and María Barranco, two of the film's leading characters are played by veterans Fernando Fernán Gómez and Juan Diego, both quintessential figures of the Spanish star system and whose long-standing acting careers span performances in both comedy and drama. In all senses, *El rey pasmado* must be considered a prime example of the popular heritage film. It was a strong commercial and critical success, winning a series of Goyas, awarded by Spanish Film Academy. This example and others like it arguably owe their success in the domestic market to a combination of period nostalgia (inscribed within a visual style articulated through high quality production values), elements of comedy and a number of intimate, culture-specific references which generated a particular appeal amid the generalised dominance of US cinema.

El rey pasmado concerns an imaginary Spanish king – clearly modelled on Felipe IV. The narrative hinges on his sexual naivety, the restrictions imposed by court etiquette and a ridiculously strict Catholicism. The queen is sent to the royal marital bed with a nightgown with a strategically-positioned embroidered hole for the purposes of procreation. However, restricted access to the queen both

Reconstructing the past

stimulates the sexual passion of the young king and drives it underground. His first vision of female nudity – on a clandestine visit to a prostitute – ironically mimics Velázquez's painting *Venus de Roqueby* and launches him on a quest with the aim of seeing the queen naked. Sexual desire is thus restored to the confines of marriage, permitting the conventional satisfactions of classic narrative closure within the period/romantic comedy sub-genre. Nevertheless, the film successfully explores a theme central to both distant and more recent Spanish experience: the invidious and absurd effects of the imposition of a rigid authority and perverse moral code.

The flood of literary adaptations encouraged by PSOE film policy during the last decade also reflected a general trend towards the recuperation of Spain's cultural past. Similar concerns had been a central feature of Francoist cultural practices, where they coincided with the regime's reaffirmation of particular notions of national identity. However, post-Franco cinema demonstrates a contradictory relationship encompassing both rupture and continuity with the past. Literary adaptations, particularly during the transition and the early days of democracy, were concerned with the recuperation of authors who had been neglected and marginalised by Francoism – such as Galdós in *Tormento* (Olea 1974), Clarín in *La Regenta* (Suárez 1974), Valle-Inclán in *Divinas palabras* (García Sánchez 1987) – or writers whose work offered critical visions of Francoism, as in the case of Cela's *La colmena* (Camus 1982), Miguel Delibes's *Retrato de familia* and *El disputado voto del Sr. Cayo* (Giménez Rico 1976 and 1986 respectively) and his *Los santos inocentes* (Camus 1984), Martín Santos in *Tiempo de silencio* (Aranda 1986) and Juan Marsé in *Si te dicen que caí* (Aranda 1989).

More recently, there has been a growing interest in adapting contemporary writers for the screen. However, it is significant that these tend almost exclusively to be novels with period settings. Torrente Ballester's novel, adapted as *El rey pasmado* (Uribe 1991), set in the seventeenth century, has already been mentioned. Arturo Pérez Reverte's *El maestro de esgrima* (1992), adapted for cinema by Pedro Olea, is set at the end of the reign of Isabel II in the nineteenth century. Buero Vallejo's *Un soñador para un pueblo* was adapted by Josefina Molina in *Esquilache* (1989) and focuses on the eighteenth-century minister's attempts to introduce Enlightenment values into the Spain of Carlos III. As outlined earlier by Riambau, all of these films appear to reproduce the standardised, quality look of a *cine polivalente*. Interestingly, it is some of the older literary classics which provide the basis for some of the most challenging and original screen adaptations of literature in the 1990s. Gonzalo Suárez's *Don Juan en los infiernos* (1991), for example, combines grandiose spectacle with an original treatment and creates challenging new images. Pilar Miró's *El perro del hortelano* (1996), breaks new ground in Spanish cinema by taking Lope de Vega's original to the screen in verse (and gaining six Goya awards, including best director, for 1996). More surprising is the fact that the film has also attracted a substantial audience in a country in which screen versions of the literary classics have tended to do badly (Cristóbal 1997: 48).

La colmena and Los santos inocentes

Whilst many literary adaptations with large budgets funded by the Ministry of Culture through ICAA have been resounding failures (and have thus brought opprobrium on government film policy), some of them figure among the Spanish cinema's greatest popular and commercial successes. The most notable of these are undoubtedly *La colmena* (1982) and *Los santos inocentes* (1984). They were both made by Mario Camus, perhaps the Spanish director most consistently associated with film adaptations of literature focused on the dictatorship. Critical reaction to these films, however, has frequently been dismissive. In *Los santos inocentes*, for example, John Hopewell identifies the film's high production values and glossy surface as unconvincing and misleading, evoking a look which runs wholly counter to the narrative denunciation of 1960s rural squalour. He would no doubt regard both films as paradigmatic examples of what Riambau calls a *cine polivalente* (Hopewell 1986: 226–8; Hopewell 1989: 408–13).

A frequent criticism of screen adaptations of literature concerns the loss of specific qualities which were central to the impact of the original. The loss or change of character point of view has a particularly important effect on discursive activity and its successful translation into film language can be crucial to the positioning of the spectator in relation to the underlying thematics of the film. This is successfully demonstrated in Víctor Erice's *El sur*, where the intimate interiorisation of Estrella's psychological perspective – her exploration of myths of identity in the passage from childhood to adolescence – present in García Morales's original, is captured in the film's visual identification strategies. By contrast, both *La colmena* and *Los santos inocentes* undergo some quite radical shifts in perspective in their translation from page to screen. Whilst these changes produce more conventionally-stuctured and accessible film versions, the powerful synthesis between formal and narrative discourse in the originals is sacrificed.

For example, the first-person narrative of Delibes's novel *Los santos inocentes* is delivered through the words of the mentally-deficient, but sharply-observant Azarías in a carefully-constructed phonetic, lexical and syntactical recreation of his language and thought processes. In the film version, however, this perspective is limited to occasional point-of-view shots from Azarías's perspective, and the establishment of psychological empathy with the character at

3   *Los santos inocentes*, Mario Camus, 1984

certain key moments such as the point at which his pet kite is shot dead by the *señorito*. The dominant point of view is that of a detached, omniscient observer, reinforced by an episodic narrative structure comprising sections, each bearing the name of its central character. The crucial sharing of Azarías's perspective on events is displaced, however, by a kind of spectatorial superiority. Point of view undergoes a similarly detrimental transformation in the film version of *La colmena*. The rich network of some 350 characters in the novel is necessarily reduced to a smaller number of protagonists and the proliferation of multiple viewpoints is largely sacrificed in exchange for the elevation of the Martín Marcos character to a more conventionally central narrative position. Furthermore, the temporal complexities of the novel are replaced by a conventional chronological order of events in the film. These alterations align Camus's film with a classic narrative model, prioritising a simplified narrative coherence over some of the essential qualities of Cela's original. Here, spatial and temporal fragmentation and disorientation and the hive-like existence of post-war Madrid inscribe a strong sense of existential futility within the form of the novel itself.

The predominance of adaptations of earlier literary works in post-Franco historical cinema also means that the historical period these films recreate is focused through a double filter: The film is a representation of a novel or play which in turn is a representation of an interpretation of the period. The distancing effect of this sort of representational layering can bring together an interesting range of temporal perspectives on the subject matter of the film. In the case of *La colmena*, for example, the film released in 1982 is a version of a novel written between 1945 and 1950, first published in Argentina in 1951 (and only some years later in Spain), which offers the multiple perspectives of a vast set of characters on their experiences of the postwar atmosphere in early 1940s Madrid. A similar effect is produced by remakes of earlier films, such as Comencini's recent recreation of the 1954 classic *Marcelino pan y vino* (Ladislao Vajda). The imposition of multiple layers of interpretation between the historical subject and the spectator introduces a series of contradictory effects – simultaneously inviting spectator identification and creating a distance which may be critical, but which also may serve to obfuscate the reality ostensibly accessed. Fredric Jameson may be correct to argue that 'intertextuality becomes a built-in feature of the aesthetic effect, and ... the operator of a new connotation of "pastness" and pseudo-historical depth, in which the history of aesthetic styles displaces "real" history' (Jameson 1993: 76).

The retro film

Jameson also argues that a similar distancing effect is created by the proliferation of *la mode rétro* in contemporary Western cinema, i.e. the recuperation of retrospective cinematic genres and styles, which, for him, approaches 'the "past" through stylistic connotation, conveying "pastness" by the glossy qualities of the image, and "1930s-ness" or "1950s-ness" by the attributes of fashion' (Jameson 1993: 75). Spanish cinema's enthusiastic embrace of historical drama clearly reflects this generalised proliferation of the 'nostalgia film' and the widespread emphasis on the surface qualities of the image. Such images of the past, particularly of the 1930s, 1940s and 1950s, are characterised by a distinctive visual style, relying largely on their accurate representation of period *mise-en-scène* in costumes and décor. It is the emphasis on style which introduces the nostalgic appeal into films which focus on historical moments and experiences which are otherwise aesthetically unappealing: war, deprivation, repression. These images of the past, however, also embody utopian notions of unity, commitment, clear moral and political choices, etc. which contrast with the *desencanto* (disillusionment) and disorientation of the transition period and after. This stress on the fictitious unity of the past and the aesthetic effacement of conflict and division, produces, according to Monterde, 'un cine del reconocimiento que no del conocimiento ... un cine que no pretende tanto la reflexión como la adhesión' (a cinema of recognition rather than discovery ... a cinema more interested in confirmation than reflection) (Monterde 1993: 23).

The aesthetics of nostalgia characterise much of Spain's period film drama from the early 1980s onwards, but it is particularly pronounced – and sometimes even self-reflexively exploited – in the style and iconography of classic Hollywood *film noir* and the recent revival of Spain's emblematic domestic film genre of the *canción española* musical. Chávarri's *Las cosas del querer* (1989) provides a particularly interesting instance of how history is treated within the genre.

Las cosas del querer

Jaime Chávarri's varied directorial career – ranging from his sharply ironic documentary examination of the Panero brothers and their mother in *El desencanto* (1976) to his 1984 adaptation of Fernando Fernán Gómez's play *Las bicicletas son para el verano*, featuring the experience of a Madrid middle-class, liberal family during the Civil War – is clearly reflected in the multi-faceted nature of *Las cosas del querer* (1989). At one level, the film ostentatiously parades period costume and décor and the music of the 1930s and 1940s (more than a dozen songs immortalised by Concha Piquer and Miguel de Molina). This is achieved by way of a sumptuous indulgence in the retro look, narratively justified by its location within the world of performance and the onstage spectacle and backstage drama of the performers. However, the film self-reflexively digs beneath the surface gloss to reveal the sordid underbelly of the world of the *canción española*. The narrative substrata of the film comprise a series of critical representations of the moral, social and political dynamics of postwar Spain.

The film concerns the triangular relationship between pianist Juan, and singers Pepita and Mario from their initial brief encounter during the war, their establishment as a performing act, the friendship of the three protagonists and the love affair between Juan and Pepita until Mario is finally driven into exile because of his homosexuality. Gender and sexual politics are addressed both through the internal narrative and formal characteristics of the film and through partial biographical reference to Miguel de Molina whose Republicanism and homosexuality also led to his exile from Spain. The film examines the double standards in attitudes towards homosexuality in the postwar period, particularly in the world of the *canción española*, where camp excess in the theatrical or musical performance context was paradoxically accepted and even encouraged despite the general condemnation and persecution of homosexuality. On several occasions, traditional cinematic practices are subverted. The visual excess and charged sensuality of the stage (and occasionally off-stage) delivery of the traditional songs is particularly emphasised. And whereas specularisation is an activity more usually associated with the imaging of the female figure, here there are notable instances of specularisation of the male figure in performance. Mario's delivery of *Te lo juro yo* (León/Quiroga) in rehearsal, accompanied by Juan on piano, clearly reveals the underlying conflict of desires and emotions between the three main male characters through the pattern of alternating shots, close-ups and framing. In the sequence in which Mario performs *La bien pagá* (Perelló/Mostazo), self-conscious point of view shots and the exchange of looks clearly establish the surrounding tensions, contradictions and hypocrisy and foreshadow the drama to follow (Morgan 1995: 159–60). Initially courted and patronised by the aristocratic family of his would-be lover, when Mario spurns his affections, the family's influential position secures his removal into exile after a severe beating by police agents. The operation of an underground sexual economy is also sharply focused through the treatment of Pepita's stage and screen career, made possible through the patronage of a series of powerful men in exchange for sexual favours.

Personalisation of Historical Memory

Monterde's criticism of contemporary Spanish historical film also focuses on its highly-personalised perspectives. However, it is important to remember that the collective cultural memory of the Civil War and Francoism from the point of view of the losers is inevitably located mainly within the private sphere. This is so since the opposition to the regime was effectively excluded from the public domain of political and economic life. Moreover, the operation of censorship severely limited its cultural production to the restricted codes of metaphor, symbolism and allusion. Following the lifting of censorship, the filmic articulation of that experience continued to bear the influence of those restricted codes, which found themselves reflected in the personalised register of much post-Franco period drama. This personalisation plays an important role in the reinstatement of previously disenfranchised subjectivities. It also carries an implicit recognition that the lived experience of historical reality is intrinsically subjective. In the 1980s and 1990s, history is overwhelmingly represented in terms of the domestic, the everyday, and focused from the point of view of the individual, the family or other small groups and communities rather than through documentary analyses and broad historical reconstructions of the epic type.

The essential model for the Franco regime was synthesised in the image of the traditional family. Its rigid patriarchal order and paternalistic operation prescribed clearly defined roles and relations of class, gender, power and authority and its sanctity and cohesion were reproduced time and again within the narratives of official cinema. It was subsequently appropriated by filmmakers of the 1970s seeking to offer alternative visions of contemporary Spain, and for whom it became a central metaphor. The ultra-conservative (Francoist) family was shown to be repressive, dysfunctional and anachronistic and was easily read as a microcosm of the state, as in Carlos Saura's *La prima Angélica* (1973), *Cría cuervos* (1975) and *Mamá cumple cien años* (1979), or Gutiérrez Aragón's *Demonios en el jardín* (1982). In post-Franco cinema, the family, made redundant by the lifting of censorship, largely loses its metaphorical dimensions and assumes its role as one of the main vehicles for the recollection of the past (particularly the period of the Civil War) from the mid-1970s with films such as *Las largas vacaciones del '36* (Camino 1976) and *Retrato de familia* (Giménez Rico 1976), through the 1980s with *Las bicicletas son para el verano* (Chávarri 1984), and right into the 1990s with films such as *El largo invierno* (Camino 1991). Whilst the family framework appears to give recognition to popular memory of the period, however, its scope is clearly limited. The families represented are predominantly middle-class and the reduction of the historical moment to the domestic and the affective, in a curious mixture of denunciation and nostalgia, obscures the unexplored political and ideological issues of the war and Francoism.

This is not to say that these films are uncritical of the social conditions of the war and postwar period. As the habit of self-censorship slowly recedes, image and narrative bring to the screen increasingly more outspoken critical denunciation of hardships, deprivations and injustices, and the repressive and often violent activities of the authorities and their impact on individuals and communities. These critical images are reproduced to both comic and dramatic effect in a range of films dealing with the family or other small community groups. Hunger is the most common indicator of wartime deprivation, whether in the shared enjoyment of scant slices of chorizo and fantasies about peacetime dishes (*¡Ay, Carmela!*, Saura 1990), the collective experience of guilt and humiliation on discovering that the whole family has been stealing a spoonful of lentils from the daily ration in *Las bicicletas son para el verano* (Chávarri 1984) or blackmarketeeering during the 'años de hambre' (hunger years) in *Pim, pam, pum ... ¡fuego!* (Pedro Olea 1975) or *Demonios en el jardín* (Gutiérrez Aragón 1982).

The authorities are usually represented through damning images of their repressive activities and abuse of power. The moral values and influence of the Catholic Church, for example, are variously presented as hypocritical, as in the behaviour of the Cardinal in *Padre nuestro* (Regueiro 1985), or absurd, as in *La corte de Faraón* (García Sánchez 1985), and police violence is denounced, as in *El Lute*. Right-wing extremism is represented through the belligerence of Falangist fanaticism, as, for example, in the case of the vulnerable individuals who are taunted and forced to sing the nationalists' emblematic song *Cara al sol* in *Las cosas del querer*, or in the background and activities of right-wing terrorists portrayed in *Camada negra* (Gutiérrez Aragón 1977). Domestic arrangements and strategies for survival offer glimpses of the dialectics of power and exploitation in operation, particularly through the dominance of the frequently interlinked underground economies of sex and privileges

Libertarias, Vicente Aranda, 1996   **4**

such as blackmarket food, professional influence, protection and recommendations as in *Pim, pam, pum ... ¡fuego!* (Olea 1975), *La colmena* (Camus 1982) or *La mitad del cielo* (Gutiérrez Aragón 1986).

Many of these films filter the recollected past from the point of view of characters who are in some way marginalised or disenfranchised. A whole range of social groups whose representation was excluded under Francoism is now recuperated into mainstream cinema: The manipulation and persecution of the gypsy community is foregrounded in *El Lute I* and *II*. Performing artists protagonise such films as *El viaje a ninguna parte* (Fernán Gómez 1986), *Las cosas del querer* (1989) and *¡Ay, Carmela!* (1990). The main protagonists of *Libertarias* (Aranda 1996) are prostitutes and nuns, and various urban casualties populate films such as Aranda's *Tiempo de silencio* (1986) and *Si te dicen que caí* (1989), or *La guerra de los locos* (Matjí 1987) where psychiatric patients are the main focus. Whilst there are major absences (particularly of ordinary urban working class people), the reintroduction of these previously excluded groups at least permits the exposure of some of divisions and conflicts which were hidden and effaced by Francoist inflections of capitalism and patriarchy.

Forming a continuum with 'the children of Franco' – the curious child protagonists of such oppositional films of the 1970s such as *El espíritu de la colmena* and *Cría cuervos*, introduced by a generation of directors, themselves children of Francoism born after the end of the War (Kinder 1983: 57–9) – the perspective on the past is often filtered through the eyes of children. Their innocent thirst for knowledge and explanations of the mysteries of adult behaviour

and events is the driving force behind films such as *El sur* (Erice 1988), *Demonios en el jardín* (Gutiérrez Aragón 1982) and *Las bicicletas son para el verano* (Chávarri 1984). Children perform a similar role in more recent films such as *Madregilda* (Regueiro 1993), where child protagonist Manuel wanders the boundary between reality and fantasy which characterises the film's sardonic perspective on postwar Madrid and Franco, or *Los años oscuros* (Arantxa Lazkano 1993) which captures the experience of childhood in the 1950s and the contrasting atmospheres of family, home and school, emphasised by the bilingual context of the Basque Country.

Politically marginalised or outlawed groups are restored to the big screen in a number of films. The continuation of resistance to Francoism after the end of the Civil War is represented in the guerilla activities of the *maquis* and the effect of their presence on local rural communities in *Los días del pasado* (1977) and *El corazón del bosque* (1979). Fernando Fernán Gómez's *Mambrú se fue a la guerra* (1986) features the phenomenon of the 'topos' (moles), Republicans who, for fear of reprisals, only began to emerge from their underground hideaways decades after the war and, in some cases, not until after the death of Franco. Political militancy is examined in *La fuga de Segovia* (1981) and *La noche más larga* (1991), political detainees in a 1970s Francoist women's prison feature in *Entre rojas* (Azucena Rodríguez 1995). In *Así como habían sido* (Andrés Linares 1986), political posturing and betrayal and a subsequent hypocritical nostalgia for the days of student militancy are contrasted with the quiet commitment of the genuine activist. Here, the psychological effects of political imprisonment turn Damián into a recluse following the amnesties of the late 1970s.

(Mis)Remembering the past

Cinema is a particularly apt medium for the expression of the subjective nature of recall and representation of the past because of the formal possibilities it offers (through editing, etc.) to disorientate the spectator in spatial and temporal terms by playing with the chronology of events or subjective points of view. These formal qualities of film had already been exploited by Carlos Saura's explorations of memory and representation in his work of the 1970s. *La prima Angélica* (1973) is yet to be surpassed for its innovative use of the flashback structure to capture the sense of stasis attributable to the repressive atmosphere of the post-Civil War period. Luis's repression as a result of his childhood experiences living with his Fascist relatives during the war – and, by extension, the repressive effect of Francoism on Spain's social, cultural and political development – are expressed visually through flashback sequences in which Luis as a child is played by the same adult (actor José Luis López Vázquez). Past and present are conflated in the psychology of Luis, who embodies the feelings of a generation who saw themselves as 'emotionally and politically stunted children' (Kinder 1983: 58), in a metaphorical representation of the inseparability of past and present in the Spanish transitional psyche.

The status of memory and testimony is also explicitly addressed by Saura's *Los ojos vendados* (1978), which questions the effect of the means of representation on the person or object represented. Based on Saura's experiences as a member of the Bertrand Russell Tribunal on the torture of political prisoners in Latin America, the film concerns a theatre director's membership of a similar tribunal where a woman wearing dark glasses and a headscarf recounts her experience in monotone. His sense of the theatricality of the event and her account lead him to reproduce it as a stage drama to draw attention to the dangers of representing reality and memory. The film questions not only the extent to which history can be faithfully represented, but also the nature and status of reality itself. These are questions which have continued to preoccupy Spanish cinema well into the 1990s.

In the transition period, the notion – both literal and metaphorical – of returning is a recurrent theme. Former exiles and other expatriate Spaniards return to Spain and visit places from their youth from which they have been long absent. This acts as an appropriate metaphor for the generalised cultural need to revisit and reassess the past. Marsha Kinder identifies Bardem's *Nunca pasa nada* (1963) as one of the first films to tentatively broach the subject of the returning exile in a small sequence towards the end of the film (1993: 280), and a number of such figures appear in films of the early seventies such as *El espíritu de la colmena* (1973) and *El amor del Capitán Brando* (1974). By the end of the 1970s, this theme had become a central narrative focus for films such as Gutiérrez Aragón's *El corazón del bosque* (1978), where an exiled Communist returns to convince a group of *maquis* to cease their activities. In broad terms, the return becomes a psychological necessity and the period of absence stands as a metaphor for the vacuum of the past which has been experienced also by those who stayed behind. For the returning exile, the *patria* (homeland) thus becomes the spatial representation of a past they hope to recapture. The therapeutic function of these attempts to recapture a lost past is as important for the fictional characters as it is as a cultural exercise for the Spanish psyche of the transition and after. In the films of the late seventies and early eighties, however, whilst the impetus to keep personal and cultural memory of the past is positively represented, regressive attempts to recreate the past are shown to be futile and destructive.

The transition period saw a plethora of films which captured the point of view of a postwar generation of men (and less prominently women) experiencing a kind of mid-life crisis directly linked to the moral and political repressions associated with their youth. With the end of the dictatorship these characters bemoaned their lost youth, and made futile attempts to recapture it through the resumption (usually unsuccessful) of sentimental relationships left unresolved from their past as in José Luis Garci's *Asignatura pendiente* (1977), perhaps the paradigm film of this group.

The most sentimental of these generational films is undoubtedly José Luis Garci's Oscar-winning *Volver a empezar* (1982), concerning the return to Spain and to his home town of Gijón of terminally sick, Nobel-prize-winning writer Antonio Miguel Albajara from the United States where he writes and lectures. The film is dedicated to this 'generación interrumpida' (fractured generation) whose lives were interrupted by the Civil War, but it is also about the brevity and fugacity of life in more universal terms. Antonio's return to Gijón is full of a sense of nostalgia and regret for a lost past, but the power of memory, recollection and symbols of the past to give back that which time (or events like the Civil War) take away is positively presented. Antonio briefly relives his youthful love affair with Elena, which both recognise can only be a precious *séjour* from their everyday lives today. The fantastical quality of their re-encounter is captured in the cinematic references of their lovers' notes to each other as 'Fred Astaire' and 'Ginger Rogers'. Antonio's recognition of the comforting function of the retreat into the past, in the words of Wordsworth's 'Intimations of Immortality', might also explain the obsessive retreat into the past in the cinema:

Aunque nada puede devolvernos los días de esplendor en la hierba, y la gloria en las flores, no debemos apenarnos. Al contrario, tenemos que buscar ánimos en el recuerdo (Though nothing can bring back the hour Of splendour in the grass, of glory in the flowers; We will grieve not, rather find Strength in what remains behind). (Quiller-Couch 1921:615)

By the late 1980s and early 1990s, a number of films demonstrate a marked preoccupation with the status of a personal and cultural history reconstructed from individual and collective memory. The flashback structure in a number of films in which characters reflect on or revisit the past specifically draws attention to the status of historical memory, showing it to be inevitably subjective, selective and unreliable. In *La noche más larga* (José Luis García Sánchez 1991) both Juan Tarna and Menéndez remark that dates and the sequences of events have become muddled as they recall events of the mid-1970s, over a meal on a train in 1990. The issue of memory is very specifically problematised in films of the late 1980s and 1990s such as *El túnel* (Antonio Drove 1988) and *El viaje a ninguna parte* (Fernando Fernán Gómez 1986) both of which focus on the inability of their protagonists to remember the past accurately. *El viaje a ninguna parte* concerns the conversations between Carlos Galván (José Sacristán), significantly a retired actor, and a psychiatrist at the old people's home in which he now resides (in 1973). A number of Galván's reminiscences, represented in flashback, are gradually revealed as inaccurate. At first, recalling the early days of his career as a member of an impoverished travelling theatre company throughout the dictatorship, they appear to be the confusions and misrememberings of an old man, but later they become imaginings and inventions. These include personal fantasies such as receiving acting awards which never happened and rubbing shoulders with stars he had only ever watched from afar in fashionable cafés. They even include inventions of 'historical' events such as the alleged visit of President Kennedy to Spain advising Franco to give up his *legionario* (legionnaire's) uniform and stop censoring the theatre! These imagined 'memories' are first presented as 'genuine' flashbacks and their unlikelihood only gradually increases to the point of obvious fantasy. The film thus draws attention to both the unreliability of memory and the disorientating verisimilitude of the moving image.

In Drove's *El túnel*, concerning the obsession of Juan Pablo Castel for a high-society woman (María Iribarne), whom he eventually marries, subjective point of view is stressed through the use of flashback. Castel's ability to recall the past accurately is severely questioned, especially by the husband of the victim. The film demonstrates the total unreliability of personal memory, a tendency towards fantasy and invention, and inability to perceive reality correctly. Castel assumes María betrays him sexually after seeing her enter the house with another man and seeing his light go quickly on and off. Blinded by *amour fou*, Castel becomes trapped in a nightmarish tunnel of jealousy and insecurity of his own making.

Fernando Fernán Gómez's *El mar y el tiempo* (1989) engages not only with the relationship between memory and the past, but also the influence on personal and collective memory of the images and behavioural models which are taken for granted. The film presents the spectator with an interestingly layered retrospection. Set in the 1960s, the film concerns the return from Argentina of Jesusín, who is Eusebio's (Fernando Fernán Gómez) exiled brother. Whilst Jesusín's encounter with Madrid in the 1960s demystifies his nostalgic recollections of the Republican Spain of his youth, the period setting of the film invites both nostalgic and critical responses to the sixties themselves and demonstrates how the identity of an era is determined by style, ideas and social behaviour. If Eusebio's children's generation and their ideological posturing oscillate between naive idealism and artificiality, the nostalgia for the alleged clarity and commitment of the 1930s is brought into sharp relief by the compromises both Eusebio and Jesusín have been prepared to make. Eusebio's livelihood and lifestyle are/were dependent on his involvement in blackmarketeering and on his share in a restaurant whose major partner is an Opus Dei member. He also turns a blind eye to his girlfriend's business affairs (including supplying prostitutes for aristocrats and various forms of wheeler-dealing and exploitation, disguised as modern, progressive initiatives). Jesusín's lifestyle in Argentina is dependent on similarly shady sources of income. Like Antonio in Garci's *Volver a empezar*, Jesusín's nostalgic return is a cathartic experience which enables him to return to his present day life in Argentina, which he now elevates to the same level of nostalgia as the memories of his youth. Stressing the displacement of reality by constructed images, his feelings of nostalgia are ironically transferred onto the stereotypical images of Argentinian national identity and the appeal of tango and *churrasco* (steak).

Relocating the past: the rural genre

Throughout the history of Spanish cinema, the rural genre has provided a focus for images of Spanish national identity for internal and external consumption. The essential characteristics of the rural context – proximity to nature, separation from urban life, cultural and economic underdevelopment and the traditional conservatism of its communities – endow it with an air both of pastness and atemporality. These qualities have made it a suitable location for various articulations of the ambiguous relationship between reality and fantasy and between linear time and atemporality.

In official Francoist cinema, Franco's notion of Spain as a timeless 'peaceful forest' (Kinder 1993: 348) was consistently reinforced by images of the rural idyll. Films such as *Nobleza baturra* (Juan de Orduña 1965), simultaneously 'naturalised' and reproduced the values and social structures of patriarchy on which the ideology of the regime rested. However, oppositional writing, and later film, appropriated the rural context for the elaboration of a critical discourse which established rural Spain as the spatial representation of stasis and repression. The rural came to be represented in terms of its material deprivation and anachronistic and repressive social structures. The feudal excesses of Francoist privilege and patriarchy have been variously explored in postwar novels such as Cela's *La familia de Pascual Duarte*, Sender's *Réquiem por un campesino español* and Delibes's *Los santos inocentes*, all of which have subsequently been adapted for the cinema. But, among non-literary adaptations, perhaps the most successful and important original film was José Luis Borau's *Furtivos* (1975).

Furtivos exposes the deceptive veneer of the Francoist rural idyll by revealing an underlying reality of ignorance, exploitation, cruelty and violence. Martina's bloody slaughter of the she-wolf prefigures the murder of the young woman who disrupts her incestuous relationship with her son and precipitates his final matricidal revenge. In similar fashion, the events of *Pascual Duarte* (Ricardo Franco 1975) subvert the harmonious utopia of the rural context and introduce the devastating effects of ignorance and matricidal violence. Both *Furtivos* and *Pascual Duarte* epitomise the 'tremendista' tradition of Spanish realism in which the ugliness, cruelty and the sordidness of reality are foregrounded both in form and *mise-en-scène*: poor-looking and dated costumes and furniture, dark interiors with dull lighting, claustrophobic framing, shooting and editing for slow pace, and even casting, e.g. the physical appearance of Martina (Lola Gaos) has been particularly commented upon elsewhere (Kinder 1993: 232–9). The raw-edged style and thematics of these films as well as their exposure of the latent violence beneath the bucolic surface introduce the radically subversive potential of the rural metaphor.

Another dimension of this subversive potential is established in films focusing on the figure of the *maquis* and the rural communities which supported them. One of the earliest films to capture the personalised point of view of the losers was *Los dias del pasado* (Mario Camus 1977). The narrative is focused from the point of view of Juana who has taken a teaching job in a small Asturian village in the hope of contacting her boyfriend who is with a group of *maquis* in the nearby mountains. The film's rhythm and pace, its scant lighting, sparse dialogues and claustrophobic framing convey the interminable waiting and the sense of stasis and emptiness which characterises the existence of those left behind and, by extension, the postwar atmosphere for the losers in the Civil War. Though lacking the self-reflexive engagement with cinema itself and the intellectual complexity of *El espíritu de la colmena* (Erice 1973), *Los días del pasado* develops its brand of historical realism through atmospheric evocation. It links the stasis and isolation of the rural community, its silence and monotony to the repressive political atmosphere of the postwar period. Juana's lost youth, her separation from her lover and the silent waiting and observation offer a symbolic psychological point of reference for young people of the same age watching the film in 1977, thus conflating the frustrations of both generations.

Los días del pasado was also the first film to introduce the previously banned subject of the *maquis* into a central narrative position. The isolation and mystique of the rural setting contribute to the elevation of these figures to the level of myth, marginally at first in such films as *El espíritu de la colmena*, and more explicitly in the transitional *Los días del pasado*. The phenomenon is developed and explored with greater complexity in *El corazón del bosque* (Gutiérrez Aragón 1978) in which *maquis* leader El Andarín – half man, half legend – is systematically mythified and dehumanised. The film's form and narrative, facilitated by the rural setting (the darkness created by dense forest, thick undergrowth and mist), reflect a blurring of the boundaries between fact and fantasy, which characterised both the image of the *maquis* and the context within which they operated.

Although retrospective images of rural repression and deprivation continue to figure in more recent films of the 1990s, from the 1980s the rural genre also begins to recover its utopian connotations – though dissociated now from the 'naturalisation' and reinforcement of patriarchal order which characterised its Francoist manifestations. John Hopewell already sees evidence of this change in Montxo Armendáriz's *Tasio* (1984):

One senses with *Tasio* that something in Spanish culture has changed. One of its key features, for example, is a sense of continuity which in the anti-Francoist cinema would have connoted monotony, a lack of vistas. Now it becomes a source of charm as characters, conversations and vistas repeat themselves from one section of the film to the next. Under Franco, the relation of environment to the individual was repressive; now it is far more symbiotic'. (1986: 235–6)

In the rural films of the 1980s and 1990s, the sense of continuity is often articulated through narratives spanning a succession of eras. *Tasio* is structured episodically around the stages in the life of charcoal-burner Tasio – as a schoolboy, an adolescent, an adult and an old man. The film stresses the centrality of the rural environment to his sense of identity, and the ageing Tasio's refusal to move to the capital to live with his daughter.

The nostalgic appeal of the rural environment as 'a source of identity and security' clearly responds to a contemporary sense of the loss of cultural roots (Hopewell 1986: 236). The rural context offers a spatial retreat from the contemporary dislocation of urban life in a range of quite disparate recent films. Víctor Erice's *El sol del membrillo* (1992), for example, chronicles realist painter Antonio López's dialogue with nature in the tranquillity of his walled garden in the heart of urban Tormellosa. In Pedro Almodóvar's urban comedies and melodramas characters escape to rural retreats. The ruined coastal village where he was born is a source of identity and comfort for Ricky in *!Átame!* (1989). The *pueblo* (home village) represents an escape from violence and materialism for grandmother and grandson in *¿Qué he hecho yo para merecer esto?* (1984) and for Leo it offers a restorative experience in *La flor de mi secreto* (1995). In *Mujeres al borde de un ataque de nervios* (1988), Pepa creates her own balcony farm in a bid to import some of the therapeutic qualities of ruralia into the urban environment.

In an era dominated by urban lifestyles, high technology, consumerism and materialism, the rural connotes appealing qualities of spirituality and continuity. The continuing gap in contemporary Spain between the social, economic and cultural realities of urban and rural communities makes this contrast all the more striking – the two worlds coexist, but remain separate as Gutiérrez Aragón demonstrates in *La mitad del cielo* (1986). In a powerful visual image of this synchronic coexistence of the two Spains, the monumentally

Tasio, Montxo Armendáriz, 1984

proportioned grandmother (Margarita Lozano), dressed in her traditional dark clothes and wooden clogs, walks determinedly down the middle of the M30, the low-angled shot endowing her figure with idiosyncratic dignity. The film seems to take a pessimistic view of the impossibility of integration, and the erosion by urban modernity of the values and spirituality embodied in the rural world. The grandmother joins her grand-daughter Rosa whose hard work, determination, enterprise and compromise have enabled her to carve out a life and successful business in the capital, but she experiences an increasing sense of incongruity and anachronism which finally drive her to leave. However, the film has a more optimistic coda as, following her death, the grandmother establishes a close spiritual relationship with Rosa's daughter Olvido with whom she converses from beyond the grave. This relationship captures the fluid movement between the mundane and the spiritual which traditionally characterises both the rural context and the world of the child. Adopting the child's perspective on reality, these conversations are presented as perfectly natural.

The particular qualities associated with the rural image, its embodiment of 'pastness' and its association with nature and spirituality connote a primitive, pre-industrial world untamed by urban consumerism. Against this background, a number of 'rural' films develop as a feature of the rural context the fluidity of the boundaries between the real and the fantastic. Such a dualism had already surfaced in some movies of the 1970s and was evident in Saura's work and in Erice's *El espíritu de la colmena* (1973). The mix

Reconstructing the past

of the real and the fantastic, the use of legends and fairytales as provocative correlatives of reality was also an integral part of the work of Manuel Gutiérrez Aragón (who also co-scripted *Furtivos*) and is evident in his *Camada negra* (1977) – an inversion of the Snow White tale (Torres 1985: 185) – *Sonámbulos* (1977), *El corazón del bosque* (1978), the magical realist *Feroz* (1984) with its human-bear protagonist, and *La mitad del cielo* (1986). In the context of this 'rural/fantasy' sub-grouping, we turn briefly to the work of one of Spain's younger directors who is fast developing a profile as an arthouse filmmaker and *auteur* in the 1990s: Julio Medem.

Redirecting the rural genre in the 1990s: *Vacas*

Julio Medem is one of the central figures of a thriving Basque cinema (see chapter 4) and his work is characteristically associated with a number of the identifying features of the rural genre: questions of continuity and change, latent violence, nature and spirituality, etc. Compared to the 'rural' films of the 1970s and 1980s mentioned above, Medem's first full-length feature film *Vacas* (1992) appears to take a more radical approach to the rural genre. The film subverts classic narrative in favour of an elliptical style within a four-part structure spanning three generations and over sixty years. It concerns the rivalry between two neighbouring Basque families, born of Manuel Irigibel's cowardly, feigned death at the Carlist war front in 1875, where his neighbour Mendiluze dies helping him to shoot at the enemy. The rivalry continues alongside Ignacio Irigibel's emigration to America with Juan Mendiluze's sister, right through to the return of Ignacio's son Pere (as a news photographer at the start of the Civil War) when Juan saves him from the firing squad. *Vacas* makes an important contribution to the post-autonomy project of cultural reconstruction, which was encouraged in the cinema by the particular funding structures established by the Basque Autonomous Government and from which Medem's debut feature film benefited. However, at the same time, the film is playfully aware of its own remystification of Basqueness. This is evident in its sardonic recycling of stereotypical images of national identity – for example, the characteristic red beret and scarf and the traditional competitive log-chopping of the *aizkolaris* – together with a self-conscious use of repetition. Notions of continuity and repetition are emphasised through the characterisation of members of the three generations, played by the same actors (including the visual joke of the 'chip off the old block'). The narrative also insists on the recurrence of strengths and weaknesses such as the *aizkolari* skills and cowardice in battle, and the immutable presence of the cows who silently witness the passage of time and the succession of events. The inscription of a range of traditional connotators of Basqueness within the narrative and *mise-en-scène* endows the film with a strong sense of cultural identity, at

Vacas, Julio Medem, 1992   **6**

the same time as whimsically drawing attention to its own recycling of stereotypes.

As with *Vacas*, Medem's subsequent films, *La ardilla roja* (1993)
and *Tierra* (1995), continue this redirection of the rural genre
whilst drawing on its essential characteristics. All three films to
some extent produce the effect of a fairytale which links them with
the whole gamut of articulations of the rural genre – from the
make-believe rural idylls of Francoist cinema to the darkly fantastical metaphors of oppositional films of the seventies such as *Furtivos*.
In all three films, this is achieved by a combination of style and
structure, most noticeably in the frequently disorientating effect of
travelling shots which adopt the point of view of animals or inani-
mate objects, or which depart from conventional narrative viewpoints to reflect more abstract motivations. In *Vacas*, the spectator
is positioned by imaginative camerawork to adopt the optical viewpoint of the cows, to follow a flying axe on its dizzy trajectory
through the air, to be sucked into the head of a cow or the hollow
trunk of a 'magical' tree, creating a world in which the unexpected
and the fantastical intrude on the realistic' (Yates 1993: 54–5). *La
ardilla roja* periodically adopts the travelling point of view of the
invisible red squirrel or follows flying objects, and in *Tierra* the
camera excavates the underground world of the insects affecting
wine production in the region where the film is set. All three films
are also characterised by the disruption of the pastoral and spiritual
tranquillity of the rural context by violence in its various forms of

war, rivalry, jealousy and madness, again forging a link with this darker aspect of both fairytale fantasy and rural genres.

With its location at the boundaries of reality and fantasy and its underlying darkness, the rural genre lends itself not only to the formal and narrative concerns of arthouse cinema, but also develops a link with more mainstream popular genres. At its simplest level, it provides a familiar context for the elaboration of tales of the supernatural, such as *El baile de las ánimas* (Pedro Carvajal 1993), *Martes de carnaval* (Pedro Carvajal and Fernando Bauluz 1991), or the TV series *Historias del otro lado*, almost invariably set in the past. In its more complex manifestations, it is capable of addressing a whole range of questions concerned with the complex nature of time and place and the elusive concept of reality itself. If the rural film has often been regarded abroad as a quintessentially Spanish genre (largely due to the international reputation of such film as *Furtivos*), its development and inflections since the mid-1970s (and beyond) clearly reflect the provisionality, fluidity and complexity of both generic classifications and their relationship to cultural identities.

Retrospective presents and contemporary pasts

Spanish film critics from a wide range of cultural and political standpoints bemoan the failure of recent Spanish cinema to address the contemporary moment. Fernando Alonso Barahona's argues that:

Lo que se echa en falta ... es una reflexión sobre los problemas contemporáneos. Esta desconexión entre el cine y la realidad actual es un grave problema creativo' (What is missing ... is a reflection on contemporary problems. This rift between cinema and contemporary reality is a serious creative problem). (1992: 188)

However, although direct engagement with contemporary issues in recent Spanish cinema is a rarity, contemporary perspectives and cultural preoccupations are very clearly inscribed within even the most retrospective film texts. The relationship between the past and the present in Spanish cinema – and in Spanish culture generally – is a complex one. Period film functions as a two-way mirror reflecting both images of the past and contemporary perspectives. The final section of this chapter examines the way in which film narratives set in the past are used as a metaphor for the present, and how cultural co-ordinates of the present have colonised films which are ostensibly representations of the past.

The practice of making oblique reference to the present by reference to the past was a well-developed strategy for commenting on contemporary issues which were otherwise taboo subjects during the Franco period. These practices were also continued well into the transition period, not only because of the delay in the abolition of censorship, but also because of the difficulty of abandoning familiar approaches and the well-established effectiveness of allusion. A number of historical films are characterised by what Monterde calls their 'presentización del pasado' (bringing the past into the present) (1993: 154) and parallels are readily implied or inferred between their period narratives and contemporary issues and situations. The conflation of past and present in this way can serve a doubly critical function, allowing the film to comment obliquely on the present whilst revealing, through the possibility of the analogy, its anachronism.

An example of this process was Pilar Miró's *El crimen de Cuenca* (1979), perhaps the most significant *cause célèbre* of military censorship during the reform period. The film was based on the true case of two shepherds wrongly condemned for murder on the strength of a confession extracted by torture. The film criticises all the agencies of law and authority, including Church, judiciary, Civil Guard and local worthies and shows highly graphic scenes of brutal torture; indeed, in this regard, Hopewell talks of Miró's images producing the effect of 'Sunday supplement sadism' (1986: 179). Although Miró claimed that the film was not a critique of the Civil Guard and, by implication, the military, these bodies thought otherwise and brought charges against the film under military law for defamation, demonstrating the continuing sensitivity of the paramilitary forces in Spain to such comparisons. When, in 1981, the Civil Guard was taken out of the jurisdiction of the military courts, the film was released to huge box-office success, demonstrating the positive effect of such notoriety on popular appeal.

The political developments of the transition and early democratic period are approached through the filter of period drama and reconstruction in both *La verdad sobre el caso Savolta* (Antonio Drove 1979) and *Esquilache* (Josefina Molina 1989). Drove's film treatment of Eduardo Mendoza's novel offers an interesting vision of the period of political transition through the prism of historical events occurring in Barcelona in 1917, where bosses keep their workers in line by hiring thugs to beat them up and if necessary, resorting to *pistoleros*. Molina's *Esquilache*, a classically filmed adaptation of Buero Vallejo's stage play *Un soñador para un pueblo*, chronicles the struggle of Carlos III's Prime Minister, Esquilache, to bring Enlightenment values to Spain in the second half of the eighteenth century and to introduce reforms which were steadfastly resisted by ingrained conservatism. Popular resistance focuses on the proclamation of a decree banning the use of capes and wide-brimmed hats in an attempt to increase safety on the street. Opposition is also fuelled by popular dislike of the fact that Esquilache was Italian. Produced in the midst of Spain's full entry into the then Common Market and the tensions within the Socialist government, there were inevitable parallels to be drawn with the present. The director refers to *Esquilache* as:

una reflexión sobre nuestro país que es válida tanto en el pasado como en el presente ... Aunque situados en el siglo XVIII, creo que los comportamientos y los personajes de la película remitirán al espectador a nuestra coyuntura actual' (a reflection on our country which is as valid for the present as it is for the past ... Although it is set in the XVIII century, I think the characters and behaviour in the film will encourage the spectator to make associations with the present moment in time). (Caparrós Lera 1992: 337)

Distancing the past

If the past appears to be colonising the present in contemporary Spanish cinema, the mark of the present (through the filtering devices that we have seen operating in the films discussed earlier in this chapter) is also clearly stamped on the film images of the past. Monterde argues that the dominant – though not exclusive – perspective on the past which emerges from post-Franco historical films corresponds to a contemporary agenda and reflects the political, cultural and production context of the transition and democratic Spain. In his study of Spanish historical cinema of the transition, he refers to the reformist climate of consensus politics in the transition period, dominated by an 'obsesivo centrismo que anulaba cualquier posición extremista (an obsessive centrism that excluded any extremist position) (1989: 56), and observed that, once censorship was lifted:

se impuso la ley de la conciliación y el consenso, aquélla que dice que nadie tuvo la culpa de nada y todos fuimos víctimas, cuando bien sabemos quienes fueron los culpables y quienes los victoriosos (curiosamente coincidentes) (the law of consensus and conciliation was imposed with the official line that no-one was to blame for anything and we were all victims, when we know very well who was to blame and who were the winners (surprisingly the same ones)). (1989: 57)

Whilst earlier political films such as *La fuga de Segovia* attempted a critical representation of ideological positions, later films appear to operate the discourse of political centrism in the democratic era. They tend to present political militancy as naive and immature (as in *La noche más larga*) or place their emphasis on the personal, emotional and psychological effects of repression or imprisonment (as in *Así como habían sido*, Andrés Linares 1986), rather than on an analysis of political and ideological allegiances.

Consensus politics and critical distance

By the 1990s a double dramatic filter and a marked sense of distance are interposed between the radicalism of the political context of the 1970s and the centrist perspectives of the democratic liberalism of the 1990s. *La noche más larga* (García Sánchez 1991), for example, recalls in flashback the events surrounding the last executions of three political militants (members of FRAP) under Francoism in 1975, through the recollections of their defending lawyer Juan Tarna and Menéndez, the *fiscal militar* (military prosecutor) of the time over a meal on a train in 1990. Familiar authenticating strategies accompany the opening credits: a montage of *No-Do* clips is ironically backed by the 1976 pop song *Mi querida España*, which simultaneously signals a critical perspective on the past and marks its temporal and ideological distance from the present. In line with Tarna's contemporary conclusion that at that time 'we were all mad', the militancy of the defendants is cast as ideologically naive, politically fanatical and organisationally incompetent. Significantly, only three of the five militants executed in 1975 are represented in the film, the absentees being the two members of ETA (Euzkadi ta Azkatasuna). Presumably the more developed political philosophy of ETA activists would have posed a greater problem for the film's discourse of political deflation than the militants portrayed (Torres 1994: 346). Menéndez's transformation from the embodiment of judicial corruption under Franco to sentimental apolitical businessman in the 1990s conforms to contemporary political metanarratives of liberalism, pluralism and centrist democracy from which extremist positions have been eradicated or rendered insignificant. An element of cynicism is introduced however in the representation of the posturing and political compromise of a 'progressive' left. The latter is portrayed as constructing its image of moderation and Europeanisation during both the death throes of the dictatorship and the complacent, self-satisfied centrism of the present.

Sombras en una batalla (Mario Camus 1993) also offers a distanced political perspective on the extremism of 1980s terrorism, referring in an oblique way to the activities of ETA and GAL (Grupos Antiterroristas de Liberación). Eschewing retrospective flashbacks, the film locates its point of view in the female protagonist who has established a new identity for herself. Her retreat from radical politics is disrupted by the reappearance of threatening figures from her militant past. However, whilst the film both condemns the politics of violence, it simultaneously promotes a vaguely ecological, utopian apoliticism which again reflects contemporary liberal centrism.

Within period film drama, set in the more distant past of the Republic, Civil War and early Francoism, the denunciation of social injustice finds itself in competition with the discourse of nostalgia inscribed within the strong visual allure of period settings and costumes and the glossy surface of high-quality production values. The fixing of the period look, however, also constitutes an important distancing device, locating repression, violence and injustice firmly in the past. Whilst images of hunger, repression, moral extremes, religious obsession, and so on present a critical view of the values and effects of Francoism, they also function as a measure of the distance which separates contemporary, democratic Spain from the repressive backwardness of the past. A discourse of self-congratulatory democratic liberalism is thus inscribed within their critique of the past. This is particularly apparent in later films, often highlighted through the use of a comic filter, which locate Francoist values and attitudes within the realms of the absurd, emphasising their excess and anachronism as in *La corte de Faraón* (García Sánchez 1985) and *La vaquilla* (Luis García Berlanga 1984). The combination of a comedy of distantiation and the nostalgic effects of period iconography create the image of a past made up of quaintly antiquated ideas and behaviour – simultaneously inspiring both fond recollection and critical laughter at its absurdity. A similar process is in operation in certain historical dramas set in earlier periods: *Jarrapellejos* (Giménez Rico 1987) offers a vision of rural *caciquismo* (the rule of local political bosses) in 1930s Galicia; in *El rey pasmado* (Uribe 1991), the hypocrisy of the moral and social codes of seventeenth century Spain is resoundingly satirised in a narrative focusing on the Church's absurd prohibition of the king's desire to see the queen naked, whilst cardinals take mistresses and the king may visit prostitutes with impunity.

An aura of pastness also characterises the shady margins of contemporary society represented in a number of recent films. The refusal or inability of their protagonists to conform to the social, moral and ethical norms of contemporary democratic society places them within an almost fantastical retrospective underworld. The socially marginal protagonists of *La madre muerta* (Bajo Ulloa 1993) inhabit a series of abandoned buildings, first a mansion and then a church with a dilapidated, period air. Their violent and unstable lifestyle is reflected and isolated within an almost gothic retrospective ambience. The underworld of *El detective y la muerte* (Gonzalo Suárez 1994) is similarly separated both from the contemporary context by its location within a spatial area characterised by its vaguely retrospective atemporality and an ambiguously fluid movement between reality and fantasy. A series of thrillers and psychological dramas with contemporary settings – including *Lola* (Bigas Luna 1986), *Intruso* (Aranda 1993) and *Mi hermano del alma* (Barroso 1993) – feature dark characters who also inhabit a symbolically dark and atemporal world. Significantly, these characters all reappear from the past life of one of the other main protagonists of the film to intrude on their present calm and ordered lifestyle, which they systematically disrupt and destroy through a combination of physical and psychological violence. Personal pasts, like historical pasts, can both be nostalgically seductive and conceal a buried memory and potential source of disruption and violence.

Synchronic reflections: *Yo soy esa* and *Belle Epoque*

Yo soy esa (Luis Sanz 1990) and *Belle Epoque* (Fernando Trueba 1992) are two of the most successful Spanish films of the 1990s and demonstrate in different modes the dialectical relationship between the past and the present and its articulation in period cinema.

Luis Sanz's *Yo soy esa*, designed as a star vehicle for Isabel Pantoja's cinema debut, was the most popular Spanish film of 1990. The film is ostensibly set in the present but the film-within-the-film structure plunges the spectator into a multi-layered narrative dominated by frequent slippages and overlap between the different planes of 'reality' and representation, past and present. The beginning of the film moves swiftly from the opening images of the Pantoja character Ana Montes's TV performance, to the première of the retrospective Spanish musical film she and her gambling, drug-addict husband, Jorge Olmedo (José Coronado) have just completed – a self-conscious homage to the CIFESA musicals of the thirties and forties. The film is introduced by real-life TV show host Carlos Herrera, thus signalling the blurring of the boundaries between reality and the film world which is characteristic of the whole movie. A series of point-of-view shots and reframings position the spectator as a member of the audience for the film-within-the-film in order to share Ana Montes's/Isabel Pantoja's curiously narcissistic contemplation of her own image on screen. This dual mode of spectatorship also parallels the interactive relationship between the film's internal narrative and Isabel Pantoja's public off-screen persona. Pantoja's personal tragedy (the loss of her bullfighter husband Paquirri), which had been a major source of interest for Spanish gossip magazines, is paralleled in her double romantic misfortune on-screen: her husband's gambling and addiction at the first level of the narrative, and, in her role as Carmen Torres, her relationship with the deceitful *galán* (handsome suitor) of the film-within-the-film. The Carmen Torres character conflates the despair of all three Pantoja personifications in her stage performance of *Romance de valentía* in the film-within-the-film as the Ana Montes character watches from her theatre seat at the premiere. *Mise-en-scène* underlines the emotive cross-references between the film personae and the star persona: the stage set is backed by the silhouette of a cross on the backdrop, Pantoja/Torres stands by a bare tree, periodically clutching the empty cape of the dead *torero* who is the subject of the song. In all three roles, Pantoja reaffirms the patriarchal role-model of the self-sacrificing female, confirming her image as 'la viuda nacional' (the nation's widow). This retrograde gender discourse is formally and narratively conveyed through the colonisation of the 'present' by the images and mores of the past (Morgan 1995: 156–8).

Fernando Trueba's Oscar-winning film offers a reversal of the *Yo soy esa* model. Although *Belle Epoque* is ostensibly set in the 1930s, the film inscribes a set of values, mores and thinking which are more readily associated with the contemporary era than with its historical context – what we might call a colonisation of the 'past' by the present. In *Belle Epoque*, Fernando Fernán Gómez's family is presented as the bohemian product of a marriage of non-conformist artists (a father who would like to have affairs, but is impotent with anyone but his wife, and a mother whose lover finances her disastrous operatic tours and meekly defers to her husband's conjugal rights on periodic visits to the family home). The film's narrative concern with the sexual initiation of the younger characters overshadows the historical context of the eve of the declaration of the Second Republic in 1931. But the emphasis on sexual experimentation as an expression of liberalism (linked to the euphoric beginnings of a new era of political freedoms) invites a number of parallels with the *apertura* of the 1970s and with the pre-AIDS freedoms of the transition period.

Trueba transforms the dawn of the Second Republic into a popular mythical space, a powerfully nostalgic representation of a Republican Spain that never was, but might have been. Despite the sobering note of the deaths which open and close the film, *Belle Epoque* remains a somewhat uncritical, indulgent celebration of a mythic libertarian Republican Spain. This invented Republic, whose citizens had the freedom to enjoy a multitude of possibilities – moral, cultural and sexual – is a far cry from the real, historical Republic of well-meaning but ineffective reformers, economic upheaval and social crisis. Hopelessly romantic and stereotypical, however, *Belle Epoque* still manages to capture some of the desires, hopes and aspirations which undoubtedly inspired and underpinned the reformist and revolutionary trends in Spain in the 1930s. The film is particularly wide of the mark in its depiction of personal and sexual relations, presenting Manolo's country residence as an almost anarchist paradise predicated on mutual tolerance and respect, free love and good food – precisely the sort of vacuous stereotypical imagery exploited and demonised by the Spanish right as the insidious creation of Jews, Masons, Communists and Moscow. Trueba's version of 1930s Spain has clearly been transfigured by social and moral revolutions that have come afterwards and this rural arcadia is a composite mixture of 1960s hippy culture, the cult of 'make love not war', plus generous helpings of 1970s and 1980s feminism as well as gender-bending and a postmodern taste for blurring political, moral and sexual boundaries. All is then projected back into the Spain of the 1930s, reproducing a luminous, attractively optimistic, joyous view of life, where one need not work, where all the bills appear to be paid and where we need only find the energy to enjoy ourselves in indulging our various libidinous appetites. This is perhaps one of the keys to the film's international

Contemporary Spanish cinema

Belle Epoque, Fernando Trueba, 1992   7

success. By transfiguring the complex, troubled historical Spanish Republic of the 1930s into an oasis of freedom, pleasure and uninhibited sexual experimentation, Trueba assigns a universality to *Belle Epoque* which is as highly attractive to the spectator as it is historically misleading. The Spain of *Belle Epoque* is not a recognisable 1930s Spain (as in Saura's *¡Ay, Carmela!*) but a myth, a joyous one which we all wish had been the case.

References

Alberich, F. (1991), 4 *años de cine español*, Madrid, Comunidad de Madrid, Consejería de Cultura, 101–29.

Alonso Barahona, F. (1992), El cine en la cultura española contemporánea in *Breve diagnóstico de la cultura española*, Madrid, Ediciones Rialp, S.A., 174–90.

Barthes, R. (1973), Mythologies, London, Paladin. 165–70.

Besas, P. (1985), *Behind the Spanish Lens. Spanish Cinema under Fascism and Democracy*, Denver, Colorado, Arden Press, 196–207.

Browne, R. B., and Ambrosetti, R. J. (eds) (1993), *Continuities in Popular Culture, The Present in the Past and the Past in the Present and Future*, Bowling Green, Ohio, Bowling Green State University Press, 87.

Caparrós Lera, J. M. (1992), *El cine español de la democracia. De la muerte de Franco al "cambio" socialista (1975–1989)*, Barcelona, Anthropos, 176–337.

Castro, A. (1996), Interview with Carlos Saura, *Dirigido*, 249, 52–67.

Cristóbal, R. (1997), La huella profunda, *Cambio 16*, 20 January 1977, 48.

D'Lugo, M. (1991), *The Films of Carlos Saura. The Practice of Seeing*, Princeton, New Jersey, Princeton University Press, 47–53.

Dent Coad, E. (1995), Designer Culture in the 1980s: The Price of Success, in Graham, H., and Labanyi, J. (eds) (1995), *Spanish Cultural Studies. An Intro-*

duction, Oxford, Oxford University Press, 376–80.

Fontenla, C. (1993), Madregilda, *ABC*, 4 October 1993, 23.

Gubern, R., *et al.* (1994), *Historia del cine español*, Madrid, Cátedra, Signo e Imagen, 209–441.

Higginbotham, V. (1988), *Spanish Film Under Franco*, Austin, University of Texas Press, 18–22.

Hooper, J. (1995), *The New Spaniards*, London, Penguin, 68–9.

Hopewell, J. (1986), *Out of the Past*, London, BFI, 9233–6.

Hopewell, J. (1989), *El cine español después de Franco*, Madrid, El Arquero, 408–19.

Jameson, F. (1993), Postmodernism or the Cultural Logic of Late Capitalism, in Docherty, T. (1993), *Postmodernism. A Reader*, London, Harvester, 62–92.

Jordan, B. (1990), *Writing and Politics in Franco's Spain*, London, Routledge, 129–71.

Kinder, M. (1983), The Children of Franco in the New Spanish Cinema, in *Quarterly Review of Film Studies*, 8: 2, 57–76.

Kinder, M. (1993), *Blood Cinema. The Reconstruction of National Identity in Spain*, Berkeley, Los Angeles and London, University of California Press, 57–348.

Labanyi, J. (1995), Postmodernism and the Problem of Cultural Identity, in Graham, H., and Labanyi, J. (eds) (1995), *Spanish Cultural Studies. An Introduction*, Oxford, Oxford University Press, 396–406.

Llinás, F. (1986), Los vientos y las tempestades, in AA. VV., *El cine y la transición política española*, Valencia, Editorial de la Filmoteca Valenciana, 2–9.

Monterde, J. E. (1989), El cine histórico durante la transición política, in *Escritos sobre el cine español 1973–1987*, Valencia, Filmoteca de la Generalitat Valenciana, 45–63.

Monterde, J. E. (1993), *Veinte años de cine español (1973–1992). Un cine bajo la paradoja*, Barcelona, Ediciones Paidós, 23–155.

Montero, M. (1993), Aún hay mucho que contar de Franco, *El Periódico*, Barcelona, 5 March 1993, 21.

Morgan, R. (1995), Nostalgia and the Contemporary Spanish Musical Film, in *Revista Canadiense de Estudios Hispánicos*, Canada, 20: 1, 151–66.

Payán, M. J. (1993), *Cine español de los 90*, Madrid, J.C.

Quiller-Couch A. (ed.) (1921), *The Oxford Book of English Verse 1250–1900*, Oxford, Oxford University Press, 615.

Sontag, S. (1977), On photography, in Sontag, S. (1983), *Extracts from Susan Sontag's Work: A Susan Sontag Reader*, London, Penguin, 349–67.

Torreiro, M. (1993), La historia extraoficial, *El País*, 21 September 1993, 34.

Torres, A. M. (1985), *Conversaciones con Manuel Gutiérrez Aragón*, Madrid, Editorial Fundamentos.

Torres, A. M. (1994), *Diccionario de cine español*, Madrid, Espasa Calpe, 346.

Tranche, R. R., and Sánchez Biosca, V. (1993), No-Do: entre el desfile militar y la foto de familia, in *Archivos de la Filmoteca*, 15, 40–53.

Yates, R. (1993), Review of *Vacas*, *Sight and Sound*, 3: 7, 54–5.

Cultural reinscription: popular genre film in post-Franco Spain

2

Introduction

In common usage, the term genre generally refers to ways of organising films according to type (Hayward 1996: 159). Genre tends to be applied most readily to popular films, products developed according to recognisable formulae, codes and conventions whereas we use terms such as 'art cinema', 'arthouse' or 'avant-garde' for films which do not 'fit' a formula. These films tend to be more experimental in narrative, thematics and film form (e.g. the disruption of time, space and point of view) and are often produced outside of or in opposition to dominant cinema systems. This sort of distinction was certainly relevant to the Spanish cinema of the 1960s and 1970s, which broadly seemed to comprise a populist, low-brow, commercial genre cinema and a more allusive, metaphorical, arthouse cinema, made by a small number of Spanish *auteurs*, for a select, mainly international audience. Over the years, such distinctions have become increasingly blurred, given that it is almost impossible to delimit the boundaries of a genre. Also, the techniques and subject matter once thought of as typical of 'art cinema' have been taken up and incorporated into popular genre films. This has led to debates about whether it is possible any longer to talk of an 'avant-garde' cinema at all (Lapsley and Westlake 1988: 181–213).

Also, by its very nature, the notion of 'genre film' or 'genre cinema' is tautologous in the sense that all cinema is genre cinema. As noted above, all films feed off, rework and reinscribe established codes and conventions, especially commercially successful ones. Yet they do so in specific ways, according to the cultures and societies in which they operate. Genres are concerned with audience experience and their memory of seeing films. They help to regulate that memory and shape the sort of expectations spectators build up in their viewing. Genres are also associated with the repetitive impulses of nostalgia and pleasure. Their determining feature is arguably the manipulation and fulfilment of audience expectations through recognisable patterns and established filmic norms and conventions, i.e. in narrative structure, character, setting, thematics, style, iconography, etc. As Schatz argues: 'a film genre gradually impresses itself upon the culture until it becomes a familiar, meaningful system that can be *named* as such' and which 'exists as a tacit 'contract' between filmmakers and audience' (Schatz 1981: 16). Once established, the pleasures offered by generic formulae are further enhanced by the familiarity engendered by their repetition. So, genres refer to combinations and articulations of filmic elements, bringing together what we have learnt to regard as baseline/required features for the genre as well as variable, innovative ones. In this sense, generic conventions are by no means static. To stay in business, the film industry must reinvent and recycle successful, crowd-pleasing generic formulae, modifying, recasting and innovating the 'mix' in order to continue to attract audiences and in so doing modify memory and expectations. A new balance in the equation between repetition and difference, familiarity and novelty, has to be struck every time.

Of course, genres are not simply a matter of textual codifications or ways of cataloguing films. As Steve Neale suggests, they also operate as systems of orientations and conventions which circulate between the film industry, the film text and the spectator's assumptions and expectations (1980: 19). In other words, genres crucially relate to matters of marketing (i.e. distribution and exhibition, how the film is placed in the market and how it is to be sold to certain audiences) and consumption (how the film is received by critics and reviewers as well as the spectator). Genres thus exist in a network of interlocking relations involving the whole system of production, commercialisation as well as reception/consumption. Finally, if genre films, such as the comedy or the thriller, rely for their appeal on the recycling of well-known, recognisable features, these conventions have to be remade in some way and adapted to the tastes and expectations of different national audiences. In the process of adaptation, genres become reshaped and it is through this reinflection that they tend to manifest their culture-specific appeal for certain types of national audiences, in our case, Spanish. Thus, while Spanish genre films respond to transnational cultural trends, they also display signs of their own cultural specificity in their various articulations. This is obvious, for example, in Francesc Bellmunt's highly polemical, futuristic, political thriller *El complot de los anillos* (1988). The film anticipated the Olympic Games held in Barcelona in 1992 and inflected their imaginary disruption by terrorist threats in terms of regional/national political tensions. The same process is also visible, for example, in the way female characters in many recent mainstream comedies, have been reimagined and reformulated in order to reflect changing perceptions of women in Spain.

Genre films in post-Franco Spain have been dominated by the comedy. Indeed, the comedy genre has been remarkably productive over the last two decades, giving rise to a number of variations, subtypes and hybrid forms, which we will try and map in the following pages. Not far behind the comedy is the equally varied area of the thriller genre which covers a wide range of film types. These would normally include *film noir*, gangster, horror, science fiction, etc., indeed any film type which tends to exploit fear, suspense or apprehension in the audience. But, rather than psychological thrillers in the style of Hitchcock, for example, thrillers in Spain have traditionally been dominated by the detective/gangster film, drawn mainly from literary sources and incorporating elements of melodrama. Melodrama, female as well as male-centred, and mainly focused on the family, sexuality and the disruptions of the domestic social order, has not been quite as prominent, though it has been very successfully inflected through the postmodern comedy, especially in association with other elements in the filmic hybrids of Almodóvar. As for other established genre categories, over the last decade in Spain, with a growing taste for nostalgia and escapist movies, the period, historical feature has done well as has the musical, which has enjoyed a significant revival. Less prominent have been fantasy, science fiction and 'adventure' films, areas which, largely because of high production costs and popular tastes (Spaniards traditionally prefer to patronise big budget Hollywood versions) have been less well developed. Finally, as noted in the previous chapter, a number of films dealing with rural Spain and the impact of modernisation have continued and developed the 'rural' genre. While providing a focus for images of a certain national identity (often predicated on atemporality and underdevelopment), the 'rural' genre also allows for an exploration of the boundaries between reality and fantasy, thus tapping into other generic fields. In other words, the boundaries between genres are never clear-cut. It is perhaps more useful to think of genres and generic conventions as capable of continual permutation and cross-over, as sets of formulae which inhabit, inform and frequently innovate not only film types and styles but our memories and ways of seeing as spectators.

The comedy

The dominance, popularity and commercial success of the comedy in post-Franco Spain clearly reflects the fact that the genre has enjoyed a long and very distinguished tradition in Spanish filmmaking. During the Franco era, alongside bullfighting and soccer, light film comedy offered convenient diversions from more disruptive pursuits such as politics and, moreover, provided an effective

Cultural reinscription

vehicle for conveying the conservative values of the regime. Under the dictatorship, the narrative structure of most mainstream comedies offered the spectator excursions into temporary social chaos, mixed with gentle titillation and emotional excess, but all safely contained within conservative resolutions which reinforced notions of patriotism, patriarchy and unassailable Catholic morality. As a result, Spanish comedy has often been dismissed as a minor genre and, arguably unfairly, has been identified with the low-budget, escapist, 'subgeneneric' movies of the Franco years (Morgan and Jordan 1994: 57–8). However, apart from being very popular, comedy also afforded (limited) opportunities for social commentary and critical reflection, as seen in Berlanga's now legendary satire of Francoist mythology in *Bienvenido, Mr Marshall* (1952). Thus, where the Franco regime appropriated popular film as a vehicle for its retrograde values, directors such as Berlanga exploited the same vehicle for rather different ends. Moreover, popular genres, such as the comedy, continue to be a site for the clash of ideas and opposing ideological standpoints. This is evident if, for example, we compare Mariano Ozores's right-wing, nostalgic, Francoist apologias with Almodóvar's 'cutre' (vulgar), 'crazy', often scandalous, postmodern comedies.

Before Franco's death, alongside other forms of output, Spanish film comedy was generally referred to pejoratively as one of a series of 'subgenres' (Vanaclocha 1974). That is, it was dominated by a whole range of substandard, low-budget, exploitative products, aimed exclusively at the home market. After 1975, the film comedy was able to deal with social, political and cultural issues far more openly and aggressively, with greater explicitness, especially in the realm of sexuality and the use of colloquial language. But even with greater freedoms and the disappearance of film censorship, we still find a series of surprising continuities with the 'sub' products of the early 1970s.

Subgeneric comedies

Sex and sexuality have long figured prominently as vehicles for humour in Spanish film comedy. Their multiple thematic inflections have frequently been linked to stereotypical notions of national identity, at the core of which has been a particularly vulnerable sense of male virility and identity. The most popular homegrown sub-genre of the early 1970s, which mercilessly satirised (but always reinforced) the Iberian male ego, was undoubtedly the 'comedia sexy' or Iberian sex comedy, immortalised in Tito Fernández's *No desearás al vecino del quinto* (1970), Pedro Lazaga's *Vente a Alemania, Pepe* (1970) and Vicente Escrivá's *Lo verde empieza en los Pirineos* (1973) (Jordan 1995: 128–31). Typically low-budget, these shamefully vulgar features, focused mainly on the hugely inflated but constantly frustrated libido of the typical, repressed Iberian male, epitomised in the figures portrayed by Alfredo Landa (Morgan and Jordan 1994: 58). In many respects, in the post-Franco period, we find obvious continuities with these sub-generic products in a host of sex comedies, though newly-inflected as 'comedias eróticas' because of their greater level of nudity and their attempt to compete more on equal terms with the wave of soft pornography emanating from Europe, principally of the *Emmanuelle* type. A few representative examples will suffice: *La lozana andaluza* (Vicente Escrivá 1976) and *Niñas ¡al salón!* (Vicente Escrivá 1977), *40 años sin sexo* (Juan Bosch 1978), *El liguero mágico* (Mariano Ozores 1980), *Agítese antes de usarla* (Mariano Ozores 1983), *El periscopio* (José Ramón Larraz 1978), *Polvos mágicos* (José Ramón Larraz 1979). The striking success, for example, of Larraz's *Polvos mágicos* depended not only on its 'soft porn' visual content, but also on the director's ability to successfully combine into one product the broad generic features of light comedy, horror and thriller with plenty of simulated sex (Torres 1994: 271). Also aware of the high returns arising from the explicit cross-generic mingling of these 'sub' comedies was the incredibly prolific Mariano Ozores (Torres 1994: 356), specialist in the sex comedy as well as in a second, important 'sub' trend, the nostalgic, right-wing, Francoist comedy.

Adopting the low-budget, fast-shooting and often clumsy editing style of the sex comedies but shifting the focus to topical political issues, the right-wing sub-comedy is seen at its most extreme in Ozores's *¡Que vienen los socialistas!* (1982), a vitriolic critique of the Socialist Party's electoral chances in 1982 and *Todos al suelo* (1982), a shameless apologia for the *tejerazo*, the attempted military coup of 1981. Pandering to an offensive jingoism and the crudest forms of sexual, political and anti-democractic prejudices, these films set out to satirise, if not demonise, the then current political situation (i.e. the transition and consolidation of democracy). They did so from a position of nostalgia for and uncritical belief in the legitimacy and desirability of the Franco dictatorship. Sociologically, perhaps, they offered a revealing though highly partial chronicle of some of the main events of the transition and the early years of the Socialist government (Monterde 1993: 131). During the 1980s, this trend had numerous followers and continuations, as in Rafael Gil's film adaptations of several of the novels of Fernando Vizcaíno Casas, literary darling of Spain's 'ultra derecha' (ultra right). Other films attempted to satirise the conduct of public officials, especially their involvement in sex scandals, sleaze, organised crime, fraud and government corruption, all titillatingly mocked in Mariano Ozores's *Disparate nacional* (1990).

A third subtrend in this area and generic spin-off from the first two is that of the historical parody, as in Fons's *El Cid cabreador* (1983), *Cristobal Colón, de oficio descubridor* (1982) and José Ramón Larraz's *Juana la Loca ... de vez en cuando* (1983). A further variant is the parodic comedy derived from the recycling and re-inflecting of formulae from successful television shows. Here, we refer to the big-screen repackaging of such popular performers as Martes y Trece in Javier Aguirre's *Martes y Trece, ni te cases ni te embarques* (1982). Later on, the same comic duo would enjoy major commercial successes with the 'comedias disparatadas' (crazy comedies) of *Aquí huele a muerto (¡Pues yo no he sido!)* (1989) and *El robobo de la jojoya* (1991), directed by Alvaro Sáenz de Heredia.

During the 1980s, the above sub-generic trends would find it difficult to prosper with changing public tastes and political circumstances. After 1982, with the rise to power of the Socialist government, the effects of the Miró film reforms and the new funding rules (which would focus public subsidies on fewer, more worthy, quality films), the Iberian sex comedy and its variants became an endangered species. Given the public availability of hard core pornographic material in designated theatres (Salas X), the cheap 'comedia erótica' (soft-core comedy) found its market increasingly under pressure. Moreover, with rising costs in the 1980s, though cheap and cheerful, these comedies were becoming harder to finance and amortise. And, as the use and sales of VCRs and video cassettes slowly increased, the market for such sub-products gradually shifted towards the home-entertainment sector. By the late 1980s, many of these films were being made for the video rental market without commercial release in mainstream film theatres.

Aside from the above sub-generic variants, Spanish film comedy of the 1980s and 1990s was dominated by the so-called 'New Spanish Comedy', which took a variety of forms. In its turn, this trend had its roots in what is usually referred to as the *tercera vía* movement of the 1970s.

The *tercera vía*

Emerging in the early 1970s, *tercera vía* (third way) films were mostly though not exclusively comedies. Initially, they were made by up-and-coming professionals who wished to distinguish themselves from their older, more traditionalist colleagues such as Rafael Gil, Juan de Orduña, José Luis Sáenz de Heredia, etc., as well as from the members of the New Spanish Cinema movement of the 1960s, such as Borau, Eceiza, Fons, Picazo and Patino, etc. The nucleus of the *tercera vía* operation is generally seen as including producer José Luis Dibildos, scriptwriter José Luis Garci and director Roberto Bodegas, the latter responsible for such early classics of the movement as *Españolas en París* (1970), *Vida conyugal sana* (1974) and *Los nuevos españoles* (1974). Within this trend, we can also include Antonio Drove's *Tocata y fuga de Lolita* (1974) and Jaime de Armiñán's *El amor del Capitán Brando* (1974). Anxious to stimulate foreign sales and offer a rather more marketable, better-made product than those of Lazaga, Ozores or Masó, these films sought to confront similar issues to those exploited in the low-budget sex comedies aimed at a mass market. However, in doing so, they left to one side the crude gender stereotyping, the tasteless, toilet humour and the reactionary moralising of the sex comedies and dealt with issues more seriously and conscientiously and with rather more critical bite. Hopewell describes them as 'a halfway house between the 'sexy Spanish comedy' and the sobriety of Saura' (1986: 82). At the same time, the *tercera vía* movement, especially in its post-Franco incarnation, also attempted to appeal to and generate a new film-viewing sector by focusing on issues of greater relevance to Spain's urban middle classes, especially the thirty-something generation and by exploiting more naturalistic settings and characters. The latter were not the caricatured, overblown, pantomimic stereotypes of the sex comedies (as represented by Alfredo Landa) but more credible, identifiable average citizens, epitomised perhaps by actor José Sacristán. These were the country's 'new Spaniards' coming to terms with their new-found freedoms and trying to cast off the repressions of a patriarchal Francoist past.

The paradigm film of this trend in the post-Franco years and arguably one of the key films of the whole reform period, was José Luis Garci's *Asignatura pendiente* (1977). Told in flashback and set against the backcloth of Franco's death and period songs of Gloria Lasso and the *Dúo Dinámico*, the film reconstructs the adulterous relationship between José, the young 'progre' (progressive) left-wing lawyer (working for the Communist trade union *Comisiones Obreras*) and his former girlfriend, Elena. Through their affair, we are offered a chronicle of the multiple frustrations felt by a thirty-something generation which grew up and was emotionally crippled under Francoism. The 'asignatura pendiente' (pending exam) of the title, of course, symbolises the pleasures, ambitions and (sexual) desires denied to the couple (and their generation as a whole) by a repressive, Francoist past, and which they now consummate in an initially carefree but increasingly frustrating adulterous relationship.

In terms of social and moral conventions, we are already some distance away from the sex comedies. It is only very late in the film that José and Elena even begin to consider that their secret liaison might be construed as an act of betrayal of their respective spouses and families, whom they still love. Their relationship thus reveals little or no angst over questions of adultery or cheating on their partners and children. Rather they grasp the moment and focus on the understandable desire to recuperate the pleasures they were denied in their youth. Such insouciance arguably reflects the situation of many middle-class people of those years in which extra-marital affairs, especially among the liberal-left intelligentsia, were deemed unremarkable, permissible and even fashionable. The downside, of course, as the film also demonstrates, is that such attempts to resurrect old love affairs are doomed to frustration and failure, for the past cannot be recuperated. *Asignatura pendiente* is thus characterised by a rather melancholy, wistful, resentful tone, conveying a tearful denunciation of the Franco regime, which denied several generations of young Spaniards their right to emotional and sexual freedoms (Gubern, *et al.* 1994: 386). The film is also a chronicle of lost illusions, illustrating quite clearly the sort of attitudes which would underlie the famous *pasotismo* (drop-out mentality) of the late 1970s in Spain. Moreover, and perhaps disconcertingly, while it is José who is called upon in the film to join the vanguard of the political reform process, he fails to take Elena along with him, for he sees no role for her. Politics is presented as an exclusively male preserve and somehow far too important and demanding to involve Elena. In terms of its sexual politics, then, the film rejects inherited notions of Francoist patriarchal order but it signally fails to take seriously the political role of women in the democratic transition.

Garci tried in vain to repeat the success of *Asignatura pendiente* in *Solos en la madrugada* (1978) and *Las verdes praderas* (1979), casting another melancholy eye over daily life in Francoist Spain on behalf of the 'niños de la guerra' (children of the Civil War). His nostalgic comedies gave rise to one or two imitations, but failed to ignite a more sustained trend. And while mainstream comedy of the late 1970s and early 1980s was still concerned with the thirty-something generation, the sub-genre became less and less fixated on a repressive past and more interested in the changing behaviour, habits and lifestyles of Spain's middle class 'progresía' (trendies) during the transition and after. In this context, we see the emergence of the New Spanish Comedy, whose nucleus was undoubtedly the so-called 'comedia madrileña'.

The New Spanish Comedy: *comedia madrileña*
The recession which had characterised the Spanish film industry in the 1970s had several notable effects: filmmaking responded more and more to market pressures; low-budget features were thus more in evidence and were virtually the only means for younger directors to enter the business. Moreover, lacking state subsidies, young aspiring filmmakers raised their capital from friends and family, created their own producer cooperatives and invariably used the open streets and friends' flats as shooting locations, as time and money allowed. Also, as Hopewell argues (1986: 219), the struggle for economic survival generated a greater degree of differentiation and experimentation in filmmaking, allowing new characters and issues to emerge: drugs, alcohol, the consequences of sleeping around, the nature of the family unit, etc., explored through figures drawn mainly from the younger generations, including students, the unemployed, ordinary people in dead-end jobs, all wondering what

might lie in store for them in an uncertain world. Out of this context, there arose a relatively sophisticated, cosmopolitan, sub-group of film comedies, aimed at the more affluent urban younger generations, which are now usually referred to as the New Spanish Comedy.

In broad terms, the New Spanish Comedy incorporated many of the features of earlier comedies of manners and customs, drawing in part on the example of *tercera vía* films. The trend also revealed the imprint of certain American and European filmmakers, notably Woody Allen, Eric Rohmer, Alain Tanner and also Andy Warhol. Perhaps the main distinguishing trait of the trend was that it exploited fresh young talent as actors and scriptwriters and above all focused on the lives of the younger generations of the 1970s, people in their twenties and thirties. Initially very low-budget projects, these films were set mainly in bustling, urban environments (particularly Madrid and Barcelona). They focused on the emotional problems (marriage, divorce, separation, bringing up children, sexual hangups, etc.) of their young adult characters. Shot in 'natural' as opposed to studio sets and based on wordy, often improvised dialogues, these films tended to exploit direct sound rather than rely on post-production overdubbing, as was the norm. In terms of their cultural politics, they virtually ignored the question of reclaiming an emotional past denied to them by Francoist repression, so central to the *tercera vía* approach and style of *Asignatura pendiente*. Indeed, if they paid attention to the past at all, it was to bury it and confidently focus on the different lifestyles and opportunities for personal development which new democratic freedoms were making possible. As Hopewell argues, these films 'tried to break with past solemnities' (1986: 223) and explore in a humorous way how ordinary people (in the main victims of *desencanto* – disaffection, depoliticisation) made sense of their lives.

The film which arguably inaugurated the New Spanish Cinema trend (and which featured so prominently at the San Sebastián Festival of 1977), was Fernando Colomo's, low-budget, off-beat satire *Tigres de papel* (1977). In 1977, Colomo was thirty-one years old and was not particularly bothered about the Franco era, its impact or its repressions. He was rather more concerned about the younger generations of the post-Franco years and in his cheap and cheerful feature took a wry, gently ironic, deflationary look at their intellectual snobberies, immaturities, emotional hang-ups and sexual exploits, etc. In the film, the characters smoke some cannabis and with a still camera in front of them, talk to camera about sex, religion, politics, etc., in an apparently slangy, colloquial, off-the-cuff, spontaneous way. In short, Colomo explored the comic potential of the immaturity and naive political correctness of these 'new Spaniards'.

Colomo's indulgence with the left 'progresía' (progressives) in the 'comedia madrileña' was also repeated in other small budget features of his, such as in *¿Qué hace una chica como tú en un sitio como éste?* (1978), *Estoy en crisis* (1982) and *La línea del cielo* (1983), shot in New York. Similar topics and issues were also dealt with in Alberto Bermejo's study of the complications arising from a *ménage à trois* in *Vecinos* (1982), in Paulino Viota's absorbing though sadly neglected *Cuerpo a cuerpo* (1982) and in the witty dialogues of Fernando Trueba's *Opera prima* (1980), one of the best of the early comedies, which launched Trueba and Oscar Ladoire on their movie careers. In the same vein, and inaugurating the early phase of the 'comedia catalana' (Catalan comedy), we find Francesc Bellmunt's homage to 1970s 'hippiedom' in *L'orgia* (1978), *Salut i força al canut* (1979) and *La quinta del porro* (1980).

Virtually all of these films, keenly aware of their status as texts for the initiated (given their many intertextual filmic references), sought to explore in humorous ways the troubling gap between unrealistic ambitions, overblown desires and cruel reality, in relation to work, jobs and particularly problems in the sexual arena. They also brought to the attention of Spanish audiences a number of young acting talents who would later become established as national and (in some cases) international stars, such as Carmen Maura, Antonio Resines, Verónica Forqué, Marisa Paredes, Assumpta Serna, Kitty Manver, Oscar Ladoire, etc.

In similar fashion, having had propitious beginnings, directors such as Garci, Trueba and Colomo would soon become established as mainstream film professionals and in Garci's case soon enjoy major international recognition for his *Volver a empezar* (1982), 1983 Oscar winner for best foreign language film. Using a typical Garci story line, the film traces the attempt by exiled novelist Antonio Albajara, on his return to his native roots, to rekindle a relationship with an old, adolescent flame, dating back to before the Civil War. Needless to say, the past proves to be irrecuperable and the attempt founders. Despite his brief moment of Oscar fame, Garci's later films failed to find critical or commercial success. Moreover, he found it very difficult to achieve financial backing for his partially autobiographical *Sesión continua* (1984) and the recycled version of his 1970s hit *Asignatura aprobada* (1987), involving a nostalgic, self-referential look at the Spanish film business. Frustrated by a lack of success, Garci moved into publishing and television for a number of years, until he remerged with the successful Goya-winning *Canción de cuna* (1994). A wistful, sentimental, saccharine-coated, light melodrama, Garci's period piece was arguably a thematic and stylistic anachronism, seriously out of step with trends in Spanish film in the 1990s. Set in a convent in Castile at the end of last century, the film shows how the relative tranquility of a closed community of nuns is transformed when they 'adopt' an abandoned baby and are forced to deal with the pressures and demands of the outside world, embodied by the agnostic country doctor don José (brilliantly played by Alfredo Landa).

As for Trueba, early success meant access to rather bigger budgets and the opportunity to make more ambitious, rather more stylised 'high' comedies of manners, as in *Sal gorda* (1984) and his *Sé infiel y no mires con quien* (1985). The latter was his first major project with producer Andrés Vicente Gómez (who would produce Trueba's next three films) and offered a star vehicle for Ana Belén and Carmen Maura. In the case of Colomo, he went on to make the highly successful pseudo-vaudeville piece *La vida alegre* (1987), set in a VD clinic, the less appealing stage-play adaptation *Bajarse al moro* (1988), concerned with drug-dealing in Morocco, again starring Verónica Forqué and *Alegre ma non troppo* (1994), classic American-style comedy concerned with the variable sexual identity of a young musician. More recently, Colomo has directed *El efecto mariposa* (1995), much indebted to his earlier *La línea del cielo* (1983) and financed by his own production company, with French and British participation. In the film, shot in the UK, Colomo playfully explores 'chaos theory', i.e. the ways in which apparently trivial events give rise to enormous consequences, the so-called butterfly effect. He does so by using the device of a young Spaniard, Luis, who is sent to London to study at the LSE (London School of Economics) and who causes major tremors by falling in love with his aunt; this incestuous relationship is further complicated by the fact that the aunt's neighbour, a *Star Trek* freak, falls for Luis's mother, who is fleeing trouble in Madrid. Though generally witty and congenial, the film's intriguing premise falls slightly short of effective realization, partly owing to unfortunate choices of casting but more to an inability to successfully combine characters, situations and dialogue into a coherent, well-paced whole. Within this more sophisticated 'high' comedy frame, we can locate the work of Emilio Martínez Lázaro including his *El juego más divertido* (1987) and *Amo tu cama rica* (1992), a highly successful tale of sexual discovery and a star vehicle for Ariadna Gil. Also, in the same frame, we must mention Almodóvar's ground-breaking, generically hybrid, crazy comedy of intrigue *Mujeres al borde de un ataque de nervios* (1988), the film which arguably launched his international career and created overseas opportunities for many other Spanish directors.

The international copro
In the early 1980s, several Spanish directors went west in search of the 'American dream' of success, international recognition and rich rewards in the huge US market. For example, Bigas Luna shot his bizarre tale of religious zealotry *Reborn* (*Renacer* 1981) in the USA; Ricardo Franco set *San Judás de la frontera* (1984) on the Mexican/American border; Fernando Colomo located *La línea del cielo*

(1983) in New York, where Gonzalo Herralde had previously shot *Vértigo en Manhattan* (1980). These pioneering directors were clearly attempting to develop the sort of americanised, hybrid products which were meant to do well at the international box office and break into the American market, going beyond the limits of the usual arthouse release. The success of their efforts was mixed, however, and it is surprising that aspiring, internationally-oriented directors of comedy who came after them did not fully assimilate the bitter lessons of attempting the leap into the international market.

One of the classic cases of market miscalculation was arguably Fernando Trueba's 1989 feature *El sueño del mono loco*. As Marsha Kinder reminds us (1993: 417–22), with this project Trueba believed he had developed the epitome of an international copro, the model of a macroregional cinema. This was a Spanish–French copro, with a medium-size budget by international standards (but very large by Spanish), shot in English, starring French, English and American actors (including Jeff Goldblum), whose script was based on a possibly over-complicated revision of the Peter Pan legend. Released in the USA under the title *Twisted Obsession*, the film did not prosper. As Kinder suggests, authored by Trueba, a Spanish director still totally unknown to international audiences, its failure partly rested on its lack of Spanish identity. For cinema audiences in Spain but especially abroad, the movie was perceived as a foreign, international, rather rootless, nondescript comedy/melodrama, perhaps too complex in its scripting. And though competently made, it was too highly stylised and polished and lacked the recognisably Spanish subject matter of Saura's *!Ay, Carmela!* (1990), for example, or the outrageous postmodern visual style, energy and bad taste of Almodóvar's hit *Mujeres al borde de un ataque de nervios* (1988).

Somewhat chastened by the experience, and perhaps following Saura's lead, for his next venture, Trueba returned to a Spanish theme (the euphoric months of freedom and optimism leading up to the Republic of 1931) and had incredible success with *Belle Epoque* (1992), culminating with the Oscar for best foreign language film in 1993. Emboldened by his Oscar success and the heightened international visibility it gave him (and clearly undaunted by his previous failure in 1989), Trueba then took the further step into the Hollywood mainstream with the screwball comedy *Two Much* (1995). Made entirely in the USA, with a largely American cast (including Daryl Hannah, Melanie Griffith, Danny Aiello as well as the newly-consecrated, modern Valentino, Antonio Banderas) and with absolutely no reference to Spain whatsoever, the film has been remarkably successful in Spain though a critical and commercial flop virtually everywhere else.

The reasons for this paradoxical and divided reception are

intriguing. As regards the film's reception in Spain, its success clearly relates in part to Trueba's high profile in the country (after the worldwide acclaim lavished on *Belle Epoque*), his enhanced standing for having 'made it' in Hollywood, as well as his use of rising megastar Banderas, one of Spain's favourite sons. Aside from this solidarity factor, there is also the fact that Spanish audiences are longstanding, avid (and slightly uncritical) consumers of American comedies and high production values, whose thematics are largely fantasy and make-believe (*Fotogramas*, 1827, January 1996, 7). On the other hand, the format adopted by *Two Much* is that of a 1940s screwball comedy, with touches of bedroom farce, i.e. an old-fashioned, rather outdated format, which Trueba fails to modernise successfully. And while the film's 'look' is glossy and sophisticated, its American stars (Melanie Griffith, Daryl Hannah) are no longer premier-league actors. Banderas, on the other hand, (who plays an exploitative, sexist character), is probably still not well-known enough among international audiences to carry the film. In its UK release, *Two Much* was showcased in only one cinema before going to video, a sign perhaps that non-Hispanic audiences did not find Trueba's visual or verbal gags sharp, witty or amusing enough (Shone 1997: 3). Intriguingly, as happened with his choice of *Belle Epoque*, after the mixed fortunes of *El sueño del mono loco*, for his next project, Trueba returns to a recognisably Spanish theme, though with an international outlook, in *La niña de tus ojos*. Scripted by the ever-reliable Rafael Azcona, this is another period piece drawing upon a little-known agreement between Hitler and Franco in 1938 to produce a number of films jointly. Trueba's story recreates the journey of a Spanish film crew to Berlin and their adventures in the Nazi capital, including an apocryphal love affair between Dr Goebbels and Imperio Argentina.

Generational rebellion

Since the mid-1970s in Spain, we have seen the rapid spread of consumerism, the breakdown of the traditional patriarchal family unit, the inexorable rise of youth unemployment, delinquency and drug-related problems and the emergence of new sub-cultural styles and behaviours which reflect an increasingly complex and problematic social stratum, that of *la juventud* (youth). It has been argued that contemporary Spanish culture is predominantly focused on the world of the young (Graham and Labanyi 1995: vii and 257-8). With numerous new, young actors and directors entering the film business in Spain, as well as the fact that film audiences are predominantly made up of young people, in recent years, films have been increasingly concerned with the issues and problems faced by the younger generation. Indeed, within the comedy remit, something of a new 'generational' comedy sub-trend has begun to define itself. Numerous film comedies have variously explored the problems of social and sexual identity, the conflicts between parents and their children, the difficulties faced by young married couples, male adolescent desire for older women as well as the traumas involved in establishing viable emotional relationships.

In this area, representative examples include Alvaro Fernández Armero's tale of adolescent disillusionment in *Todo es mentira* (1994), Eugenio Martín's *La sal de la vida* (1995) as well as Emilio Martínez Lázaro's *Los peores años de nuestra vida* (1994). Despite the ironies of the title, this latter movie offers a relatively upbeat, 'rites of passage' story mixed with elements of the cautionary tale. It features the highly bankable young star Gabino Diego who, in competition with his more confident brother (the even more bankable Jorge Sanz) kicks against impossible role models and high expectations with regard to love and romance. In *Los hombres siempre mienten* (1994), Antonio del Real introduces a similarly sensitive character who finally fulfils his professional and emotional goals but only by (apparently) sacrificing his integrity. Martín (again played by Gabino Diego) is a student of creative writing whose success on his course depends on him producing one high-quality, end-of-course piece of work. Unfortunately, his desire to seduce fellow student Alicia proves stronger than his dedication to literary activity. In order not to flunk the course, Martín steals part of the manuscript of an unfinished novel from a professional writer (Antonio Resines) who lives next door. Here, del Real appears to suggest that, given the many pressures to succeed and 'have it all' in an increasingly acquisitive, consumerist age, his young protagonist's theft and plagiarism of another's work is understandable though not to be condoned outright. Martín may have betrayed the confidence and trust of his successful neighbour by appropriating his work, but his actions are seen as in keeping with survival in a modern, competitive environment.

In *¡Por fin solos!* (1994), Antonio del Real exploits an intriguing reversal of the theme of youth emancipation. The long-suffering representatives of the older generation (including a father figure splendidly played by Alfredo Landa) are desperate to achieve more time and space for themselves. They manage to persuade their offspring to abandon the family nest and leave them in peace only to have the youngsters return. Though frustrated and diverted from their objective, the parents willingly sacrifice their happiness and convenience for the sake of their children. Cutting against the grain of family fragmentation and youth revolt, the film thus provides a reassuring closure which reaffirms the notion of the close-knit, stable non-oppressive family unit.

The *esperpento* tradition

If the above subgroups of Spanish film comedies represent some of the more innovative and challenging strands of the genre in post-

Franco Spain, a third main trend draws upon already well-established filmic and broader popular cultural traditions. We refer to the *esperpento* tradition in Spanish cinema, that is the filmic exploitation of a long-standing aesthetic of Spanish black humour, vulgarity and bad taste. Over the last century or so, the latter has been developed chiefly in art, literature and drama (particularly Valle-Inclán) and has promoted a view of Spain as a laughable distortion, a crude deformation of European civilization. In contemporary Spanish film, the use of caricature, the grotesque, the farcical and the absurd as tools to mock national customs and institutions arguably has its origins in the work of Berlanga, Ferreri and Fernán Gómez in the 1950s and 1960s (Hopewell 1986: 59–61). This comic tradition has been maintained and developed during the 1970s and 1980s. And it is Berlanga above all, always faithful to techniques and comic styles developed in earlier work, who has continued to dominate this sub-genre. This is particularly true of his famous satirical trilogy dealing with the absurdities of Spain's decadent aristocracy, represented by the Leguineche family in *La escopeta nacional* (1977), *Patrimonio nacional* (1980) and *Nacional III* (1982). Such films, especially the first of the series, offered a resounding and effective critique of politics and the ways of power under Francoism.

As is well-known, the idea for the story line of *La escopeta nacional* came from that fateful, real-life hunting party of 1 February 1964 when Manuel Fraga Iribarne accidentally shot Franco's daughter Nenuca in the bottom. By presenting a satirical, black-humoured view of a similar 1960s shooting party in his film, Berlanga was unashamedly drawing recognisable parallels with an incident which had seriously embarrassed the Franco dynasty. Moreover, he was also fitting into a tradition of Spanish film making, from *La caza* to *Furtivos*, which had taken the hunt as a metaphor for human relations though giving it a new series of parodic, satirical twists. At the same time, the film was clearly a comment on the nature of transition politics suggesting that whatever shifts in power might occur in Spain, those same power elites (as satirised in the film) would remain intact and continue to dominate and exploit the lower orders.

In the film, Canivell is Berlanga's parodic version of the tight-fisted Catalan businessman, prepared to suffer all manner of indignities and compromises in order to strike a deal. He is also the spectator's guide to the bizarre and degenerate world of Spain's ruling elites, especially its weird, discredited, parasitic aristocracy, portrayed as a band of sexual perverts and fetishists. No less objectionable and venal, however, are the politicians and civil servants (all on the take) and the Catholic Church, represented by a foul-mouthed, traditionalist, xenophobic priest. The film proposes a wholesale, indiscriminate condemnation of Francoist politicians, civil servants and power brokers of whatever institutional stripe. If

Canivell's business dealings with the power elites are viewed as a metaphor for the transition, then the film clearly regards any political change as motivated by economic and not democratic concerns and thus simply a question of those elites re-adapting to new times. There is thus a strong, underlying note of cynicism projected towards transition politics, a plague on all houses.

Perhaps the most striking feature of the film is that, in the liberal, post-Franco context, Berlanga takes much further than before the crudity and salaciousness of the portrayal of old Marquis, a sexual pervert who collects pubic hair and whose perversions are handed down to his son. Also given greater verbal license is the foul-mouthed, blasphemous, priest, who rails against the topic of Catalan separatism and sees the 'Virgin of Montserrat fucking up Spain' (a line which would not have been approved by Censorship in 1976). Surprisingly, perhaps, such verbal rawness and directness are not matched on the visual level. Indeed, there is very little *destape*, nudity or stress on male voyeurism. However, from a predictable Berlanga, there is much toilet humour and many of the jokes and references have to do with bodily functions, especially urination, flatulence and so on. The film was certainly the best of the trilogy, with the satire and black humour accurately hitting all the main targets.

The two sequels to *La escopeta nacional*, though commercially reasonably successful, were rather dull and repetitious and largely recycled the topics and gags contained in the first of the series. It was only with *La vaquilla* (1984) that Berlanga once again hit upon a successful comic formula of populism (with those memorable war songs) and black humour (showing the absurdity of war), which did reasonably good business at the box office. However, in later comedies and despite the success of *La vaquilla* (1984), Berlanga was arguably less effective, repeating without reinventing the same old slapstick and tiresome toilet humour of *Moros y Cristianos* (1987) and more recently *Todos a la cárcel* (1993). Here, once again, in a rather laboured skit on ex-political activists under Francoism (who attend a prison reunion), predictable scatological gags are underpinned by the very same general political cynicism for which Berlanga's cinema is renowned. In much the same vein, but with a more modern, post-Franco, 'Euro' focus, Manuel Estéban (*Los mares del sur* 1991) satirises Spain's 'eurofilia' and its continuing commitment to compulsory military service in *Historias de la puta mili* (1993). Based on a strip cartoon by the graphic artist Ivá, the film follows the antics of a batch of raw recruits, under the control of a sergeant (Juan Echanove), as they stumble into and eventually subvert a NATO military exercise.

Similar comic styles drawing on the *esperpento* tradition of subversive black humour and bad taste are evident in the work of Valencian film maker Carles Mira. Grounding his satire of Francoism in the lunatic figures of a Spanish imperial tradition, Mira typically contrasts a dark, repressive, austere Christian tradition with a Moorish celebration of sensuality and earthiness. His films also exploit musical numbers, choral protagonists and foreground a specific concern with Valencian culture, especially the Fallas (the spectacular fiestas of the Valencia region) as in *Con el culo al aire* (1980), *Jalea real* (1981) and *¡Que nos quiten lo bailao!* (1983). Also, in a similar *esperpento* vein, seeking to satirise the dictatorship by revealing the vulgarity and absurdity of its servants, are García Sánchez's *Las truchas* (1977) and *La corte de Faraón* (1985) as well as Francisco Betriu's *Furia española* (1974), *La viuda andaluza* (1976) and *Los fieles sirvientes* (1980). Notable for its exploitation of indigenous styles, such as the *sainete* (low-life sketch) and *zarzuela* (operetta), but drawing heavily on the same satirical tradition is of course Fernando Fernán Gómez's *Bruja, más que bruja* (1976) and *Mambrú se fue a la guerra* (1986), his sharply-observed commentary on the losers of the Civil War and transition politics.

As a film director, Fernán Gómez has maintained the scepticism, pessimism and satirical bite typical of the *esperpento* tradition with *7000 días juntos* (1994), his resounding vote of no-confidence in the institution of marriage. The film charts the midlife crisis of a university medical technician, Matías (José Sacristán) who, no longer prepared to put up with the stultifying tedium of his marriage, leaves his unemployed musician wife Petra (Pilar Bardem) – who threatens to stay with him until death – for a dizzy shop assistant Angelines (María Barranco). After the euphoria of a passionate, whirlwind love affair with Angelines and in order to gain his freedom, Matías vows to murder his wife. He does so, although the crime (supported by his friend Luis-Agustín González) is presented in a fairly unremarkable, deadpan, subversively indifferent manner. By contrast, and revealing the deliberate exploitation of an 'estética feísta' (a delectation in blood and gore), the scenes involving the disposal of the wife's body are deliberately stomach-churning and disgusting. But, given Fernán Gómez's longstanding passion for sarcastic, unpredictable finales, Matías's crime does not go unpunished. Indeed, the world he represents is one in which happiness and the fulfilment of desire are fleeting and ultimately deceptive. In a society based on greed, jealousy and villainy, characters such as Matías and Angelines end up as losers. Incisive and deeply critical of a marriage that has outlived its usefulness, by contrast, the film is remarkably indulgent towards its middle-aged males and their attempts to transform their sexual fantasies and desires for sexual freedom into reality. A similar concern with such dangerous desires, but this time emanating from the representative of a very different social stratum, is evident in Fernán Gómez's more recent feature *Pesadilla para un rico* (1996). The film follows the tribulations of Alvaro, a fifty-year-old business executive who, having reached the very pinnacle of his career, comes close to putting it all into jeopardy. A young woman, Mane (thirty years his junior), evades a rapist by jumping into Alvaro's car; the businessman's offer of a lift culminates in a night of love-making, after which Mane fails to wake up. As in *7000 días juntos*, the question again arises as to how Alvaro is to dispose of the woman's body without rousing suspicion or scandal. And as before, Fernán Gómez casts a sarcastic though indulgent eye over the ageing hero's attempts to dig himself out of a hole of his own making.

La España eterna: Recycling stereotypes

As indicated in other chapters, a number of recent film comedies have demonstrated a strong fascination with the essential peculiarities of national identities and the underlying spirit of an enduring, eternal, 'deep' Spain. A number of directors have recycled, updated and ironized many of those stereotypical figures, topics and filmic cliches which were once proudly paraded to represent the 'España es diferente' jingoism of the Franco era. As we mention in the chapter on Catalan cinema, José Juan Bigas Luna has been one of the foremost exponents of a cinema increasingly populated by 'Hispanic prototypes' and their often, bizarre, but always overdeveloped, insatiable appetites and desires. Bigas Luna has a long track record in capturing on film these libidinal curiosities, most notably in *Bilbao* (1978) and *Las edades de Lulú* (1990), rather dark, detailed studies of mainly male sexual obsessions, perversions and denied gratifications. More recently he has chosen to organise his filmmaking according to trilogies, the first of which is already complete: *Jamón Jamón* (1992), *Huevos de oro* (1993) and *La teta y la luna* (1994). All three films offer different but complementary views of Hispanic machismo and delight in revealing the troubling effects of unregulated, male libidinal desire on friends, lovers, the family and the social order. More broadly, they also suggest that, in the modern age of obsessive consumption, our relations with other people tend to be lived in increasingly shallow, superficial, reified ways. And as our egos, driven by insatiable appetites, seek constant reinforcements and new disguises, human relations degenerate into role play and fakery. Such are the apparent negative consequences of uncontrolled masculine drives. Interestingly, rather than subject his hispanic prototypes to serious critique, Bigas Luna appears to endorse, if not celebrate, their fantasies as well as their foibles, their excess or deficit of testosterone. Indeed, while their behavioural excesses usually lead them to disaster (and some form of catharsis and renewal of self-awareness), his Iberian archetypes are treated in a warm, indulgent, affectionate manner, which tends to undercut their parodic function.

Having completed his trilogy on Hispanic machismo, Bigas Luna embarked on a second trio of films concerned with women, that is, with the irrational, obsessive, sexualised responses women supposedly provoke in the opposite sex. This time Bigas has focused not only on Hispanic women, but (following the Euro-friendly outlook of *La teta y la luna* and the generous financial input from the European Council via its media arm Eurimages) on the fundamental energies underlying a wider 'Mediterranean' sensibility, including French and Italian female national stereotypes. The first instalment is *Bambola* (1996), shot in Italy, a story which recycles the director's earlier obsessions with the excesses of human appetites, in which restaurant-owner Mina (nicknamed Bambola) becomes the focus for male rivalries and sexual gratification. The next two pieces are to be *Marie, la camarera del Titanic* (on the love story between a man and a waitress on the ill-fated liner) and *Carmen* – Spain's feminine prototype par excellence.

Operating in similar territory and again concerned with exploring the essential features of 'homo hispanicus' are relative newcomers from Madrid, Santiago Aguilar and Luis Guridi, alias La Cuadrilla. Adopting the triology format and seeking in turn to explore the worlds of bullfighting, football and the police, so far (apart from several comic shorts) they have produced the extraordinary *Justino, un asesino de la tercera edad* (1994) and its follow-up, *Matías, juez de línea* (1996). Low-budget, shot in black and white and surprise Goya winner in 1995 for the best film from a newcomer, *Justino* cleverly recycles the best film traditions of the Spanish *esperpento* of the 1950s and 1960s, represented by Berlanga, Ferreri and Fernán Gómez. A troubling, sardonic, vicious black comedy, this curious 'retro' film follows the macabre activities of a retired bullfighter (puntillero). Rejected by society after thirty years of dedicated service administering to bulls the *coup de grace*, in order to retain a sense of professional identity and personal self-worth, he reinvents his bloody profession by becoming a serial killer. With its anachronistic 'look', its precise observation of social customs and manners, its cold and clinical portrayal of Justino's new part-time profession, the film seeks to avoid pastiche. And with its detached, unemotional portrayal of murderous activity, it raises intriguing questions concerning the relations between humour and screen violence.

The second instalment, *Matías juez de línea*, connects with the first through the figure of Matías, who is the son of Justino. Football linesman as well as judge in his local community, Matías's problem is that he is scrupulously honest and fair, both in his footballing duties and in his role as local judge. Unfortunately, the economy of his coastal village depends on the traffic of stolen liquor and the success of a major, forthcoming scam. Predictably, Matías's obsessive integrity threatens to undermine the livelihoods of his neighbours and indeed the whole local economy. Highly reminiscent of Alexander McKendrick's *Whiskey Galore* (1949), and

8　　　　　　　　　　*Justino, un asesino de la tercera edad*, La Cuadrilla, 1994

indebted to the Ealing comedies as well as Berlanga, this choral comedy offers a sarcastic, sideways look at hispanic attitudes towards moral probity. And by contrasting Matías's imperturbable honesty with the venal pragmatism of the villagers, the film comments incisively on the nature of innocence as well as the power conflicts that can arise between individual and community. Such issues are to be further examined in the forthcoming third and final instalment of the trilogy *Atilano, presidente*, in which a worker in a crematorium becomes prime minister.

Very much in the same vein, combining road movie and picaresque adventure is José Luis García Sánchez's *Suspiros de España (y Portugal)* (1994). With its title based on a *pasodoble*, this sympathetic, episodic satire on 'eternal Spain' and its institutions (landowners, clergy, military, law, etc.) is again recycled in his follow-up film *Almas de Dios* (1995). Here, two priests wander the byways and backwaters, sampling the simple pleasures and rustic delights of rural Spain in pursuit of an inheritance. And with *Siempre hay un camino a la derecha* (1997), a mordant skit on 'reality shows', García Sánchez offers a second instalment and continuation of his *Suspiros*.

The post-modern comedy
With the death of the dictator in 1975, Spain embarked on a dizzying, headlong rush to join the communications revolution and the global capitalist marketplace. Spain was no longer so 'different' and

in order to affirm their rejection of past repressions, Spain's younger generations seized upon, reworked and translated into their own terms numerous contemporary American and European trends in music, fashion, identity politics, drug cultures, etc. Against a background of a resurgence in regionalist politics and a recognition of the diversity of languages and cultures in Spain, the famous *Movida* occurring among Madrid's marginal groups began to develop. As noted elsewhere, a new pop culture, unsupported by government institutions with its roots in 1960s New York underground and 1970s punk, hit the capital, increasingly visible in everything from music, fashion, art, design and graphics to photography and film. Without Franco around, Spain's rebellious youngsters decided to explore alternative identities, sexualities and values in an orgy of experimentation and hedonistic pursuit of pleasure. Madrid's all-night clubs and cafés, pumping out punk and heavy metal, alongside flamenco and sevillanas, offered the nocturnal arena for what came to typify Spain's peculiar brand of (post) 'postmodern' culture, i.e. a fetishism of the frivolous, captured so successfully in his early comedies by Pedro Almodóvar (Vernon and Morris 1995: 6).

This is the territory occupied by what we might call the postmodern comedy, which in part emerges from but also breaks significantly with previous trends (Morgan and Jordan 1994: 57–8). The notion of postmodern comedy arguably resists any clear definition as a discrete filmic style or practice precisely because of its ostentatiously hybrid, cross-generic character and its contempt for established filmic aims well as other cultural and social boundaries and hierarchies. Its humour tends to arise as much from the wilful disruption of the spectator's reading expectations as from narrative and generic incongruities and the juxtaposition of the bizarre and the banal. Moreover, the humour usually tends to focus on the hedonistic pursuit of visceral pleasures, involving grotesque, deluded, obsessive characters and their outlandish behaviour. At bottom, the postmodern comedy may be seen as a comedy of excess, deliberately designed not only to disrupt conventional notions of filmic logic but to scandalise the sensibilities of its viewing publics. Historically, this postmodern impulse formed part of a wider movement in Spanish film comedy, the so-called New Spanish Comedy, which, between the mid-1970s and 1980s, capitalised on and exploited the new-found freedoms of the Franco era. Films such as Colomo's *¿Qué hace una chica como tú en un sitio como éste?* (1978), Bellmunt's *L'orgia* (1978) and Mira's *Con el culo al aire* (1980) signalled a significant break with a filmic past in that their narratives were based on the cathartic effects of sexual and social experimentation. The same was true of films which evolved from the so-called 'comedia madrileña' of Trueba and Colomo into the type of work produced by Bigas Luna and particularly Almodóvar. The postmodern comedy has clearly developed within this latter strain and it is the early work of Almodóvar which will briefly concern us here, particularly his first feature *Pepi, Luci, Bom y otras chicas del montón* (1980).

For all their scandalous novelty, Almodóvar's early films did not arise in a vacuum. Indeed, apart from the obvious debt to Warhol in his first feature, other significant elements such as the focus on sexual experimentation, the foregrounding of marginal groups and relationships, the use of choral characters, the recourse to parody, caricature, distortion and farce, the appeal to crudity, toilet humour, *tremendismo* and 'shock tactics' to scandalise the spectator, etc., had all been exploited before in varying degrees in the work of Colomo, Mira, Berlanga and Bigas Luna (Vernon and Morris 1995: 14-15). In his early social comedies then, Almodóvar was not starting from scratch. But what was distinctive about his work, especially the pioneering *Pepi, Luci, Bom ...* (1980), for example, was that he pushed these narrative, thematic, intertextual and stylistic elements to filmic excess, to levels of crudity, explicitness and self-consciousness hitherto unseen in Spanish filmmaking.

In his first major feature, he deliberately set out to create a bizarre, subversive, outrageous piece, a lesbian love story in which a repressed housewife, having experimented with the option of a lesbian *ménage à trois*, returns to her brutal husband in search of a more muscular, masculine brand of sado-masochistic pleasure. With such a 'politically incorrect', farcical story line, Almodóvar's irreverent 'crazy comedy' was in some ways doing for Madrid's gay and lesbian subcultures what Warhol had done for the fashion world and gay scene in New York. Moreover, he was also tapping into elements of Madrid's famous *Movida* of the late 1970s, anxious to record (as well as promote) a set of heterodox lifestyles and a raucous, uncompromising attitude to sexual experimentation (Hooper 1995: 344–5). In the film, the comedy and humour arise from the clash between images of banal domesticity (the knitting scene) and perverse sexual practices (the famous 'meada' or urination). Above all, his film style was highly self-conscious, not only in the way his marginal characters became foregrounded and the dirty, 'cutre' elements were pushed to excess. His developing trash aesthetic was also seen in the manner of his filmic construction: the continual disruption of filmic logic and continuity editing; the representation of anti-naturalistic characters in an often disjointed, discontinuous manner; the packaging of stories of sexual pleasure and perversion in lurid sets, ham acting and lumpy scripts, all within the framework of farce. (Many of these 'aesthetic' features were of course partly a response to low-budgets, weekend shoots and post-production inexperience. But in other ways, narrative disruption certainly reflected the director's disdain for dominant social, cultural and moral values). Moreover, Almodóvar was deliberately and wilfully engaging in generic confusion, mixing and juxtaposing aspects of cine *verité*, melodrama, situation comedy, pornography, advertising, pop music, *zarzuela* (operetta), etc. into a unique *mélange*, which would become an unmistakable Almodovarian trademark.

The main thrust of Almodóvar's early features, including the cult movie *Laberinto de pasiones* (1982) and the convent comedy *Entre tinieblas* (1983), was clearly the desire to challenge both sexual and cinematic taboos, to reach a new level of visual and verbal explicitness, to offend the sensibilities of mainly heterosexual audiences and affirm a frivolous exuberance and delight in the freedom of expression. There was also a desire, one might argue, to rewrite the rules of film syntax and editing, although in some respects, what were taken as signs of a radical new film style often consisted of the director's errors and poor camera work. Leaving aside these technical shortcomings, the early Almodóvar affirmed the power of the senses, the pursuit of pleasure and the anarchic pulse of libidinal drives. Politically, of course, such hedonism not only mocked the repressions of the traditional Francoist right but also the moral dilemmas of liberal, left-wing progressives.

With the early Almodóvar, notions of sexual and political identity were thus being re-invented. Sex and gender roles were being represented as highly fluid and mobile; indeed, life was frequently portrayed as one long orgy and was expressed as a series of role plays in which no one role was given any significant authority or status, politically or morally. In such a relativistic world, it was difficult to assert any serious notion of identity or sense of self, since one self, one role could be regarded as just as pleasurable or desirable as any other. Moreover, the editing and collage effects of Almodóvar's films tended to call into question any authoritative diegetic voice and reaffirm the idea that identity was provisional, discontinuous and subject to opportunistic transformation. As Paul Smith has argued, in his early films, Almodóvar swung between crazy farce and social comedy, adopting no single genre, but specialising in hybrids (1994: 18–20). After *¿Qué he hecho yo para merecer esto?* (1984), Almodóvar revamped his generic parameters towards the melodrama and highly stylised thriller, as in *Matador* (1986) and *La ley del deseo* (1986), culminating in *Mujeres al borde de un ataque de nervios* (1988). With *Átame* (1989), *Tacones lejanos* (1991) and *Kika* (1993), however, he seemed to recuperate the generic features of the high comedy and, in the case of *Kika*, blended them with a serious critique of the role of the communications media. *La flor de mi secreto* (1995) marked something of a change in his trajectory. It totally set aside the hedonism, overblown stylisation and *auteur* as interior decorator of previous farces in favour of a rather drab naturalism and a confusingly real 'reality effect'. And despite the *trompe l'oeil* at the beginning of the piece (the 'bogus' training session, apparently no more real than the rest of the film), the film seemed to take itself more seriously, revealing a more sober, reflective Almodóvar. Indeed, his introspective, mature, 'rootsy' analysis of a middle-aged woman rediscovering her identity was arguably a cry to be taken seriously. But given the rumours concerning his forthcoming feature *Carne trémula* or *Carne de cañón* (an extremely 'free' adaptation of a Ruth Rendell triangular thriller/love story between a cripple, ex-convict and the delectable Francisca Neri), we can be assured that Almodóvar will be seeking to confound his critics and regain by reinventing that delirious, postmodern edge he is supposed to have lost.

One might argue that Almodóvar transformed the genre film into a peculiar *auteur* style of his own. Moreover, as a marketing device in selling his pictures abroad, his 'auteurish' identity, stamped on films carrying his particular personal vision and outlook, has been very successful (Vernon and Morris 1995: 14–15). Indeed, outside of Spain, his movies have usually been coded as art pictures which are aimed at an initiated, international, culturally elite audience. His camp cultural and generic hybridism have mirrored particularly well his affirmation of a sexual and cultural relativism, visible not only in his own later features but in rather similar, internationally-acknowledged hits such as Bigas Luna's *Jamón Jamón* (1992) and *Huevos de oro* (1993), as well as the developing output of newcomer Manuel Gómez Pereira.

Operating within the framework of the Americanised, 'high' comedy tradition, Gómez Pereira is perhaps one of the most prolific and successful younger directors of comedy to emerge in recent years. Highly bankable, very much in the Almodóvar mould, with his flashy, stylised, strong visual content and his apparently risqué sexualised subject matter, though politically conservative in his res-olutions, he has since his *ópera prima Salsa rosa* (1991), established a formidable *oeuvre* with *¿Por qué lo llaman amor cuando quieren decir sexo?* (1992), *Todos los hombres sois iguales* (1994) and *Boca a boca* (1995), in which Javier Bardem works in the telephone sex busi-ness, though surprisingly, despite its subject matter, the film offers little in the way of visual spectacle to titillate the spectator. The more recent and remarkably successful *El amor perjudica seriamente la salud* (1996) marks a further advance in Gómez Pereira's career, indicating a shift towards a more ironic, self-conscious, sophisti-cated form of comedy. Set in Paris, the film charts the thirty-year sexual relationship between a security guard and a high-society, independent woman (Ana Belén) who controls the 'affair' accord-ing to her own needs and preferences.

Más que amor, frenesí (1996), directed by a young triumvirate (Alfonso Albacete, Miguel Bardem and David Menkes) and produced by Fernando Colomo, arguably constitutes a less successful recy-cling of the crazy, postmodern, Almodovarian comedy, complete with dead bodies and *crime passionel*. Scripted in committee, dealing with a group of twenty-year-old men seeking sex and excitement, this urban choral *comedia frenética* seeks to provoke and scandalise very much in the manner of the early, naively *cutre* (vulgar) Almodóvar. However, its crazy characters (including a lesbian madame, drag queens, junkies and assorted bisexuals and homosexuals), its absurd, confusing situations and its tired topics and clichés fail to create a minimally connected narrative or a viable form of (post) postmodern humour. In very similar 'crazy comedy' territory, with its thriller structure and McGuffin is Félix Sabroso and Dunia Ayaso's gay whodunnit *Perdona bonita, pero Lucas me quería a mí* (1996).

Other takes, other trends

Since the 1990s, within the broad field of Spanish film comedy, several other sub-trends have (re)appeared. These include: the slapstick-oriented 'comedia disparatada' or crazy comedy as in Jaime Chávarri's *Gran Slalom* (1995), in which a Civil Guard is forced to dress in drag. The religious satire has also made a comeback, as in José Luis Cuerda's pythonesque *Así en la tierra como en el cielo* (1995) and Ricardo Franco's *¡Oh cielos!* (1995), in which a (female) guardian angel guarantees life to a publicity executive on condition that he promote family values. A number of comedies have engaged in a critique of economic conditions under the Socialist administration: José Luis Cuerda's *Crisis* (1993) and *Tocando fondo* (1993), Carlos Suárez's *Adiós tiburón* (1995), Joaquín Trincado's *Sálvate si puedes* (1994) and the silent movie by the theatre collective El Tricicle, *Palace* (1995). Also, surprisingly, there has been something of a reprise of the old, sub-generic sex comedy in Javier Elorrieta's *Demasiado caliente para ti* (1996) and Javier Rebollo's *Calor* (1996). Interestingly, perhaps indicating a wider trend, Joaquín Orìstrell, scriptwriter and collaborator on several 1990s features for Gómez Pereira, has directed his first comedy *¿De qué se ríen las mujeres?* (1996), star vehicle for Verónica Forqué and the up-and-coming Candela Peña.

Conclusion

Since the mid-1970s, the Spanish film comedy has undergone a series of profound thematic and stylistic transformations. To a large extent, these have developed alongside social and cultural changes arising from the political realignment of Francoism after the dictator's death, the new freedoms ushered in by democratic reforms and the long period of Socialist government. The Iberian sex comedy, for example, which had been a bulwark of the commercial cinema up to 1975 gradually disappeared, being overtaken initially by a flood of international soft porn films, banned under Franco. Moreover, all the major thematic, stylistic and ideological principles upon which the Iberian sex comedy had been founded were rapidly abandoned or reinflected. Francoist repression was dead or so it seemed and post-Franco film making appeared to reflect a nation-wide cathartic obsession with sex and sexual experimentation; an 'anything goes' mentality. This was the case not only in Almodóvar's early comedies but also in other film examples mentioned in this section, including the work of Garci, Colomo, Berlanga, Trueba, Bigas Luna, etc. Indeed, traditional notions of order, nation, patriarchy, family, machismo, gender roles, Francoist fantasies of cultural 'difference' and Spanish 'otherness' were already being questioned in many *tercera vía* (third way) films and in examples of the New Spanish Comedy. However, they were most self-consciously and systematically subverted, especially sex and gender roles, in the crazy, *cutre* (vulgar) early comedies of Almodóvar. Here, a series of marginalised 'others', including lesbian and gay identities (anathema to Francoist/Catholic principles) were recuperated as the centre of attention and put on display. And where the iberian sex comedy had denied or tried to repress the dizzying effects of sexual desire, increasingly in Colomo, Berlanga and above all in Almodóvar, unregulated desire was celebrated, reaffirmed and used to mock and subvert repressive social convention of whatever ideological persuasion. Of course, if those embarrassing sex comedies of the early 1970s could be criticised for recycling and repeating stock situations, gags, toilet humour, farcical set pieces, etc., the same might also be said of other types of work mentioned above. In fact, Berlanga, Almodóvar and others have also been criticised for repeating themselves, for offering in their work a series of often bland simulations of already manufactured material. This may be the ultimate fate of all generic or cross-generic film products, especially those marked by the tag 'postmodern'. In other words, they may set out initially to destabilise the familiar, invert hierarchies, bring the marginal to the centre, play intertextual games and shock the spectator into new ways of seeing. But while they have great fun in deflating the absurd egos of their stereotypes and fabulous eccentrics, they may end up simply recycling and reaffirming those very Hispanic repressions and fantasies they set out to mock.

The thriller

In the case of Spanish, there is no single concept in the language which adequately covers and translates the idea of 'thriller'. Nowadays, most Spanish critics tend to use the English term anyway. But even here, the notion of 'thriller' itself is by no means easy to pin down although, in most cases, thrillers do seek to excite anxiety, apprehension and fear in the spectator (i.e. the 'thrill'), in part by attempting to exploit our infantile sexual fantasies (Hayward 1996: 111). In the Spanish context, the term 'thriller' normally takes into account what is usually referred to as *cine policíaco* or *cine negro* as well as *cine de suspense* and *cine de misterio*. Given this variety of material, the 'thriller' in Spain operates as a macro-genre which comprises all those films dealing with crime, detection and the police, while also including elements of mystery or suspense. However, at bottom, what tends to characterise the 'thriller' is its connections with criminal behaviour; indeed, crime, of one sort or another, arguably represents the thematic core of the genre (Valentí 1996: 44).

This section is concerned mainly with the modern thriller of the 1980s and 1990s in Spain. Of course, when talking of the 'modern' thriller, we need to understand that recently-made thrillers may well exploit and recycle classic narrative codes of the 1930s and 1940s, the heyday of the American gangster/crime movie, which helped give rise to the genre. Equally, other films may be set in the past and seek to give a strong period inflection to the narrative, *mise-en-scène*, camerawork, etc. Yet others may take certain thematic or iconographic elements (instances of murder or kidnapping; desolate, marginal urban settings, claustrophobic interiors) and work them into films which reinflect these features by combining them with other generic features and styles to produce something rather different (e.g. Almodóvar's postmodern parodies or Alex de la Iglesia's generic hybrids, which exploit *noir* conventions alongside many other elements). In other words, the modern Spanish 'thriller' can take a wide variety of forms. Moreover, while the Spanish term *cine negro* (after the French *film noir*) is perhaps the one which comes nearest to our modern understanding of thrillers, it is by no means the whole story. Thus, for our purposes, Spanish *cine negro* might best be seen as a sub-category within the macro 'thriller' genre as a whole.

Cine negro during the dictatorship

In broad terms, *cine negro* has long been cultivated and variously reinflected during Spain's own film history, both under as well as after the Franco dictatorship. According to Antoni Lloréns, Spain's indigenous *cine negro* or crime movie first emerged in the early 1950s with such features as Ignacio F. Iquino's *Brigada criminal* (1950), Julio Salvador's *Apartado de correos 1001* (1950), José Luis Sáenz de Heredia's *Los ojos dejan huellas* (1952) and *El ojo de cristal* (1955) by Antonio Santillán (Lloréns 1988: 3).

Following Lloréns, Marsha Kinder argues that, during the 1950s, such crime movies offered a potential vehicle for social and political critique of the Franco regime from both left and right-wing positions (Kinder 1993: 60). This may well be so in certain cases. However, in more general terms, such attempts at political critique were necessarily muted. As Freixas argues, censorship and the state control of the film business in Spain made it virtually impossible to offer a realistic filmic portrayal of delinquency, the police or corruption (Freixas 1996: 49) In fact, the Spanish crime/detective/

police movie was effectively prevented from seriously exploring and exposing the interface between crime, the police services and the state. Given these institutional limitations, most *noir* movies were almost obliged to portray police work in highly positive, even glowing terms. Spanish detectives in the 1950s and 1960s were invariably kind, considerate, swift-acting and efficient, never venal or corrupt. Moreover, references to police or government incompetence or corruption were officially banned. As Hopewell persuasively argues: 'Spanish audiences could see a film about police corruption in New York, but were barred from watching "anything remotely contrary" to "the internal security of the country", which would include a film about police corruption in Madrid'. (Hopewell 1986: 37–8).

These constraints remained in force until the death of Franco. In general, under the dictatorship, the overwhelming majority of Spanish *noir* films were predominantly of the B-movie type cheap and unpretentious, with no star names, produced mainly in Barcelona and Madrid, and with few if any exceptions (possibly Borau's *Crimen de doble filo*, 1964), they offered low-key apologias for the police services (Monterde 1993: 143). Despite these limitations, by the early and mid-1970s, a reasonably solvent, indigenous *noir* tradition had been established and was being developed in Barcelona, for example, by Gonzalo Herralde's uneven *La muerte del escorpión* (1975) and Bigas Luna's rather bland adaptation of Vázquez Montalbán's *Tatuaje* (1976). Meanwhile, in Madrid, Bardem was making *La corrupción de Chris Miller* (1972) and *El poder del deseo* (1975), Eloy de la Iglesia was producing his erotic noirish thrillers such as *El techo de cristal* (1970) and *La semana del asesino* (1971) and Borau was overseeing the Spanish-Swiss, copro thriller *Hay que matar a B* (1973) (Kinder 1993: 351–7). Needless to say, filmmakers in Spain could not exploit the full critical and subversive potential of the *cine negro* subgenre until after the death of the Franco and the lifting of censorship.

Codes, conventions and the *femme fatale*

One of the enduring appeals of *film noir/cine negro* rests on its surface look. This is usually conveyed through the repetition of generic codes and conventions relating particularly to the use of *mise en scène*, camerawork and especially lighting. Indeed, *film noir* is identified principally by its visual style, whose main features include: the use of claustrophobic interiors (such as cars, trains, etc.), tightly-framed shots, chiaroscuro lighting (originating in German Expressionism, this involves the use of strong sources of directional light, such as neon signs, table lamps, etc., surrounded by deep shadows), silhouettes and other dark images, exaggerated camera angles and frequent close-ups. Settings are predominantly urban, the more desolate, seedy and rainwashed the better. These formal, iconographical features are also indicative of theme, mood and psychology, invariably suggesting marginality, alienation, pessimism, social malaise, corruption and danger. As regards characters, these tend to be seen according to the way they are lit and include many male neurotics and obsessives. Moreover, protagonists tend to be neither wholly good or bad, but morally ambiguous, questionable, flawed but also with possible redeeming features. Ostensibly, *film noir/cine negro* has to do with the search for knowledge and truth, the pursuit of a solution to an enigma or riddle, involving an investigation usually headed by a male lead protagonist. However, as Hayward has recently argued, the very quest for knowledge and justice may sometimes be called into question and derailed or at least seriously diverted by the intervention of the *femme fatale*. (Hayward 1996: 119–20; see also chapter 3 on Gender and Sexuality). And it is the latter's assertiveness and bid for sexual empowerment which can threaten the male quest for a resolution to the enigma and by implication the foundations of male identity. Thus, female power may need to be contained or exorcised in some form. In short, female sexuality may become the underlying goal of the investigation since it threatens the male quest for knowledge and thus the affirmation of male identity.

Investigating the transition

By the end of the 1970s in Spain, we find a proliferation of films being made in the thriller/*cine negro* tradition. The increase in the popularity of the genre no doubt reflected the excitement arising from post-Franco freedoms and the desire to broach topics, such as police and government corruption, which had been taboo and virtually untouchable under the dictatorship. Corruption had been at the very heart of Francoist civil society and endemic in its political system. And given the backstairs 'management' of the transition process by the Francoist political class, it was widely acknowledged that post-Franco politics were inevitably tainted. The Spanish transition was seen as more a product of smoke-filled rooms than of open, democratic assemblies. Indeed, in many ways, democracy brought with it the removal of national politics from open debate and public scrutiny. Thus, the early euphoria attaching to democratic change during the transition soon gave way to a sense of growing disillusionment with democracy (de la Cuadra and Gallego Díaz 1981: 21–44).

The corruption and cynicism at the centre of classic American *noir* movies thus found a resounding echo in contemporary Spain and in Spain's own *cine negro*. Also, recalling Italian political cinema of the late 1970s and with the example of the highly successful fictional television series *La huella del crimen* in the background, a number of real-life, high-profile political scandals in Spain (involving both politicians and police) became prime filmic subjects.

These were repackaged sometimes in terms of historical chronicles or reconstructions as in Pedro Costa's *El caso Almería* (1984) and *Redondela* (1987); in other cases, they were reinflected according to sensationalist *noir* conventions in such films as *Matar al Nani* (1988) by Roberto Bodegas (Gubern, *et al.* 1994: 426–7). Other cases of real-life criminal activity given the big-screen treatment included: Santiago Lapeira's *Asalto al Banco Central* (1983), Santiago San Miguel's *Crimen en familia* (1984) and Victor Barrera's *Los invitados* (1987).

If classic American *noir* of the 1940s and 1950s evoked postwar disillusionment, political insecurity, Cold War paranoia and male concern at the economic and sexual emancipation of women (Hayward 1996: 120), its appropriateness to the cultural mood of Spain in the 1980s is self-evident. This can be seen in a large number of thrillers which, by exploiting more conventional *noir* features (criminal activity as backbone of the plot, narrative structured according to the crime, its investigation and its consequences), also offered critical readings of the transition and its effects. These include Paulino Viota's *Con uñas y dientes* (1978), Jordi Cadena's *Barcelona sud* (1980), José Antonio Zorrilla's *El arreglo* (1983), José Luis Garci's *El Crack I* and *II* (1980/83), Carlos Balagué's *Adela* (1986), Luis José Comerón's *Puzzle* (1986), Francesc Bellmunt's *El complot de los anillos* (1988) and Eduardo Campoy's *A solas contigo* (1990) and *Demasiado corazón* (1992).

Zorrilla's *El arreglo*, for example, despite its rather schematic plot and flat, underdeveloped police inspector Crisanto Perales (Eusebio Poncela), was one of the first films to explore the institutional workings of the police (Monterde 1993: 145; Benet 1989: 130) and to probe state corruption from the inside (Hopewell 1986: 221). A classic of the same period, Garci's *El Crack*, follows the more conventional path of the private detective/ex-police inspector, Germán Areta (splendidly played by Alfredo Landa), on the trail of the sixteen-year-old daughter of an international financier linked to Spain's political elites. Rather unsatisfactorily, the case is finally resolved in New York, thus downplaying and diverting attention away from the theme of corruption in Spain and the links between the political establishment and the security services. Despite these concessions to political sensitivities (Hopewell 1986: 221), so successful was Garci's first excursion into the *noir* genre that he made *El Crack II* (1983). Here, Garci shows a similar reticence towards probing the Spanish political situation in a film in which sleuth Areta is finally persuaded by multiple death threats to drop the case and take a holiday.

Other films of the period focused on marginality and the social causes of juvenile delinquency, issues prefigured in Gutiérrez Aragón's *Camada negra* (1977) and *Maravillas* (1980) and in Juan Antonio de la Loma's *Perros callejeros* (1977). Notable among the more searching excursions into these problematic areas are: Saura's reprise of *Los golfos* (1959) in the part-fiction, part-documentary *Deprisa, deprisa* (1980) and also Eloy de la Iglesia's violent family melodramas such as *Navajeros* (1980) *El pico I* and *II* (1983/84) and *La estanquera de Vallecas* (1987). As Hopewell points out, Eloy's films 'made Spanish delinquents and the culture they embodied such attractive figures for Spaniards troubled by their past and the doubts of *desencanto*' (Hopewell 1986: 223; also, Smith 1992: 129–62).

The literary connection

The post-Franco resurgence of *cine negro* formed part of a process which witnessed a publishing boom in detective fiction in Spain (mainly American classics in translation) linked to the remarkable rise of indigenous Spanish crime fiction, which enjoyed soaring output and sales between 1975–85. Clearly, as noted earlier, underlying this literary phenomenon was a particular mood in the country, a deep cynicism and mistrust of politics, institutions and authority, which was symptomatic of a wider public *desencanto* (disillusionment) with the political system as a whole. The *novela negra* offered Spanish writers a popular vehicle with which to comment on official corruption as well as the venality of politicians and public servants. Writers such as Manuel Vázquez Montalbán, Jorge Martínez Reverte, Andreu Martín, Juan Madrid and Eduardo Mendoza produced numerous titles reflecting not only a deep disillusionment with transition politics, but an awareness of the difficulties of achieving justice and making sense of a stubbornly indifferent, chaotic and unanswerable system. Through marginal, cynical, uncommitted anti-heroes such as Carvalho, Areta and investigative journalist Gálvez, Spanish readers could perhaps find some reassurance that someone somewhere (fictional or not) was able to cut through official smoke screens and provide the ordinary person with some semblance of truth, justice and possibly retribution.

Such literary sources were highly attractive to filmmakers, with the work of Vázquez Montalbán, as the best known of the *novela negra* writing fraternity, heading the list of film adaptations. Apart from *Tatuaje* (Bigas Luna 1976) and the RTVE Carvalho television series, these include: *Asesinato en el comité central* (Vicente Aranda 1982), *Los mares del sur* (Manuel Estéban 1991), *El laberinto griego* (Rafael Alcázar 1992) and *Galíndez* (Imanol Uribe 1996). There were also several screen adaptations of novels by another specialist in the genre, Andreu Martín, including *Fanny 'Pelopaja'* (Vicente Aranda 1984) and *Adiós pequeña* (Imanol Uribe 1986). Martín was also responsible for the script of *Barcelona Connection* (Miguel Iglesias 1988), until his own debut as a director with *Sauna* (1990), based on a story by María Jaén. Jorge Martínez Reverte, creator of reporter/sleuth Gálvez, has also had several of his novels adapted: *Demasiado para Gálvez* (Antonio Gonzalo 1980) and a version of the novel *Gálvez en Euskadi* retitled *Cómo levantar mil kilos* (Antonio Hernández 1991). Other adaptations include: Eduardo Mendoza's own novel *La verdad sobre el caso Savolta* (Antonio Drove 1979), as well as Antonio Muñóz Molina's *Un invierno en Lisboa* (José Antonio Zorrilla 1991) and his *Beltenebros* (Pilar Miró 1991), Juan Benet's *El aire de un crimen* (Antonio Isasi 1987) and Juan Madrid's *Al acecho* (Gerardo Herrero 1987).

The thriller in the 1990s

The 1990s have seen a quite remarkable volume of film output within the thriller/*cine negro* remit, revealing a wide diversity of film subtypes and a clear recognition by filmmakers of the fluidity and flexibility of generic boundaries. We find many directors working within the macro genre, happy to recycle established conventions of the detective story, murder mystery, action or psychological thriller, etc., in period or contemporary settings. Examples include: José Luis Gonzalo Suárez's *El detective y la muerte* (1994), in which Javier Bardem is hired (unwittingly) to murder the wife of an industrial tycoon; *Amores que matan*, star vehicle for Carmen Maura, involving fraud and embezzlement (Juan Manuel Chumilla 1995); Ana Díez's murder mystery *Todo está oscuro* (1995), as well as several features from younger directors: Xavier Ribera Perpinyá's study of exploitation and deceit, *Puro veneno* (1995), Carlos Pérez Ferré's *Best-seller (El premio)* (1996), Joaquín Jordá's thriller set in rural Catalonia *Un cos al bosc (Un cuerpo en el bosque)* (1996), Carlos Amil's *Blanca Madison* (1996) and Koldo Askarreta's *Rigor mortis* (1996). We also find filmmakers working on the outside of the genre, borrowing, reinflecting and grafting thriller elements onto/into other filmic frames, and giving rise to new hybrids. Often this can result in an ironic, parodic, postmodern perspective, as seen in the early Almodóvar (*Pepi, Luci, Bom* ...) as well as in more recent features, such as *Kika* (1993). Elsewhere, a film may begin within one recognisable, dominant frame, only to develop towards or exploit the conventions of another (as in Bajo Ulloa's mixing of thriller and horror elements in his early features such as *Alas de mariposa* (1991) and *La madre muerta* (1993) or in Alex de la Iglesia's generic parodies such as *Acción mutante* (1992).

Within the thriller macro-framework, we can identify a number of subtrends, which we attempt to outline below.

The crime/action thriller

Here, we refer to the more conventional crime thriller, the sort of film in which criminal activity forms the backbone of the story and where the narrative is reasonably clearly structured according to the comission of the crime, its investigation and its consequences.

While films in this category are concerned, to some extent, with the background to criminal behaviour, the main interest lies in the narrative drive to unravel the plot complications in a satisfactory, though perhaps not legally-defensible, manner. A particularly striking example of this sub-type is Enrique Urbizu's action thriller *Todo por la pasta* (1991) (see also Basque cinema in Chapter 4).

Set in the Basque Country, in the modern day, the film deals with the violent theft of the takings from a Bingo hall and the frantic pursuit of the money by various interested groups. Narrative complications arise immediately with some of the gang members slaughtering each other, allowing the youngster Ruedas to disappear with the loot. Enter Azucena (María Barranco), an exotic dancer at the Zado night club, whose boyfriend (and gang member) has been murdered by Ruedas and who is determined to retrieve their share. She is joined by Verónica (Kitty Manver) – corrupt administrator of an Old People's Home. Like Azucena, (from whom she learns of the heist and will befriend and exploit) she is also desperate to recover the money. Initially, Ángel (Antonio Resines) is the investigating officer in the case, though he is soon replaced by colleagues from a rival unit. The reason, we soon learn, is that the robbery has been organised by these plain-clothes detectives in league with a local drug gang.

Urbizu pulls no punches in this fast-paced, hard-hitting, truculent thriller which, despite an oversupply of plot elements, manages to avoid confusion and incoherence. The marginal settings for the film (seedy clubs, garish smoky interiors, derelict suburbs) are clearly contemporary and emphatically sordid, suggesting a situation of social decay and the breakdown of law and order. The Zado club, for example, is a microcosm of marginalia: a den of prostitution, gambling, drug dealing and perverse sexual practices. Its popular floor show depicts disturbing simulations of bondage, fellatio and sado-masochistic sex; it is also the meeting point for local drug dealers, gangsters and corrupt policemen. Equally sordid and problematic and frequently juxtaposed to the latter, is the police station/precinct, where hard-nosed, aggressive officers from different units compete with each other for the best turf and most lucrative returns from their own criminal activity. In short, the boundaries between the law and the criminal fraternity have become totally blurred. Moreover, human relations are reduced to fear, betrayal and the double-cross. Unfortunately, within this fearsome human jungle, at times Urbizu overstates his case. The use of sensationalist violence and excessive vitriol in the dialogues at times tend to transform the action and character portrayal into lurid caricature (witness Resines's devastating assault on the woman in the tenement block, his interrogation of Azucena and the wild, random shooting of the freakish (Buñuelian?) blind man). At the same time, the final shoot-out in the club is arguably weakly choreographed, with an excess of blood and gore, with rather lame special effects, all of which detract from the reality-effect of the slaughter. Yet, despite these shortcomings, *Todo por la pasta* is a very competent, watchable and highly-engaging thriller, with enthusiastic acting performances from the main cast. However, the film concludes with a welcome but perhaps too topical, narratively improbable and politically correct dénouement for the 1990s: Azucena and Verónica manage to outwit and outgun all the male competition, join together and escape with the money.

The 'retro'/period thriller

As noted in the previous chapter, a number of films have exploited the thriller framework in order to repackage and reinflect their testimony of a certain historical past, for example, Antonio Drove's *La verdad sobre el caso Savolta* (1979), Imanol Uribe's *La fuga de Segovia* (1981), Jaime Camino's *Dragon Rapide* (1986) – framed by the intervention of the fictional investigative journalist – Aranda's *El Lute I* and *II* (1987/88) and José Luis García Sánchez's *La noche más larga* (1991). Other films working within other generic frames, such as Francisco Regueiro's satirical/historical fantasy *Madregilda* (1993), have also exploited thriller elements, such as the grim 1940s settings and atmospheres and the intimidating underworld locations. Other period features, such as Pedro Olea's *El maestro de esgrima* (1992), whose story of love, vengeance and corrupted political idealism is infused with mystery and intrigue, emerge as fully-developed thriller vehicles in their own right. In part, the purpose of such 'retro' settings is to achieve a visually striking, nostalgic reconstruction of a certain historical situation relevant today, in which the narrative enigma may be located as well as a social or political parable. But, just as important as the narrative, the film will seek to indulge the spectator in the specular pleasures of the 'retro' look (through period costume, décor, music and iconographic elements denoting the past). We find both of these aspects strongly represented in recent thriller features by Pilar Miró.

In *Beltenebros* (1991), based on the novel of the same title by Antonio Muñoz Molina, Miró weaves a complex tale of equivocal political loyalties, betrayal and revenge. Shot in English, with an international cast (including Terence Stamp, Patsy Kensit and Gerladine James) and firmly rooted in the conventions of classic *noir*, *Beltenebros* tells of the double attempt by Captain Darman (Stamp) to eliminate Communist Party traitors in Madrid, the first (mistaken) effort set in 1946 and the second in 1962. These parallel missions allow Miró to draw a variety of comparisons, contrasts, symmetries and role inversions between the younger and older party hit man Darman. She also presents us with various versions of the Rebeca Osorio character (James/Kensit), party agent in the 1940s, striptease dancer in the 1960s and in both settings, sub-

Beltenebros, Pilar Miró, 1991　　　　　　　　　　　　　　9

missive object of sexual desire for Darman as well as his nemesis, police chief (and ex-communist agent) Ugarte/Valdivia. In both missions, it is Ugarte, not Darman's ostensible quarry, who turns out to be the traitor and who is finally eliminated after the shootout in the burning shell of the derelict cinema.

In *Beltenebros*, Miró faithfully captures the settings, atmospheres and oppressive conditions of life under Francoism. She also coolly explores the narrative's 'return of the repressed', i.e. Darman's fear of making the same mistake in 1962 as he did in 1946 and (like his victim Walter) killing another innocent man (Andrade). However, Miró's adaptation is complex and demanding; its temporal shifts sometimes puzzling; characters and roles intermingle, creating a play of repetition and 'doubling' in which, for example, the younger Rebeca/*femme fatale* (Kensit) offers a more explicit, sexy 1960s simulacrum of Rita Hayworth's legendary musical 'striptease' taken from *Gilda* (Charles Vidor, 1946). This is just one of many cinematic and intertextual citations which punctuate the film and which, while of obvious interest to film *aficionados*, tend to complicate an already complex story line. Indeed, the filmic dénouement (the discovery that Ugarte/ Valdivia is the traitor) is set against a suggestive, multi-layered background, involving the fire in the projection machine, the melting of the film stock and the blaze in the film theatre. All of these images may be symbolic of the need for a purifying conflagration to consume not only the many classical Hollywood images cited in the film but even Miró's own

example of filmic deception, betrayal and make-believe (see Rolph 1995: 125).

In *Tu nombre envenena mis sueños* (1996), Miró's more recent, period murder mystery and her ninth feature to date, rather than betrayal, the director focuses on female revenge. Mainly set in 1940s Spain, based on the novel by Joaquín Leguina (whose title is taken from a line of a poem by Neruda, talking of Spain from the position of exile), and again exploiting classic *noir* conventions, the film is narrated by male protagonist, police inspector Ángel Barciela. Structured around three clearly-delineated temporal segments, reflecting different historical moments, the narrative follows Barciela's investigation of a triple murder of so-called 'fifth columnists', who operated in Madrid during the Civil War, eliminating left-wing militiamen. These murders were committed apparently at the hands of a female assassin, whose victims include the Civil Govenor of Guadalajara. At various moments, Barciela is pressurised by his superiors to close the case, though it is not clear why; political reasons may well be answer. Moreover, in a number of instances, the spectator is faced with an excess of unnarrated story material, i.e. a lack of data. While satisfying the demand for mystery and intrigue, this narrative parsimony (as well as other narrative ellipses) create a degree of confusion over certain actions, historical events as well as character motivation. On a wider scale, Miró sets her tale of revenge, murder and obsessive love, against a much larger canvas of political and economic intrigue during the Civil War and after, a period of insecurity, fear and impossible passions. Therein, Julia Buendía, an unusually modern, politically-uncommitted, cold, calculating young woman wreaks bloody revenge on those responsible for liquidating her lover during the Civil War. But in an apparent compulsive repeat performance of the same affair, she fatally falls for the detective who is destined to accuse her of murder. The film thus combines a powerful, highly-charged story of impossible passions between two insignificant people with a parable concerning the absurdities, tragedies and personal disasters of an insane war.

Youth culture, delinquency, drugs

A third, wide-ranging subtrend relates to issues of juvenile delinquency, crime and the devastating effects of drugs on contemporary youth cultures in Spain. It covers films which acknowledge the effects of the massive and growing youth unemployment crisis in the country and its tragic consequences, including family and generational conflict as well as social breakdown, drug abuse, prostitution and the problematic situation of marginal groups and their identities.

Occupying the more populist, sensationalist corner of this subtype, we find Javier Elorrieta's *Cautivos en la sombra* (1994), a challenging though crude and very violent recycling of an American 'genre' drug movie. Curiously anachronistic, Elorrieta's film also recalls the down-market, truculent, subgeneric, *thriller a la española*, current over two decades ago, which was (arguably unfairly) associated with the work of Eloy de la Iglesia, among others. Set against a now clichéd background of dilapidated brothels, crumbling billiard halls, dingy bars and ubiquitous 'yonquis' (junkies), Elorrieta relates a sordid, though (supposedly) everyday story of deceit, petty theft, armed robbery, murder, prostitution, drug dealing and gang warfare among the dregs of a hispanic urban jungle. Echoing Urbizu's *Todo por la pasta*, his treatment of social marginalisation and urban decay is rendered in a no-nonsense, excessively graphic and voyeuristic manner. In particular, Elorrieta concentrates on 'strong' themes and topics (prison rapes, sexual perversion, drug abuse, violent revenge killings). Unfortunately, as noted above, his set-ups, treatments and locations are rather too derivative of American examples of the subtype. Moreover, his 'americanised' dialogues sound doubly clichéd and unreal, his action sequences are poorly choreographed and the perfomances of his actors rather stilted and artificial. Uncannily reminiscent of many of the subproducts of the 1960s and 1970s, *Cautivos en la sombra* is nonetheless an intriguing example of a thriller formula one assumed had died out.

A rather more more effective vehicle for the exploration of Spain's contemporary drug culture is José Antonio de la Loma's *Tres días de libertad* (1996), where a prisoner on weekend parole from jail is forced to confront his past and is drawn back into the drugs underworld by local criminal gangs. Taking a rather different line is Imanol Uribe's no less hard-hitting but far more compelling *Días contados* (1994). Based on the novel by Juan Madrid, set during the period of the capital's famous *Movida* and spectacular Goya winner for 1994, Uribe's film successfully blends a love story and drug abuse with elements of the political thriller, all set against the background of an attempted ETA bombing in Madrid. Having arrived in the capital to set up the explosion, Antonio (Carmelo Gómez) develops a passionate sexual relationship with junkie prostitute Charo (Ruth Gabriel). Aware of his prodigious sexual appetites, the other two members of the ETA team or 'comando' fear his excess libido might compromise the operation (in fact, senior figures in ETA's high command already take this view). Charo, on her side, inhabits a sordid, violent, unforgiving world of junkies, dealers, gangsters and pimps, in which she sells sex to local shopkeepers to earn drug money. She belongs to a group of junkie misfits, including Vanessa (Candela Peña) and the volatile Lisardo (powerfully and convincingly played by Javier Bardem). Two very different worlds thus collide and intermingle. The drug wars in the 'barrio' – the murder of dealer 'el Portugués' by a rival gang – stand as a small scale coun-

10   *Días contados*, Imanol Uribe, 1994

terpoint to the equally deadly political conflict between ETA and the Spanish state. However, what is significant is the way in which Uribe tends to play down the ETA story line, using it more as a means of establishing the marginality of his characters than as a vehicle for political critique. What stands out is the sexual relationship between Antonio and Charo, which gradually develops into a stronger emotional attachment. However, the finer feelings of the two lovers do not obscure numerous highly explicit images of sexual activity, including simulations of fellatio, as well as clearly visible examples of drug abuse and needles piercing veins. While not altogether gratuitous, Uribe's deliberately 'hot', 'sexy' and 'graphic' verisimilitude could be seen as bordering on the sensational and exploitative, a matter of commercial rather than filmic imperatives. By contrast, the film's political back-story is minimised and if *Días contados* affirms a political 'thesis', then this emerges indirectly rather than by way of any heavy or discursive dialogue. In the end, arrested and taken to Police Headquarters for her drug activities, Charo is an unwitting victim of the very bombing campaign planned by Antonio. This represents an ironic twist, perhaps, to the adage that the personal is always political, though it is the personal that Uribe deftly foregrounds in an otherwise harrowing though highly effective thriller.

Family breakdown, gang culture, gender differences and the search for male identity figure prominently in Mariano Barroso's *Extasis* (1996), a film which takes some of its bearings from the more metaphorical cinema of Camus, Gutiérrez Aragón and Miró during the transition. Here, Rober (Javier Bardem), lacking a father figure and any economic means or prospects, stupidly and cynically betrays his family in pursuit of his own 'ecstasy', his own selfish, individuated quest for success. Pedro Olea's much-praised *Morir en Chafariñas* (1995) is set in a military barracks in Melilla and concerns a criminal investigation into the murders of three soldiers, the third of whom is homosexual. The narrative comprises a number of promising threads: the story of the friendship betwen two young recruits (Javier Albalá and Jorge Sanz) who are suspected of involvement in drugs and murder; the relationship between Sanz and the wife of his captain; the relationship between the captain and his business associates; the link between Albalá and the sister of the third victim; the investigation process. Well-paced, set in exotic locations, mixing classic American *noir* elements with Hitchcockian suspense and complicated by the issue of homosexuality in the armed forces, Olea's thriller is an impressive piece of work. Unfortunately, its many intriguing narrative elements are combined in perhaps too predictable and mechanical a fashion. Also, though not explored very deeply, the movie hints that homosexual jealousy and the fear of betrayal may explain the motivation behind the three murders.

The definition of masculine identity and the shaping of male emotional relations underlie Montxo Armendáriz's *Historias del Kronen* (1995), based on the novel by José Ángel Mañas. The Kronen of the film title refers to a tapas bar of the same name, a meeting place in which a 'lost generation' of middle-class youngsters engage in various sorts of antisocial activity, punctuated by sex, drugs, alcohol and violence. The film is memorable for its topical exploration of young male identities and their need for emotional security and support. However, it is not clear whether the instances of male friendship should be construed as old-fashioned machismo or signs of a developing same-sex attachment. Similar ambiguities underlie Ernesto del Río's disturbing *Hotel y domicilio* (1995), which graphically explores the public/professional as well as the private/intimate lives of young male prostitutes.

A less lurid view of modern Spanish youth culture, this time focusing on the limited horizons available to working-class youngsters is found in Alfonso Ungría's *Africa* (1996). Reappearing in a directorial role after an absence of some fourteen years, Ungría focuses on family relations and oedipal anxieties in a marginal, working-class district of Madrid (San Blas). Intent on anatomising the relationship between a father and son, Ungría contrasts an untrustworthy, unreliable, violent father figure with a son who, in order to bolster his self-esteem and separate existence, trains as a long distance runner. The running motif acts as an obvious though no less powerful metaphor for the youngster's desire for escape from a desperate world of unemployment, drugs and family violence. In the end, pushed to the limit, the youngster attempts to overcome patriarchal violence by murdering the oppressive father figure. And in so doing, he opens the window to his mythical goal of 'Africa', symbol of freedom but also replete with complex notions of cultural and racial difference.

Here, it is perhaps worth mentioning two recent films which develop the themes of racism and xenophobia within a thriller format. Firstly, Carlos Saura's *Taxi* (1996), which deals with a group of taxi drivers, committed to persecuting blacks, homosexuals and other marginal groups, who are regarded as enemies of certain eternal, national values. Obviously reminiscent of Scorsese's *Taxi Driver* (1973) and the memorably chilling figure of loner Travis Bickle, as well as echoing his own earlier *Deprisa deprisa* (1980), Saura's collective approach to racism shows a group of night-time drivers, led by an ex-policeman, linked to extreme right-wing groups, who murder passengers of whom they disapprove. Ultimately, their scheme is put into jeopardy when the daughter of one of the drivers discovers the truth of their grisly nocturnal business. Despite its laudable and powerful denunciation of intolerance and xenophobia, Saura's study of modern fascism among those who scapegoat and persecute racial/sexual minorities is arguably flawed. Its heavy-handed condemnation of racial prejudice tends to overdetermine narrative logic; this results in a thesis film whose anti-fascist message is less effectively conveyed for being too emphatically presented.

The same difficulty arises in Imanol Uribe's feature *Bwana* (1996), a film adaptation of the play by Ignacio del Moral (*La mirada del hombre oscuro*) which deals with racial prejudice among otherwise well-meaning Spaniards. Here again, a taxi driver (Andrés Pajares) and his wife (María Barranco) and family, on holiday, encounter a destitute black man on the African coast. The encounter becomes the premise for a display of racist topics and clichés about blacks, accepted and parroted by the Spanish family (including Barranco's clichéd, erotic dream about sex with black men). The film represents another denunciation of racism as well as a condemnation of the cowardice and inherent xenophobia of the typical middle-class Spanish family. Unfortunately, the portrayal of the family and their ideas is exaggerated and caricatured to a point where any fair-minded spectator could easily distance him or herself and feel morally superior, and thus immune to any serious self-examination about the issues raised. Moreover, this is another thesis film, in which the message is rendered largely ineffective by its constant repetition and overstatement.

Finally, within this category, several films in the 1990s have brought their female protagonists centre stage and explore their responses to issues of family responsibilities, female friendship and love, in marginal social settings, dominated by drugs, crime and the ever-present possibility of personal oblivion. For example, Daniel Calparsoro's first full-length feature *Salto al vacío* (1995) explores a day in the life of Alex, a twenty-year-old misfit who supports her family through dealing in drugs and arms and looks to her gang for muscle as well as meaning. Calparsoro's second film *Pasajes* (1996), less impressive than the first, is also concerned with a delinquent youth culture but now in terms of a female thief who develops a troubled love relationship with an older and wiser woman. And in a rather different vein, within the frame of the road movie, Manuel Huerga's provocative *Antártida* (1994) charts the decline and fall of a once vibrant female rock star through drugs and subsequent alienation. However, her eventual salvation and redemption are secured through female solidarity.

Psychological thriller

The subcategory of what we might call the psychological thriller was represented in the late 1980s and early 1990s by features such as Jesús Garay's *Pasión lejana* (1987), Ricardo Monleón's *Baton rouge* (1988) and Antonio Chavarrías's *Una sombra en el jardín* (1989) and *Manila* (1991). More recently Chavarrías has returned to the genre with *Susana* (1996), a piece which explores one woman's response to the complex interaction between three different social strata: the Catalan petit bourgeoisie (represented by Susana), her contact with members of low-life criminal gangs and her discovery of African immigrants. Taking a rather different slant on the degree to which Spain's middle classes are aware of their prejudices and shortcomings, Mario Camus's *Adosados* (1996) analyses the domestic crisis of a model family. The death of a family pet is the trigger which leads to recriminations, withdrawal of emotional support, a lack of communication and eventually the break-up of the family. Camus manages to expose the false stability at the heart of the family unit, where the deceitful gaze and subtle lie substitute genuine communication.

Approaching issues of lying, pretence and role playing from a rather different perspective is Julio Medem's *La ardilla roja* (1993). Arguably over-hyped as a trail-blazing effort from one of the younger generation of Spanish filmmakers, the film is nonetheless an important contribution to the subtype. By way of the device of feigned amnesia, Medem's rather cerebral, complex feature contains a parodic, postmodern send-up of personal as well as cultural 'origins' and 'roots'. Indeed, the film invites the spectator to reflect on the ways in which we construct our notions of self, cultural heritage and national identity, which can be seen as potentially fanciful, always provisional and subject to transformation. Dealing with similar issues of personal indentity and cultural roots, Agustín Díaz Yanes, in his first award-winning feature *Nadie hablará de nosotras cuando hayamos muerto* (1995) follows Gloria, a prostitute (Victoria

Abril) caught up in the violently masculine world of bullfighting and Mexican gangsters. With her husband having been in a coma for three years as a result of being gored, the film charts Gloria's return to Madrid, her attempt to rebuild her life through blackmailing a drug gang, the spiritual crisis of the gunman sent to kill her and her relationship with her mother-in-law (an old Communist Party militant). The movie focuses upon constructions of female identity and angst as well as male; and, as in Huerga's *Antártida*, it also shows how an older generation, through self-sacrifice, is able to help its younger counterpart to escape violence and exploitation and reach some form of inner freedom and spiritual redemption.

At the harder, more troubling end of the pyschological thriller spectrum is Gerardo Herrero's provocative international copro *Desvío al paraíso* (1994), starring Charles Dance as Quinn, the impostor handyman, and Assumpta Serna as María, single mother of Sara. The film focuses on the relationship between a twelve-year-old-girl (Sara) and an amoral, enigmatic adult (Quinn), following the youngster's forced abduction. The relationship between paedophile Quinn, Sara and her young male companion Gus is a menacing combination of simulated sadism and symbolic torture (represented by the murals). And while Herrero handles the nightmarish threat embodied by Quinn in a controlled, skilful manner, the spectator is always kept aware of the disturbing nature of paedophilia and the potential for the abuse of power from the deranged outsider. In the same context, and adopting a more truculent, *tremendista* approach to his subject matter, we are obliged to recall here the first two features of Juanma Bajo Ulloa. His *Alas de mariposa* (1991) and *La madre muerta* (1993) reveal an apparent concern with the causes and effects of psychological disturbances and infantile neuroses and the nature of violent behaviour. While *Alas de mariposa* analyses the disintegration of a working-class family-unit through the destructive effects of infantile sexual repression, *La madre muerta* follows the disturbingly paradoxical behaviour of a thief turned psychopath, capable of brutal murder but at the same time, remarkable tenderness and compassion. Bajo Ulloa raises compelling questions regarding such dysfunctional, violent behaviour, but provides few answers. He is one of several directors who have looked at the figure of the psychopath, including José Luis Acosta, whose *Gimlet* (1995) explores the figure of the 'stalker'. While clearly paying homage to classical American *noir* and Chandler's Marlowe (seen in the character of the gumshoe, played by Antonio Resines), Acosta updates his thriller by observing Angela Molina's relentless persecution by a sex stalker, in a dark, doomed non-relationship, highly reminiscent of Bigas Luna's *Bilbao* (1978).

In many ways, the figure of the psychopath acts as the bridge which connects us to the 'serial-killer' film, a subtype inaugurated internationally by Jonathan Demme's *The Silence of the Lambs*

La madre muerta, Juanma Bajo Ulloa, 1993   **11**

(1990) and continued in David Fincher's *Seven* (1995). The main interest provided by this sort of film lies in the visual representation of sickeningly violent and repellent male behaviour which we regard as deeply disturbing and which has awesome repercussions on the public as well as the police professionals. Moreover, as a means of exploring the pathology of the killers, such films tend to focus on the grisly, bloody handiwork of the serial killer, as if the murderer's unspeakable treatment of his victims (including the inevitable mutilation of the bodies) were viewed as the essence and absolute expression of evil. 'Serial killer' films thus attempt to transcend the sensationalist spectacle of *cine gore* in order to explore the dark side of humanity and the background and motivations for this indescribably evil behaviour. In Spain, while numerous films have looked at the figure and behaviour of the psychopath, so far, those featuring the serial killer are few in number and this subgroup remains relatively undeveloped. Indeed, apart from Almodóvar's highly stylised *Matador* (1986), Bigas Luna's *Angustia* (1987) and Pilar Miró's *Tu nombre envenena mis sueños* (1996), which explores the motivations behind an apparent female serial murderer, the main contemporary example of the subtype is the parodic *Justino, un asesino de la tercera edad* (1994) by La Cuadrilla (Santiago Aguilar and Luis Guridi). Here, the issues raised above concerning the killer's background, the impact of his activities on his victims and their loved ones and the more serious question of moral evil are all undercut by the film's corrosive black humour. However, we do have an example of a film in which male violence, torture, mutilation and murder are dealt with in a more serious though no less

Tesis, Alejandro Amenábar, 1996

commercial manner. This is Alejandro Amenábar's *Tesis* (1996).
Amenábar stresses the criminality and illegality surrounding his
subject matter, the 'snuff' movie. He also registers the alarming fascination such material can exert over the viewer. This is seen in
Ángela's divided relationship towards her thesis material and particularly towards Bosco, who appears in the murder scene in the
stolen video. However, Amenábar's attempts to explore the implications of his subject and elucidate the nature of the evil attachment to acts of murder and mutilation are perhaps left rather
vague. There is also the obvious contradiction betwen the film's
rejection of male violence and aggression and the clear commercial
potential arising from showing (simulated) examples of such behaviour.

The erotic/sexual thriller

A salient feature of the Spanish thriller over the last two decades
has been its unrestrained attitude towards the explicit portrayal of
sex and violence, seen as a key to its viability and commercial
potential. Though this trend recently appears to have been attenu-
ated somewhat (witness Gómez Pereira's *Boca a boca* (1995) – in
which the visual representation of telephone sex is significantly
toned down) – a number of recent thrillers/melodramas have
included strong and highly-revealing sexual or erotic elements.
Obvious precedents include Almodóvar's *Matador* (1986) and *La ley
del deseo* (1986), Bigas Luna's *Bilbao* (1978) and *Lola* (1986) and
Juanma Bajo Ulloa's noirish/horror hybrid *La madre muerta* (1993).
However, the now notorious *Amantes* (1991) by Vicente Aranda,

based on a real historical case (the so-called 'Tetuán de las Victorias'), is arguably the film which has done more than most to foment the (international) public perception of contemporary Spanish cinema as invariably hot, sexy and very explicit. As noted in another chapter, if one of the main themes of *Amantes* is the destructive potential of obsessive passion and sexual desire, in order to make its point Aranda's cautionary tale still requires the graphic display of stylish and very explicit screen sex. Such erotic exhibitionism has become a strong selling point of his recent output, visible in *El amante bilingüe* (1993), *Intruso* (1993) and *La pasión turca* (1994), based on the novel by Antonio Gala. Here, the main female protagonist Desideria, after the failure of her marriage, is driven by her single-minded pursuit of sexual pleasure to return to her Turkish lover, Yaman. 'Soy una guarra' (I'm a slut), remarks Desi, confidently asserting the legitimacy of her appetites. However, those same appetites lead to her obsessive dependence on Yaman, her willingness to prostitute herself for her lover's business clients and ultimately her own degradation. The price of love, it seems, is the total collapse of Desi's self-esteem and her eventual suicide (according to the novel, though not in the film). The criminal element in *La pasión turca* is small compared to Aranda's focus on explicit scenes of coitus which, perhaps in deference to the traditions of Islam, always seem to involve the female in subordinate positions.

Also exploiting the commercial potential of explicit sexual behaviour, we find Imanol Arias's *Un asunto privado* (1995), a complex, highly-charged erotic thriller in which sexual experimentation (including same sex) again structures the narrative and informs the central theme. Other films within the category which explore various aspects of sexuality with very strong and explicit scenes, include: Antonio Chavarrías's *Susana* (1996), Antonio Farré's romantic thriller *Razones sentimentales* (1995), Elio Quiroga's *Fotos* (1996) and Enrique Gabriel Lipschutz' *Desgracias personales* (1996).

Following an argument advanced by Marsha Kinder (1993: 432–3), we could say that the contemporary Spanish thriller, in its multiple guises, provides yet another powerful example of that 'eroticised marginality', which has come to epitomise much of post-Franco film output, especially in the perceptions of foreign audiences. Indeed, what many of the films mentioned above appear to do is to bring centre-stage marginal behaviours, practices and social issues (drugs, terrorism, homophobia, etc.) and refigure them as both local/national as well as international/global problems.

The musical

Alongside the comedy, the musical film has been one of Spain's most consistently popular domestic genres. The golden age of the Spanish musical was undoubtedly the 1930s and 1940s, during which companies such as Cifesa produced numerous so-called *españoladas*. These were hybrid products, a mixture of comedy, musical and *relato costumbrista* (stories of social customs), invariably remakes of silent movie versions or screen adaptations of popular stage plays, as in such classics as *María de la O* (Francisco Elías 1936), *Carmen la de Triana* (Florián Rey 1938) and *Suspiros de España* (Benito Perojo 1938) (García Fernández 1985: 63 and 102). It was these films that established Spain's first national star system, with such immortal figures as Manuel Luna, Antonio Moreno, Miguel Ligero, Imperio Argentina, Estrellita Castro and Concha Piquer (Morgan 1995: 152). And it is to this era that the revivalist movies of the 1980s and 1990s look back and pay homage.

After the Civil War, such films became the embodiment of escapism and the vehicle par excellence of the *mitología franquista* (Francoist mythology), offering a seductive but false notion of Spanishness for both internal and external consumption. Their themes and narratives were inextricably associated with the arch-conservative ideology of the Franco regime, reflecting and promoting patriarchal attitudes towards nationalism, class, the family, gender and sexuality and celebrating romanticised myths about love, honour, religion, morality, the social order, etc. As Hopewell indicates, the appeal of such films had to do with the instability of the period. They offered audiences easy identifications and solidarity with national archetypes and stock racial models. And in the difficult postwar years, they also offered a comforting, if illusory, alternative to shortages, rationing and political repression as well as a sense of defensive patriotism (1986: 15–16). Little wonder then, that their mythical vision of 'deep Spain' has provoked almost blanket critical derision for decades.

In the 1950s and 1960s, the musical tradition was continued by a younger generation of *tonadillera* (light songs) stars such as Lola Flores and Rocío Jurado, but in the early 1970s the genre was virtually absent from Spanish screens, until a revival of interest in the mid-1980s. The peaks of the genre's popularity are thus historically associated with periods of instability, turmoil and fear. Conversely, the musical's virtual disappearance from the cinema from the mid-1970s to the mid-1980s coincides with a period of optimism and hope evoked by the transition to democracy and the return of political freedoms. Intriguingly, the revival of the genre over the last decade coincides with a period of *desencanto* (disillusionment) and a widespread cynicism towards party politics in Spain. And against this background, some of the retro-musicals of this period appear to reproduce both the stylistic and ideological conventions of the classical genre. By contrast, other films take advantage of the nostalgia value of the retro styles and iconography to introduce more challenging narratives and critical themes for contemporary audiences.

The viability of the musical film was arguably revived in part by the international success of Carlos Saura's 'dance' trilogy, beginning with *Bodas de sangre* (1981) and followed by *Carmen* (1983) and *El amor brujo* (1986). (Saura has continued his dance and musical interests with *Sevillanas* (1992), *Flamenco* (1995) and *Tango* (1997), exploring the way in which Spanish dance traditions have been adapted and reformulated in the New World). Also, starting with the success of José Luis García Sánchez's *La corte de Faraón* in 1985, the retro-musical tradition has been successively refashioned and relaunched. This trend has included Jaime Chávarri's period piece *Las cosas del querer* (1989), Luis Sanz's incredibly successful *Yo soy esa* (1990) – which drew on the classical traditions of the Spanish musical and turned *tonadillera* Isabel Pantoja into a film star – as well as *El día que nací yo* (1991) by Pedro Olea and Joséfina Molina's remake of the 1940s classic *La Lola se va a los puertos* (1993). A number of other retrospective features such as Saura's *¡Ay, Carmela!* (1990) and the sequel to *Las cosas del querer* (1995) clearly indicate the sub-genre's continuing popularity and business potential.

The reasons why the retro or revivalist musicals should have renewed their appeal so successfully over the last decade are not difficult to fathom. As noted above, with one or two exceptions perhaps (*La corte de Faraón, Las cosas del querer, La Lola se va a los puertos*), in times of uncertainty, economic pessimism and political *desencanto*, as under Franco, such films broadly efface complexity and contradiction and in their artificial vision of a stereotypical Spain, they offer a comfortably familiar world, far removed from the realities of the contemporary moment. Films such as Luis Sanz's *Yo soy esa* not only trade on the nostalgia value of their retro styles, they also reproduce both the stylistic and ideological features of the classical 1940s hits of the genre. In the subsequent Pantoja showcase film *El día que nací yo*, though set in the early 1940s, it again offers an overly sanitised view of the period and a highly retrograde view of female sexuality. By contrast, other films such as *La Lola se va a los puertos* and *Las cosas del querer* have challenged such stereotypes and taken a more critical, searching attitude towards social and sexual identities (Morgan 1995: 158–62).

The fantasy/science-fiction/horror/adventure film

As noted at the very beginning of this chapter, generic features and conventions are remarkably fluid and can be found in all sorts of intriguing combinations. For example, in Medem's *Tierra*, elements of fantasy and magic coexist within a nominally realist portrayal within the rural genre; Gonzalo Suárez's *El detective y la muerte* combines a thriller format with features of a dark, gothic fantasy underworld, as does Pablo Llorca's *Jardines colgantes*; also, Juan Pinzás's *La leyenda de la doncella* (1996), blends a period cautionary

Cultural reinscription

tale with elements of gothic horror and black magic. So, when we talk of the 'fantastic', science fiction and horror movie, we are dealing with unstable categories, which are inevitably informed by elements and features drawn from other generic groupings.

Following the catastrophic failure of Fernando Colomo's *El caballero del dragón* (1985) – which cost 264 millions and only managed box office takings of 71 million) (Gubern, *et al.* 1994: 435) – Spanish efforts in the fantasy/fantastic genre came to a complete halt for nearly a decade. However, one of the few positive features to emerge from official funding initiatives since the Miró reforms of the 1980s has been modest support for younger filmmakers to enter the business via the production of shorts (e.g. Santiago Segura, Pablo Lloréns) and financial support for scriptwriting endeavours. This backing has created the conditions in which certain types of genre films, such as fantasy, adventure, science fiction, etc. (which were rarely exploited by Spanish filmmakers before the 1980s) have seen something of an upturn since the early 1990s. A combination of more positive promotion of such material at Film festivals (such as the *Semana de Cine Fantástico y de Terror*, at Sitges and San Sebastián – the 1995 San Sebastián event was the subject of a recent short by Juanma Bajo Ulloa), plus the remarkable success of Alex de la Iglesia's futuristic, science fiction/comedy/thriller (produced by Almodóvar) *Acción mutante* (1992), have had a significant effect on the willingness of producers and directors to chance their arm in areas traditionally monopolised by Hollywood.

Generically, de la Iglesia's award-winning *Acción mutante* is a complex hybrid, a multi-layered *mélange* of narrative conventions and stylistic features lifted from different genres. Science fiction is probably the dominant frame of reference (in film but also in comic and cartoon form), but within this area we find elements of the kidnap/hijack movie, the postmodern musical (the wedding ceremony) and the western-style shoot out finale. Also, certain plot features such as Yarritu's release from jail and the grisly murder of his colleagues on the spaceship strongly recall *film noir* as well as the black farce of the *esperpento*. Yet, in the middle section of the film, during the journey to Axturias, several scenes are reminiscent of drawing-room comedy and bedroom farce. Above all, the effectiveness of the film relies on the consistent exploitation of filmic excess and bad taste, as much as from its promiscuous raiding of other genres and texts. For this purpose, the film seeks to establish a certain look: 'sucio', 'roñoso', 'cochambroso', i.e. dark, filthy, earthy, scabrous, reinforced by the graffiti in the space ship, the clothes on the washing line, the gallons of brake fluid used to simulate spurting blood and, overall the parody of the 'working interstellar vessel' of the *Alien* series. All this is contrasted with the chic, futuristic, designer look evoked by the guests in the wedding scene.

Building on his 1992 success, Alex de la Iglesia developed his

Acción mutante, Alex de la Iglesia, 1992   **13**

more recent parodic *El día de la bestia* (1995), mixing elements of
The Exorcist, *The Omen* and *Don Quijote*, space opera, serial killer
movies and rock videos. In it, a Basque priest and his heavy metal
sidekick seek to eliminate the anti-Christ at Christmas before he
destroys the world (see Basque cinema in Chapter 4). Following his
patron Almodóvar, de la Iglesia appears to have reinvigorated the
trend in the parodic, postmodern, 'grungy', hybrid comedy. For
along very similar lines, we find Alberto Sciamma's *La lengua asesina*
(1996), a 'road/prison' movie incorporating a *pot pourri* of generic
clichés and film citations, incuding Stephen King and Almodóvar;
Estéban Ibarretxe's *Sólo se muere dos veces* (1996), in which a dead
actor finds work playing a zombie; Alvaro Sáenz de Heredia's
hugely successful *Aquí llega Condemor* (1996), crazy mix of horror
movie and spoof western; Elio Quiroga's fantasy *Fotos* (1996), Oscar
Aíbar's *Yo también fui alienígena adolescente* (1997) and Jess Franco's
trash movie *Killer Barbies* (1996).

In the 1990s, exploiting the more traditional, classical norms of
the horror/fantasy film, we find a remarkable volume and variety
of output. Juan Pinzás's *La leyenda de la doncella* (1996) is a reworking of the Dracula story set in the 1930s against the backdrop of
rural Galicia and its myths and legends. Gonzalo Suárez pays
homage to the Jekyll and Hyde myth in *Mi nombre es sombra* (1995)
and Arantxa Lazcano's *Como ala de cuervo* (1995), is a ghost story
combining elements of Poe and Basque legends. Also, in the manner
of *The Witches of Eastwick*, in *Brujas* (1996), Alberto Fernández
Armero develops a contemporary, fantasmagorical comedy about a
day in the bizarre lives of three women. On more purist horror
movie terrain, we find the unexpected return of Spain's horror

Cultural reinscription

specialist of the 1970s, Paul Naschy, with cameo parts in Arturo de Bobadilla's *Los resuscitados* (1995) and Francesc Javier Capell's Chrichtonesque *Científicament perfectes* (1995). And finally, against the current background of increasing levels of activity in virtually all types of genre film, Spanish movie making even hits the world of Tron and the Internet with Rafael Alcázar's *Hackers, corsarios del chip* (1996), an ambitious though not totally convincing attempt to compete with the American 'kids/computer nerd' movie.

References

Benet, V. J. (1989), Notas sobre el film policíaco español contemporáneo, in Benet, J. V., *et al.*, *Escritos sobre Cine Español 1973–1987*, Valencia, Filmoteca de la Generalitat Valenciana, 125–31.

Caparrós Lera, J. M. (1992), *El cine español de la democracia. De la muerte de Franco al "cambio socialista" (1975–1989)*, Barcelona, Anthropos.

de la Cuadra, B., and Gallego Díaz, S. (1981), *Del consenso al desencanto*, Madrid, Editorial Saltés, 21–44.

Fernández, Valentí, T.,(1996), El thriller moderno, *Dirigido*, 252, 42–51.

Freixas, R. (1996), review of *Apartado de Correos 1001*, Centenario del cine español, *Dirigido*, 248, 49.

García Fernández, E. C. (1985), *Historia ilustrada del cine español*, Planeta, Madrid, 63–102.

Graham, H. and Labanyi, J. (1995), *Spanish Cultural Studies. An Introduction*, Oxford, Oxford University Press, 257–8.

Gubern, R., *et al.*. (1994), *Historia del cine español*, Madrid, Cátedra, Signo e Imagen, 386–435.

Hayward, S. (1996), *Key Concepts in Cinema Studies*, London, Routledge, 111–59.

Hooper, J. (1995), *The New Spaniards*, Middlesex, Penguin, 344–5.

Hopewell, J. (1986), *Out of the Past. Spanish Cinema after Franco*, London, BFI, 15–223.

Hopewell, J. (1989), *El cine español después de Franco*, Madrid, Ediciones El Arquero.

Jordan, B. (1995), Genre cinema in Spain in the 1970s: the Case of Comedy, *Revista Canadiense de Estudios Hispánicos*, Canada, 20: 1, 127–41.

Kinder, M. (1993), *Blood Cinema. The Reconstruction of National Identity in Spain*, Berkeley and Los Angeles, University of California Press, 60–433.

Lapsley, R., and Westlake, M. (1988), *Film Theory: An Introduction*, Manchester, Manchester University Press, 181–213.

Lloréns, A. (1988), *El cine negro español*, Valladolid, Semana de Cine de Valladolid.

Monterde, J. E. (1993), *Veinte años de cine español (1973–1992). Un cine bajo la paradoja*, Barcélona, Ediciones Paidós, 131–45.

Morgan, R. (1995), Nostalgia and the Contemporary Spanish Musical Film, *Revista Canadiense de Estudios Hispánicos*, Canada, 20: 1, 151–66.

Morgan, R., and Jordan, B. (1994), Jamón, Jamón: A tale of ham and pastiche, *Donaire*, 2, 57–64.

Neale, S. (1980), *Genre*, London, BFI, 19.

Payán, M. J. (1993), *Cine español de los 90*, Madrid, J.C.

Rolph, W. L. (1995), Desire in the Dark: *Beltenebros* goes to the Movies, *Revista Canadiense de Estudios Hispánicos*, Canada, 20: 1, 117–25.

Schatz, (1981), in Browne, R. B., and Ambrosetti, R. J. (eds) (1993), *Continu-*

ities in Popular Culture, The Present in the Past and the Past in the Present and Future, Bowling Green, Ohio, Bowling Greet State University Press, 16.

Smith, P. J. (1992), *Laws of desire. Questions of Homosexuality in Spanish Writing and Film 1960–1990*, Oxford, Clarendon Press, 129–62.

Smith, P. J. (1994), *Desire Unlimited. The Cinema of Pedro Almodóvar*, London, Verso, 18–20.

Torres, A. M. (1994), *Diccionario del cine español*, Madrid, Espasa Calpe, 271–356.

Vanaclocha, J., *et al.*. (Equipo Cartelera Turia) (1974), *Cine español. Cine de Sub-géneros*, Valencia, Fernando Torres.

Vernon, K. M., and Morris, B. (1995), *Post-Franco, Postmodern. The Films of Pedro Almodóvar*, Westport, Connecticut and London, Greenwood Press, 6–15.

3 | Gender and sexuality in post-Franco cinema

Introduction

Spanish cinema is known for producing more explicit images (of both sex and violence) than most other contemporary European cinemas. On the wider international circuit, this reputation has been fuelled by legal and media controversies surrounding the US release of films such as Vicente Aranda's *Amantes* (1991) as well as Pedro Almodóvar's *¡Átame!* (1989) – which a US court attempted to ban – and *Kika* (1993), which was released unclassified. The prominence of sexual thematics in contemporary Spanish film and the explicitness and eclecticism of its imagery are no doubt partially due to commercial considerations, although erotic content is no guarantee of large returns in the international market. It is also clearly the product of a certain historical context which, despite the vastly different reality of contemporary Spain, has left its mark on Spanish cultural production and reception and ensures a continuing association between the sexual and the political.

Francoism, let us recall, operated on the basis of highly traditional and retrograde concepts of gender and sexuality. This led to the conflation of sexual and political repression in the cultural life of the dictatorship. Along with other forms of cultural opposition to the regime, oppositional cinema was quick to exploit the metaphorical possibilities of the thematics of sexual repression. This was particularly evident in a number of films by Carlos Saura, including *El jardín de las delicias* (1970), *Ana y los lobos* (1972), *La prima Angélica* (1973) and *Cría cuervos* (1976). Also, the relations between politics and sexual repression were often articulated through the perspective of a child protagonist, as in *El espíritu de la colmena* (Víctor Erice 1973) and *A un dios desconocido* (Jaime Chávarri 1977), as well as Saura's *Cría cuervos* (1976). In such films, the dual concept of the precocious child and the stunted adult produced, as Marsha Kinder suggests, a model of the divided self which encapsulates 'the tragedy of lost potential' (Kinder 1983: 74). Issues of gender and sexuality thus became inextricably linked and highly politicised.

By the early 1970s, the regime's regressive sexual politics had begun to modify, allowing for a slight liberalisation of what could be shown on cinema screens. This ushered in a flood of so-called *destape* film products, featuring images of (exclusively female) nudity, such as Carmen Sevilla's appearance in *La loba y la paloma* (Gonzálo Suárez 1973). However, such films merely reinforced the traditional specularisation of the female form, which had characterised mainstream cinema since its inception. At the same time, such concessions to screen nudity and bad language were superficial and cosmetic, aimed at buying off increasing popular pressures for political and sexual freedoms. If the consequent proliferation of more explicit sexual imagery appeared to indicate some form of moral and sexual liberation, then this was misleading. In fact, as we have noted in other chapters, the so-called *destape* of the early and mid-1970s was simply part of a wider diversionary strategy to deflect attention away from growing political tensions. Moreover, as indicated above, the underlying gender politics of the resulting images were just as retrograde as before.

Despite this predominant sensationalist trend, a small but nevertheless persistent undercurrent of films continued to operate a more critical, questioning sexual discourse which gradually found its way into more mainstream cinema through the work of the *tercera vía*. In Jaime de Armiñán's *El amor del capitán Brando* (1974), the ground-breaking, full-frontal shot of Ana Belén, which links the spectator with the small boys spying on their teacher in an invasive act of infantile voyeurism, is a case in point. Such critiques of a system which had enforced sexual repression and ignorance also fed into what might be regarded as a second-wave sexualisation which swept through both arthouse and mainstream cinema, often producing more reflective or provocative representations of gender and sexuality.

This chapter will seek to explore such representations in the context of post-Franco cinema. After considering the impact of the so-called *Movida* on cultural and cinematic trends, we will focus particularly on the increased profile of women both behind and in front of the camera. We then attempt to deal with representations of patriarchy and masculinity and the contradictory images these can produce. We also explore the evidence of a more radical questioning of traditionally-erected gender boundaries and the promotion of a more eclectic range of models for sexual orientation and personal and family relationships.

Gender and sexuality

Post-Franco freedoms: the *Movida*

Spain's rapid modernisation and social, economic and legislative changes since the end of the dictatorship have had a major impact on social values, structures and patterns of behaviour. The availability of contraception, maternity rights, the introduction of equal opportunities at work, together with the impact of recession and extended unemployment, have changed the composition of the workforce so that by 1990 women represented 35 per cent of the active population (Barañano 1992: 14). State intervention in the organisation of private and domestic affairs and the previously pervasive influence of the Catholic church have dramatically receded. Other changes such as the decriminalisation of homosexuality have led to the proliferation of a series of alternative lifestyles. These changes have a powerful bearing on the whole gamut of interpersonal relations and the articulation of the relationships between the individual, society and the state. As Spanish cinema became more familiar with post-censorship freedoms, the relationships, lifestyles, structures and orientations represented on screen became more adventurous and eclectic. In the Spanish cinema of the 1980s, a whole range of sexual orientations and practices, which had been variously banned or marginalised under Francoism, could now be explored in mainstream as well as arthouse films (Monterde 1993: 165–6).

The *Movida* and the *fenómeno Almodóvar*

Some of the most radical challenges both to traditional values and to accepted notions of cultural radicalism in the 1980s came from Madrid's *Movida* movement which, among its leading figures, produced Spanish cinema's *enfant terrible* Pedro Almodóvar. The protagonists of the *Movida* seemed to espouse a radical apoliticism and practised a kind of 'cultural transvestism', trying on and casting off the range of different identities which suddenly became possible after the end of the dictatorship and which caused some commentators to regard post-Franco Spain as 'the epitome of the postmodern, the incarnation in practice of European theory – from its multilingual, multicultural mix to its alleged toleration of drugs, pornography and homosexuality' (Vernon and Morris 1995: 10). This interpretation perhaps overstates the impact of the *Movida*; the notion of a fully liberated Spain in the democratic era also begs a number questions. What for some indicated the introduction of progressive attitudes and tolerance, for others signalled either a dangerous abandonment of political commitment and submission to the values of consumerism or merely confirmed their worst suspicions of democracy and the freedom of expression, provoking a further retrenchment of conservative attitudes and a reassertion of traditional patriarchal values. However, the influence of Pedro Almodóvar's work – which is as much a product of the *comedia madrileña* and long-standing traditions of the *esperpento* as of the *Movida* – has certainly had an iconoclastic effect on Spanish cinema.

In terms of its sexual politics, Almodóvar's cinema has always been controversial. His early work was as dismissive of the limits of conventional sexuality as it was of distinctions between high art and popular culture, good and bad taste. It is his flamboyant visual style and his treatment of gender and sexuality which have stamped an overarching identity on his films. Conventional social structures and patterns of behaviour are parodied or ignored and displaced by a parade of alternative lifestyles and relationships presented through hilarious subversions of popular film genres. The convent comedy *Entre tinieblas* (1983) hinges on the lesbian attachment of the mother superior to her protegée Yolanda and *La ley del deseo* (1986) is a thriller based on compulsive homosexual love and pursuit. But the apparent sexual ambiguity of these characters is more than mere whimsical game-playing. In line with his generally deconstructive approach to artificial categorisations, these representations are a means of subverting the traditional roles and patterns that shape patriarchal society. Almodóvar's characteristic appropriation of family melodrama challenges conventional configurations of the family to replace them with unorthodox alternatives such as the homosexual brother and transsexual sister partnership of *La ley del deseo* and the eminently more secure and effective parental role they fulfil for Ada than her natural mother (played by real-life transsexual Bibi Andersson). Conventional gender roles are similarly dismantled in a quite radical way. In *Tacones lejanos* (1991), it is the concept of justice that comes under attack through Almodóvar's play on gender and sexual ambiguity. The judge takes on a number of deliberately ambiguous guises, including the role of transvestite cabaret artist, Letal (Morgan 1992a: 28–9). In *Matador* (1986), first impressions suggest a resurrection of the old Freudian penis-envy saga but mere role-reversal is displaced by the more radical thesis of the fluidity of traditionally gendered characteristics (Morgan 1992b: 399–404).

Given his actively deconstructive approach to dominant representations of cultural production, sexuality, authority, religion, justice, etc. and his self-declared pro-feminist position, the fact that Almodóvar's films are most often about women in a cinema dominated by male characters and problems has positioned him as a 'women's director'. The rounded and sensitive characterisation of his female protagonists and the positive representation of female relationships and support networks contrast markedly with the critical and underdeveloped portrayal of many of the men in his films (Holden 1992: 99–100). Nevertheless, some of his representations of women have also provoked considerable criticism. *Mujeres al borde de un ataque de nervios* (1988), for example, has been attacked

14   *Tacones lejanos*, Pedro Almodóvar, 1991

on the grounds that it portrays women as empty-headed neurotics. Alternative readings of these female characters stress their superiority to the male characters in terms of their solidarity and moral integrity. *¡Átame!* (1989) has been taken to task for the dangerously negative interpretations its resolution seems to imply when Marina falls in love and drives off into the sunset with the man who held her hostage. For Almodóvar, this ending is a demonstration of love rather than evidence of perversity. A similar situation is explored in *La ley del deseo*, where the pursuing lover goes to equally violent and reprehensible lengths to win over his male lover and, though the pursuit ends in his own self-destruction, he too succeeds in winning the love of the object of his desire. The mismatch between Almodóvar's apparent intention and critical perceptions of his films seems to be rooted in the 'liberal' approach underpinning his treatment of all social structures. His defence of *¡Átame!* hinges on arguments in favour of freedom of choice. These might work within the film world which Almodóvar constructs, free from the constraints of dominant ideological concepts. However, his audiences inhabit a world in which the repression of women is too deeply entrenched within social and psychological consciousness for such representations to be entirely free from misogynistic interpretation. Whilst there is no eroticism in the bondage scenes in *¡Átame!* and Antonio's violence towards María distances her rather than acts as a perverse kind of attraction, it would be naive to ignore the troubling effect this kind of representation can produce (Morgan 1995: 113–27).

    Almodóvar's work since the success of *Mujeres al borde de un ataque de nervios* has often been regarded as less original and thought-provoking. *Kika* (1993) clearly attempted a return to the more provocative register of his early work. However, setting out to deliver a study of obsession and a critique of media exploitation and 'seguridad ciudadana' (urban safety), the film appears to fall foul of its own critical thesis. The intrusive media exploitation of violence is epitomised in Kika's rape at the hands of half witted, exporn-star Paul Bazzo, which is videoed by a voyeur from a building opposite and relayed by Andrea Caracortada in her TV Reality Show *Lo peor del día* (The Worst of the Day). Despite the narrative condemnation of both violations, the protracted length and comic register of the rape sequence provoked vehement criticism of the film's own exploitative intent and renewed accusations of the trivialisation of rape and sexual violence which had greeted the treatment of this theme in his earlier *Matador* and *¡Átame!*. This, together with *Kika*'s complex and fragmented plot and a series of over-familiar comic strategies, snippets of dialogue and stylistic idiosyncracies, ensured the film's critical failure and may partially explain the filmmaker's quite radical change of direction in his next film. In *La flor de mi secreto* (1995), the characteristic Almodóvar strengths of style and female characterisation are directed towards a more effective – if in some ways more conventional – narrative, focused on the personal melodrama of marriage failure and mid-life crisis from the perspective of a mature woman. The protagonist's process of recuperative self-determination and the film's positive resolution recover the potential demonstrated in the sensitivity and insight of Almodóvar's earlier films.

Claiming the frame: women in contemporary Spanish cinema

The role and status of women have been at the epicentre of the social, economic and legislative changes which have reverberated throughout contemporary Spanish society since the end of the dictatorship. Although experience of these changes is shaped and qualified by such factors as age, class and the continuing gap between rural and urban milieux, there has been a radical and irreversible shift in the role and perceptions of women in contemporary Spain. Their changing socio-economic roles have been accompanied by significant changes in consciousness and, in contrast with their traditionally passive role, Anny Brooksbank Jones argues that in many respects women have become 'the motor of contemporary social change' (1995: 387). This increased cultural presence and profile is reflected in contemporary Spanish cinema where, particularly in the 1990s, the creative contribution of an increasing number of female film professionals (writers, directors, producers, craftswomen, actors) is matched by the greater prominence of female issues and perspectives in both the arthouse and popular mainstream film.

Women filmmakers

The massive influx of female directors which has occurred since the late 1980s and particularly in the mid-1990s, has clearly been a significant development for the representation of women in Spanish cinema and marks a huge contrast with their former scarcity. Spain's particular cultural, political and industrial context has meant that its domestic film production has historically constituted a magnified example of the male domination of the film industry internationally. The under-representation of women has always been particularly severe in the crucial areas of production and direction. The almost total absence of women from film production and direction in the early years of the cinema mirrored the exclusion of women from Spanish public life in general.

It was not until the 1930s that women's rights became a public issue and the subject of some reformist legislation under the Second Republic. These changes and the Republican cultural impetus, which gave rise to the most successful and productive moment in the history of Spanish cinema, provided more favourable conditions for the emergence of the first Spanish female director, the Catalan Rosario Pi. Pi's career demonstrates the professional acumen and entrepreneurial spirit which was to become typical of those few women able to carve out a career in cinematography during the early years of the industry and within the adverse cultural and industrial context of Francoism. Having started out in the fashion world, together with Pedro Ladrón de Guevara, she co-founded and headed the Madrid-based Star Film, one of the first new production companies to spring up in response to the introduction of sound cinema in the early 1930s. Her creative film work began in scriptwriting, most notably for Fernando Delgado's *Doce hombres y una mujer* (1934) and finally led her into direction, focusing mainly on mainstream genres such as her popular *zarzuela* (light opera) adaptations *El gato montés* (her first film in 1935) and the subsequent *Molinos de viento* (1937).

The Second Republic was, of course, short-lived and, following the end of the Civil War, the patriarchal traditionalism of the Franco years ensured the continuing scarcity of female directors. The work of those women filmmakers who did overcome the professional, social and ideological obstacles in their career paths is typically characterised by its eclecticism, and often, significantly, by a marked political consciousness. Ana Mariscal, already well-established as an actress in the 1940s, subsequently turned her hand to both production (setting up her own company, Bosco Films) and direction. Joining a number of young filmmakers influenced by Italian neorealism and anxious to provide alternatives to the dominant escapist outlook of institutional cinema, Mariscal's debut social realist film, *Segundo López, aventurero urbano* (1952), focuses on the slum *chabolas* (shacks) of Madrid and her subsequent *Con la vida hicieron fuego* (1957) is a testimonial representation of postwar hardship through the narrative focus of a returning exile. Although, ironically, Mariscal's work is usually dismissed as mediocre, folkloric material because of her later movies, such as the folkloric *Feria en Sevilla* (1960) or the musical melodrama *Vestida de novia* (1966), its commercial orientation enabled her to become the only continuous female director in 1950s Spain.

Josefina Molina, the first woman to graduate from the Escuela Oficial de Cine (National Film School) began her directorial career in television drama, later moving into both theatre and cinema and becoming the only female film director of the early 1970s, making her cinema debut with her early Gothic horror movie *Vera, un cuento cruel* (1973). Like Molina, Pilar Miró's directorial career began in TV drama where she established and continues to build on a distinguished career alongside her work in film, theatre and opera. Undoubtedly Miró has been the most outstanding woman in the Spanish film industry to date, not only because of her relatively successful career in filmmaking, but also through her prominent and frequently controversial political role particularly in her post as Directora General de Cinematografía in the first PSOE government of the 1980s. Both Miró's and Molina's work is characterised by its eclecticism and a distinct critical edge, and both filmmakers are frequently referred to as 'feminist'. Molina's films range from experimental to populist and span such varied genres as her contribution to the collective film *Cuentos eróticos* (1979), the documentary *Función de noche* (1981), *Esquilache* (1989) – a period adaptation of the Buero Vallejo play *Un soñador para un pueblo* – the *canción española* musical remake of Juan de Orduña's 1947 *La Lola se va a los puertos* in 1993 and the contemporary drama *Lo más natural* (1990). Miró's work embraces such varied generic forms as historical docudrama (*El crimen de Cuenca* 1979), period melodrama (*La petición* 1976), a drama inspired by Goethe's *Werther* (1986), the feminist realism of *Gary Cooper, que estás en los cielos* (1980), the noirish thrillers *Beltenebros* (1991) and *Tu nombre envenena mis sueños* (1996), and her recent adaptation of Lope de Vega's *El perro del hortelano* in verse (1996).

Women filmmakers in the transition

The end of the dictatorship permitted a more explicit articulation of political discourse and women were amongst those to take advantage of the new freedoms. It was, of course, the notorious case of Pilar Miró's dramatised historical reconstruction *El crimen de Cuenca* (1979) which both spectacularly demonstrated the continuing difficulties encountered by politically sensitive films beyond the official end of Francoist censorship in 1977 and represented the final legal and symbolic battle in its eradication. Cecilia Bartolomé's *Después de ...* (co-directed with brother Juan José in 1981) made an ambitious, if ultimately unsuccessful, two-part attempt to chronicle the period immediately following the death of Franco. Ana Díez's later first film *Ander eta Yul* (1988) is typical of the personalised approach to political subjects which characterises Spanish cinema in the 1980s and 1990s in general, focusing on the outer margins of society and examining the clash between the drugs culture and the highly disciplined world of ETA.

Significantly, much of the social and political critique contained in films by women filmmakers focuses on marginalised sectors of society and, unsurprisingly, this critical edge is sometimes centred on gender politics. Spain has never produced a strong body of feminist counter cinema – cinema that uses radically different forms to break away from the male-constructed codes of conventional filmmaking. To some extent this reflects the lack of a significant feminist activism in Spain in general. Rosa Montero explains this phenomenon as the result of the silencing of public debate on such issues under Francoism, and the fact that the end of the dictatorship and subsequent cultural changes for women in Spain coincided with a period of crisis in the international women's movement (Montero 1995: 382). As far as feminist or feminine discourses in the cinema are concerned, contemporary film theory now places greater emphasis on the the the active role of spectators in constructing meanings as they view films rather than on the relationship between the director and the film text. A specifically gendered discourse is clearly not limited to the gender of the filmmaker (Kuhn 1982: 3–18). It is important, nevertheless, that women are adequately represented behind as well as in front of the camera and women filmmakers undoubtedly contribute particular insights to the treatment of female thematics and the construction of female identity in the cinema.

Cinema functions like a language (Monaco 1977: 121–42) and, given the gender binaries which are inscribed within language and the fact that cinema is a largely male-dominated practice, women filmmakers have often developed specific formal and narrative strategies which work together to privilege a specifically female voice. The transition period in particular produced a number of films by women which challenged the formal and ideological foundations of male-dominated mainstream film in a number of ways and revealed particularly strong feminist discourses.

Cecilia Bartolomé's *Vámonos, Bárbara* breaks radically with mainstream thematics in 1977 by focusing on a woman who, together with her daughter, leaves her husband and embarks on a journey of self-discovery in which she explores independence, sexual freedom and mother–daughter relations from a specifically female perspective. Both Miró and Molina produced some of their most significant reflections on women's issues in the transition period, challenging the conventions of both patriarchy and traditional film form and genre. Pilar Miró's challenge to class, gender, sexual and generic conventions in *La petición* (1976) provoked the wrath of the Board of Censors, resulting in the film only securing a release after a high-profile press campaign by professional colleagues. The ninteenth-century setting and the classic look of a conventional costume drama provide a dramatic contrast to the film's radically subversive narrative featuring the protagonist's hedonistic indulgence of sexual pleasures with a taste for sadism. The final resolution leaves her unpunished for the accidental death of her lover and for the cold-blooded murder of the man who helps her dispose of his body. By the end of the film, she is poised to claim a third victim in her society marriage. Miró's later *Gary Cooper, que estás en los cielos* (1980) eschews mainstream generic forms in pursuit of stark realism and the development of a powerful feminine discourse 'in the marginal space of Andrea's silence and her experiences' (Rabalska 1996: 175). Protagonist Andrea struggles to communicate within the alienating contexts of her male-dominated profession, as well as enduring a floundering relationship and the prospect of a life-threatening illness.

Josefina Molina delivers a powerful denunciation of the situation for women under the repressive patriarchal order of the Franco era in her experimental documentary *Función de noche* (1981). The film draws on the traditions of *cinéma vérité* to address gender roles and relations of power through its examination of the relationship between theatre actress Lola Herrera and her soon-to-be-divorced husband Manuel Dicenta. The extent of her frustration in the marriage is epitomised in a particularly raw-edged, fly-on-the-wall sequence where she reveals that her husband has never given her an orgasm.

Women filmmakers in the 1990s

The late-1980s and particularly the mid-1990s have seen a sudden burgeoning in the number of women filmmakers achieving releases and, in some cases, significant critical and popular success. A *Fotogramas* feature listed eighteen active women filmmakers: Marta Balletbó-Coll, Cecilia Bartolomé, Ana Belén, Icíar Bollaín, Isabel Coixet, Ana Díez, Chus Gutiérrez, Mónica Laguna, Arantxa Lazcano, Eva Lesmes, María Miró, Pilar Miró, Josefina Molina, Gracia Querejeta, Azucena Rodríguez, Mireia Ros, Mar Targarona and Rosa Vergés (1995: 36). With the exception of veterans Miró, Molina and Bartolomé, and twenty-seven-year-old Bollaín, all of these women are in their thirties and early forties and more than two thirds of them made their debut film in the 1990s. In another feature on talented young Spanish directors, six of the sixteen mentioned were women (Trashorras 1996: 57–63). Not only do these facts mark a stark contrast with the 1970s and 1980s, but the irruption of these women into the industry has occurred during one of the most difficult periods for young filmmakers, particularly in the absence of a National Film School (which closed down in 1971, to be resurrected in 1995). Faced by the general problems of funding and production in Spain, these contemporary women filmmakers demonstrate a continuation of the flexibility, determination and initiative which characterised their predecessors, both in terms of the range of their preparatory training and experience and their strategies for creative survival.

Some have come from an acting background, such as Ana Belén and Icíar Bollaín, both of whom made their debut as children. Belén began as a child singing star in the sixties in Luis Lucía's *Zampo y yo* (1965) and Bollaín's most famous screen interpretation continues to be her role as Estrella, the child protagonist of Erice's *El sur* (1983). Like Ana Belén, several of these women have parallel careers in popular music: Chus Gutiérrez with the group Xoxonees and Mónica Laguna with the Santa Sede rock group. Many of them, like Molina and Miró, have worked in television and advertising (Lesmes making medium-length films, didactic programmes and advertisements, as has Coixet) or other film-related areas – Arantxa Lazkano, whilst working as a teacher, was also a dubbing artist for Basque television. Although Mónica Laguna graduated in Media from Madrid University and worked as an *auxiliar de cámara* (assistant camera operator) before making *Tengo una casa* (1996), Marta Balletbó-Coll studied film in the United States, as did both Chus Gutiérrez and Eva Lesmes – in New York and the American Film Institute in Los Angeles respectively. This range of backgrounds clearly has a bearing on the type of films these women make.

Women filmmakers have adopted flexible and imaginative approaches to the major problem of film finance both by taking a realistic and inventive approach to funding limitations and by actively pursuing those funding opportunities which exist. Despite its New York setting, Chus Gutiérrez's first film *Sublet* (1992) managed to keep its costs down by confining its action largely to interiors, especially the sublet apartment of the title. The narrative and thematics of Mónica Laguna's *Tengo una casa* (1996) fortuitously focus the action of the film on the single location of a hut in a forest. Despite its 1950s period setting, the small-scale, intimate style of *Los años oscuros* (Lazkano 1993) kept it within a budget of 75 million pesetas. *Sexo oral* (Gutiérrez 1994), consisting of a series of interviews with people from a range of age groups talking to camera about about their sexual experiences and attitudes, claims to be the cheapest Spanish film ever made. Although it is frequently argued that creative quality is inevitably compromised by financial limitations, the high standard achieved by many of these films is acknowledged in their critical and popular success and awards, such as Mónica Laguna's prize for her first Super 8 short and Icíar

Bollaín's award for *¡Hola! ¿Estás sola?* (1995) at the Festival de Comedia de Peñiscola in 1996.

This new generation of female filmmakers demonstrates a clear understanding of the combination of artistic and commercial imperatives which nowadays influences filmmaking, as Eva Lesmes points out: 'si no se conecta con la gente, es que algo ha salido mal. Esto es arte y una industria, está claro' (something's wrong if you don't get through to people. This is clearly both art and industry) (Yráyzoz 1996: 18). Strategies to actively encourage audiences and simultaneously secure higher budgets include the conscious appeal to wider audiences (at national and international level). Within the totality of the industry, a relatively larger proportion of female directors seems to have embraced the possibilities offered by co-production and collaboration. Such strategies have inevitably prompted questions about the loss of the Spanish cultural specificity of such films. Ana Díez's Spanish-Colombian co-production *Todo está oscuro* (1996) is set in Bogota, for example, and Isabel Coixet's film *Cosas que nunca te dije* (1996) was made in English in the USA with an almost entirely American cast and has no narrative or thematic connection with Spain. Many of these collaborative productions nevertheless maintain their cultural specificity through their narrative and thematics. Marsha Kinder's detailed examination of Rosa Vergés's directorial debut *Boom boom* (1990) gives an intriguing account of how this film, set in Barcelona, with its modern look, popular generic form and international cast, aimed at an international audience, attempts to deliver an international, cultural reinscription of its Catalan specificity (Kinder 1993: 422–3). Like that of Isabel Coixet, Chus Gutiérrez's work is heavily influenced by US independent cinema but, although her first film *Sublet* was set in New York, it concerned the experiences of a young Spanish woman living in the city for the first time. The narrative setting for Pilar Miro's *Beltenebros* (1991), a film made in English (and later dubbed into Spanish) and starring Terence Stamp and Patsy Kensit, is the Communist underground in post-Civil-War Madrid, but its international cast, retro style and thriller genre are clearly targetted at an international audience. Marta Balletbó-Coll, whose work is also closely connected to US independent cinema, filmed her debut *Costa Brava (Family Album)* (1995) in Spain with a Catalan cast but performing in English to gain access to foreign markets (Smith 1997: 43).

If films by women in the 1970s and 1980s tended generically and thematically towards the arthouse, where they often attracted considerable critical recognition, their generic characteristics tended to limit their appeal to mainstream audiences. In terms of their numbers and popularity, therefore, women filmmakers continued to remain on the margins. Female filmmakers of the 1990s are clearly predominantly opting for the mainstream. This is not to

15   *Things I never told you/Cosas que nunca te dije*, Isabel Coixet, 1996

say, however, that they have abandoned the critical and reflective mode which has characterised much of the work by women in the past. Indeed, whilst women directors are not exclusively concerned with female issues, and the films by the new filmmakers do not have overtly feminist discourses, many of them introduce an important focus on gender politics and the thematics of womanhood either directly or indirectly through their narrative focus. The articulation of such perspectives within popular genres such as period drama, the thriller, the musical and comedy, creates a vitally important space within mainstream cinema for the representation of female subject positions and redefinitions of femininity for the 1990s.

Drawing on autobiographical experience, both Arantxa Lazcano and Azucena Rodríguez introduce a specifically female focus into examples of the continuing trend in historical drama, set in the Francoist period. *Entre rojas* (Rodríguez 1995) is set in the political wing of a women's prison in the 1970s and *Los años oscuros* (Lazkano 1993) focuses on the experience of a young girl growing up in Euskadi in the 1950s. Both films concern the negotiation of adolescence and identity in the face of conflicting and contrasting pressures – political, linguistic and social. The Civil War provides the historical setting for Pilar Miró's stylish retro thriller *Tu nombre envenena mis sueños* (1996). Concerning the return of Julia Buendia to Madrid in the early 1950s and the revival of a 1942 investigation into the murder of three left-wing underground militants, the film overturns the conventional male protagonism of films concerning violence and revenge by placing a woman at the centre of the narrative (Ponga 1996: 109–10). The musical genre which, more than any other, exemplifies the traditional cinematic objectification of the female image in film (Mulvey 1989: 14–26), and which constitutes one of Spanish cinema's classic popular genres, is taken up by Josefina Molina in 1993 in a remake of Juan de Orduna's 1947 *La Lola se va a los puertos*. However, Molina reappropriates the genre to deliver a critical expose of exploitation and manipulation in the world of performance and patriarchal society in general, and reverses the conventions of the genre by making the female singer-performer (Lola/Rocío Jurado) the desiring subject. Chus Gutiérrez's *Alma gitana* (1995) also draws on the musical and dance film tradition, but again redirects it toward a reflection on racial and cultural intolerance and the position of women in gypsy society.

In line with the general trend in Spanish cinema, comedy is a major genre for women directors. Their humour typically relies on scenarios constructed and exploited comically from a specifically female viewpoint: role-reversals, for example, and strategies to deal with intransigent men and other gender relations in such films as *Pon un hombre en tu vida* (Lesmes 1996), *Puede ser divertido* (Rodríguez 1995), *¡Hola! ¿Estás sola?* (Bollaín 1995), *Cómo ser mujer y no morir en el intento* (Belén 1991), *Cosas que nunca te dije* (Coixet 1995). All of these films focus on strong, central female protagonists and raise a range of issues and specifically female perspectives on gender and the experience of womanhood.

Screening women

The gradual increase in the 1980s and 1990s in the number and range of films (by both male and female directors) which focus on female characters as subjects and privilege specifically female viewpoints plays an important part in raising gender awareness in general. In Spanish cinema, it is particularly significant that it has created a representational space for subject positions previously absent, marginalised or reduced to a rigid set of gender stereotypes and paradigms. Although traditional patriarchal values and role models persist in the narrative and formal discourses of much contemporary cinema, a significant number of contemporary reformulations of these genres and styles are subverted or redirected in subtle or – as in the case of filmmakers like Pedro Almodóvar – in quite flamboyant ways. A substantial number of these films offer an encouraging indication of changing realities and perceptions of women in contemporary Spain. Many of them have been widely-viewed, popular successes and represent a significant shift towards more progressive representations of women by constructing positive images focused on equality and independence, recognising and celebrating difference, and increasing the range and presence of female subject positions on the cinema screen. Equally important are those films which offer a critical representation of female marginalisation and discrimination and reveal the social construction of gender identity.

Narrative agency

The more prominent profile of women in contemporary Spanish cinema is reflected in the role and narrative function of female characters. Women now regularly asssume the narrative agency conventionally associated with male characters, so that the hermeneutic drive of the film is dependent on the psychological development and actions of a central female figure in a wide range of roles and generic types. Women now protagonise road movies such as ¡Hola! ¿Estás sola?, (Bollaín 1995), prison dramas such as Entre rojas (Rodríguez 1995), political thrillers such as Sombras en una batalla (Camus 1993), Tu nombre envenena mis sueños (Miró 1996) and action thrillers such as Nadie hablará de nosotras cuando hayamos muerto (Díaz Yanes 1995). It is women who ultimately 'save' male characters in distress in Almodóvar's Mujeres al borde de un ataque de nervios and, arguably, ¡Átame!, who do the investigating in Tu nombre envenena mis sueños, and wronged women who take the law and/or revenge into their own hands in El pájaro de la felicidad (Miró 1993) and Dispara (Saura 1993), where female rape victims seek out and punish their attackers, and in La pasión turca (Aranda 1994), where Desideria exacts a bloody price for her lover's infidelity. The power and control of women who continue to represent the 'dark continent' is now represented positively. It is Lisa's manipulation of the past, reality and fantasy, which for the most part controls the development of the narrative in La ardilla roja (Medem 1993) and both narrative and destiny are powerfully guided by the supernatural powers of the grandmother in La mitad del cielo (Gutiérrez Aragón 1986). Whilst traditional heterosexual romantic endings are still highly popular, a number of contemporary narratives conspicuously posit the achievement of female independence and self-assurance – as in La flor de mi secreto, El pájaro de la felicidad, Nadie hablará de nosotras cuando hayamos muerto – or the triumph of female solidarity as in Rosa rosae (Gómez Pereira 1992), Puede ser divertido (Rodríguez 1995) and Mujeres al borde de un ataque de nervios – as equally satisfying resolutions in both psychological and narrative terms.

Female (re)generations

The development over the last ten to fifteen years of a new and highly successful star system from within the Spanish film industry has been an important factor in more progressive representations of gender and sexuality in contemporary domestic cinema. Peter Evans observes that this new star system has produced a series of 'filmic prototypes of the Spanish "New Woman" (Evans 1995: 329)

La flor de mi secreto, Pedro Almodóvar, 1995

16

closely associated with the generation of female stars established in
the early eighties such as Carmen Maura, Laura de Sol, Assumpta
Serna or even earlier in the case of Ana Belén. Belén's profile has
evolved through a series of constructions from the squeaky-clean
child singing star of the 1960s to the more mature political consciousness and gender awareness of her performances in such films
as *El amor del capitán Brando* (Armiñán 1974), *La colmena* (Camus
1982), or *Cómo ser mujer y no morir en el intento* (Belén 1991), etc.
The vast range of characters these actors have brought to the
screen have done much to deconstruct traditional unidimensional
notions of femininity in Spanish cinema. This generation is particularly well-placed to articulate the contrasting and often conflicting
roles which have faced women whose adult years have spanned
both dictatorship and democratic eras. They consistently represent
women as complex, multidimensional, thinking subjects in their
negotiation of the social, professional, emotional and sexual
changes which have characterised post-Franco Spain in such roles
as Carmen Maura's transexual adoptive mother in *La ley del deseo*
(Almodóvar 1986), bored middle-class housewife in search of fantasy in *La reina anónima* (Gonzálo Suárez 1992), tranquilliser-pop-
ping working-class housewife, mother and cleaner in *¿Qué he hecho
yo para merecer esto?* (Almodóvar 1984), ex-terrorist vet in *Sombras
en una batalla* (Camus 1993), etc.

The maturity of these women, now in the mid-1990s, and the
characters they embody constitute a significant shift towards the
representation of a broader range of female subject positions and
the destabilisation of the iconographic status of youth. A number of

Gender and sexuality

recent films provide central narrative spaces for the representation of more mature female subjectivities previously unexplored or relegated to marginal characters. Pedro Almodóvar's *Tacones lejanos* (1991), for example, and especially *La flor de mi secreto* (1995), have accredited fifty-year-old Marisa Paredes with a shooting-star status previously reserved only for younger talents. Other recent examples of mature Spanish actresses who are finally receiving long-overdue attention and whose performances make a crucial contribution to the screen recognition of mature female subjectivities include Pilar Bardem's incorporation of Doña Julia in *Nadie hablará de nosotras cuando hayamos muerto*, Concha Velasco in *Más allá del jardín* (Pedro Olea 1996) and Ventura Pons's *Actrices* (1996), which engages in a fascinating interplay between the internal narrative, in which a young actress draws on the memories of three older actresses in her research on the now-dead megastar Empar Ribera, and the extra-filmic personae of veteran stage actresses Nuria Espert, Rosa María Sardá and Anna Lizaran who embody her former colleagues.

The massive irruption into Spanish film of young acting talent has also been crucially important to the construction of positive representations of female identity. Work by such actresses as Ariadna Gil, Maribel Verdú, Mari Carrillo, Cristina Marcos, Emma Suárez, Icíar Bollaín and Anna Torrent and a younger clutch of new names including Candela Peña, Penélope Cruz, Ingrid Rubio, Ruth Gabriel, Silke Klein, Lucía Jiménez and others articulates the very different formative cultural experience and concerns of a generation of young women born into the postmodern and postfeminist Spain of the democratic period. The simplicity and naturalness of their acting styles and the *despreocupación* (nonchalance) which characterises many of their roles, marks a visible distance from the more dramatic and traumatic roles of the older generation, weighed down with the personal historical baggage of Francoism. These actors consistently represent young women who are socially, professionally and sexually independent and, whilst still having to negotiate conflict and contradiction, do so with a greater sense of confidence and self-sufficiency as the career of Ariadna Gil demonstrates through a range of roles such as the lesbian Violeta in *Belle Epoque* (Trueba 1992), sexually independent Sara in *Amo tu cama rica* (Martínez Lázaro 1991), María in *Los peores años de nuestra vida* (Martínez Lázaro 1994) and the title role in *Malena es un nombre de tango* (Gerardo Herrero 1996) .

Independent women

Spanish cinema's 'new Spanish woman' is socially, economically and sexually independent. Mirroring the class characteristics of the average contemporary cinema audience, these women are predominantly well-educated, liberal and middle-class, working as dentists (*Boom Boom*), vets (*Amo tu cama rica* and *Sombras en una batalla*),

Malena es un nombre de tango, Gerardo Herrero, 1996   **17**

translators (*Todo es mentira*, Fernández Amero 1994), dubbing actors (*Mujeres al borde de un ataque de nervios*), freelance writers (*La flor de mi secreto*), broadcasters (*Tacones lejanos* and *Puede ser divertido*), lawyers (*Matador*), businesswomen (*Todo está oscuro*) and so on. In contrast to the repressive discourses of Francoist cinema, the modern Spanish woman – often single or separated – is sexually active and frequently takes the initiative in relationships: the seductive tactics of Silke Klein's sensual Mari are ultimately more successful than the more conventional reserve of Emma Suárez's Ángela in establishing a permanent relationship with Ángel in *Tierra* (Medem 1995); Trini (Candela Peña) nonchalantly suggests sharing her friend's new lover in *¡Hola! ¿Estás sola?*; the four daughters (Ariadna Gil, Maribel Verdú, Penélope Cruz and Miriam Díaz Aroca) of Fernando Fernán Gómez's bohemian fantasy family take it in turns to seduce the adolescent Jorge Sanz in *Belle Epoque*, where a contemporary morality is superimposed onto the superficial 1930s period setting; Sara (Ariadna Gil) unproblematically initiates relationships and her multiple partners, despite the frustration and threat they represent for her would-be suitor in *Amo tu cama rica*, never become a moral issue.

Whilst representing both psychological strength and practical independence, the construction of these strong images of women can also be problematic in a number of ways. The fact that their freedom hinges so crucially on class, professional category and financial independence demonstrates both a strength and weakness in Spanish cinema's response to contemporary social realities. The reduction of financial worries and the logistical difficulties of domestic arrangements permit these women and the films they protagonise to focus attention on the psychological and philosophical problems associated with a range of female experiences, but they fail to address the more pragmatic obstacles to female autonomy, which are the reality for the vast majority of women. In *El pájaro de la felicidad* (Pilar Miró 1993), for example, Carmen's career as an art restorer permits her the luxury of moving from Madrid to the south whilst she works through her personal experience of alienation and trauma following a violent attack in the street and disillusionment with the relationship with her partner. Freelance writer Leo is able to retreat to her mother's *pueblo* (home village) to recover from the emotional shock of facing the long-denied truth of her failed marriage and reconsider her professional future in *La flor de mi secreto*. Similarly, a comfortable middle-class lifestyle enables recently divorced María to ponder the philosophical vagaries of chance in *Un paraguas para tres* (Felipe Vega 1992); Desideria to fly off to rejoin a holiday lover in Turkey in pursuit of the passion and excitement lacking in her well-heeled conventional marriage in *La pasión turca* (Aranda 1994) or Sara to live alone and enjoy her sexual independence from the comfort of a smart Madrid apartment in *Amo tu cama rica* (Martínez Lázaro 1991).

No such luxuries are available to Pedro Almodóvar's Gloria in *¿Qué he hecho yo para merecer esto?* whose drudgery and exploitation are barely alleviated by the *minilips* (tranquillisers) or, on a really bad day, a few moments of oblivion courtesy of a deep inhalation of the cleaning fluid or the glue pot. The representation of female subjectivity in the less privileged, but arguably more representative experiences of working class women is much less common. When it occurs, however, it is all the more striking. Against the oppressive background of male social, sexual and economic chauvinism, exploitation of the hidden labour force, overcrowded housing, etc., Gloria's survival strategies and, finally and spectacularly, her murder of husband Antonio with a hambone are a monumentally pleasurable celebration of female initiative, self-reliance and strength of character in the most adverse of social circumstances. The location of strong female characters and images of empowerment within working class contexts where the economic, social exploitation and disenfranchisement of women is arguably most acute is important both for the generation of positive images and because of its challenge to conventional assumptions about working class women.

Another unusual and powerfully positive representation of female initiative and determination at the margins of conventional society is embodied in the character of another Gloria (Victoria Abril), returning to her in-laws' house and her comatose husband in Spain after working as a prostitute in Mexico and stealing money from the gangsters for whom she worked in *Nadie hablarán de nosotras cuando hayamos muerto* (Díaz Yanes 1995). Here the spectator is positioned through the formal and narrative manipulation of

Nadie hablará de nosotras cuando hayamos muerto, Agustín Díaz Yanes, 1995   **18**

humour, suspense and other strategies, to empathise with the socially unacceptable female character of a crooked, alcoholic prostitute as she makes various attempts to rebuild her life – initially with the money stolen from the Mexican gangsters. The final shots of the film show her seated in an examination hall sitting for the *bachillerato* (baccalaureate) her mother-in-law longed for her to pass. This narrative resolution clearly privileges the notion of female empowerment through education. Gloria's final achievement is perhaps only undermined by its dependence and submission to the values and demands of the establishment. In such filmic representations, images of independence and strength of character are less dependent on external factors such as job, money, etc. than on inner strength, determination, ingenuity and these also occur in a range of other films of quite different generic styles.

Mothers and matriarchs

Some of the most striking images of strong women have undoubtedly been those of the matriarchal figures dominating such films as *Ana y los lobos* (Saura 1972), *Mamá cumple cien años* (Saura 1979), *Camada negra* (Gutiérrez Aragón 1977) and *Siete días de enero* (Juan Antonio Bardem 1978) in Spanish cinema of the 1970s, and in some later period pieces such as *Demonios en el jardín* (Gutiérrez Aragón 1982) or *La casa de Bernarda Alba* (Camus 1987). The specific economic and social effects of Civil-War casualties and exile, industrialisation, rural migration and emigration led to the frequent absence of the traditional male head of family in certain social groups and geographical areas and, in his place, the consequent emergence of the matriarchal figure in some of Spain's otherwise most conservative communities. This cultural phenomenon provided a rich source of images for oppositional cinema whose focus on the perversity at the heart of the arch-conservative Francoist notion of the family was enhanced by the occupation of the authoritarian patriarchal role by a female. As Marsha Kinder points out, these women were often exaggerated into phallic, castrating mothers who stunted, perverted or traumatised their (male) offspring in the process of their usurpation of traditional male authority (Kinder 1993: 214–15). In *Furtivos* (Borau 1975), the perversity of matriarchal dominance was exaggerated by incest; in *Ana y los lobos*, it produced a series of social and personal 'defects' and 'abonormalities' in Mamá's (Rafaela Aparicio) sons; and in *Camada negra*, it became a major factor in Blanca's (María Luisa Ponte) son's fanatical right-wing terrorism. The matriarch was thus marked as a perverse distortion – of both traditional notions of the feminine and the maternal, and of the patriarchal order itself. Consequently, although this image was highly effective in political terms, it also attached further negative connotations to the image of the strong, powerful woman.

A number of recent films have produced far more positive images of benign matriarchs whose power and status are less dependent on assumed patriarchal authority or financial power than on the wisdom they impart and the protective influence they exert in films such as *El mar y el tiempo* (Fernando Fernán Gómez 1989) where Rafaela Aparicio (who, significantly, previously embodied the overbearing matriarch of Saura's *Ana y los lobos* and *Mamá cumple cien años*) is transformed into the apparently confused grandmother who nevertheless dispenses perceptive words of wisdom as well as warnings to her sons about self-deception and living in a (false) past. If the castrating matriarchs of the 1970s were usually constructed in terms of their relationships with their sons, the protective and empowering influence of the benign matriarchs of the 1980s and 1990s thus often focuses on mother–daughter relationships. Unlike their devouring predecessors, the matriarchs of contemporary films such as *La mitad del cielo* and *Nadie hablará de nosotras cuando hayamos muerto* are giving rather than demanding. Although they often die within the narratives, their deaths are both practical and symbolic contributions to the empowerment of the next generation of women. The grandmother in *La mitad del cielo* protects her granddaughter Rosa from exploitation by eliminating her opportunist fiancé and later, once Rosa has opted for a form of independence based on compromise, she recognises her own anachronistic incongruity in her granddaughter's new life. She takes herself off to die, posthumously establishing spiritual communication with her great-granddaughter Olvido in and through whom she continues to exert a protective influence. In *Nadie hablará de nosotras cuando hayamos muerto*, strong mother figure Dona Julia (Pilar Bardem) encourages her daughter-in-law Gloria (a strong character who is, nevertheless, at the mercy of male sexual exploitation, violence and crime) to take control of her life. Her ultimate sacrifice is the termination of her comatose son/Gloria's husband's! life, to free her from the situation which had precipitated her into a life of alcoholism and crime in the first place. In *Tacones lejanos*, Becky assumes her daughter's guilt in order to protect her from punishment for the murder of her husband.

Female subjectivity/audience identification

If cinema has traditionally addressed the male spectator, as some film theorists have argued (Kaplan 1988: 22–35), what is also important (for both male and female spectators) about more progressive contemporary representations of women is the establishment of spectatorial identification with female psychological viewpoints and the centrality of female subject positions. A significant feature of a number of contemporary films in a range of popular genres is the prominence they give to relationships between women. The major cultural importance of female support networks is reflected in several high-profile films by Pedro Almodóvar such as *¿Qué he hecho yo para merecer esto?* and *Mujeres al borde de un ataque de nervios*. The vicarious experience of female complicity also characterises the recent spate of female 'buddy' movies, a subgenre more traditionally associated with *male* bonding. The shared complications and problems of Carmen and Alicia's common domestic situations as single parents separated from their husbands is at the heart of their complicity in *Puede ser divertido*. This is reinforced by the frequent use of two shots often in close-up, followed by shared point-of-view shots which extend their complicity to include the spectator. Similar strategies are evident in *¡Hola! ¿Estás sola?* and *Rosa rosae*, where female bonding (like its erstwhile male counterpart) becomes more important than romance. Female bonding is shifted into the more rarely represented province of lesbian affairs in films such as *Pepi, Luci, Bom y otras chicas del montón* (Almodóvar 1980), *El pájaro de la felicidad* (Miró 1993) and *Costa Brava (Family Album)* (Balletbó-Coll 1995). Most commonly, the cinematic representation of female complicity is represented within the context of comedy and continues to focus on female strategies for dealing with various products of the social legacy of patriarchy such as the intransigence or unreliability of unreconstructed men. Prime examples of this arise in *Todos los hombres sois iguales* (Gómez Pereira 1994) and *Salsa rosa* (Gómez Pereira 1991) – or the juggling of the multiple competing (and often conflicting) female roles of mother, wife/partner and worker as in *Cómo ser mujer y no morir en el intento* and *Puede ser divertido*.

For female audiences in particular, effective spectatorial identifi-

Gender and sexuality

cation may be achieved by giving narrative prominence to details of common patterns of behaviour and private emotional reactions normally hidden from view but which are instantly recognisable to female spectators. These might take the form of Carmen's physical and emotional need to shower following her violation in the street in *El pájaro de la felicidad* or, in a more light-hearted vein, the expression of emotional reaction through ostensibly irrational actions – such as Ann's kneejerk response of swallowing a bottle of nailvarnish remover in self-destructive defiance and anger at being jilted in *Cosas que nunca te dije* (Coixet 1996), or her desperation when the local store runs out of her favourite chocolate-chip icecream. Such details eloquently capture the defence mechanism of transference which displaces physical and emotional responses from one context to another.

Autobiographical discourse, particularly when it is conveyed through some form of direct address, is perhaps unsurprisingly one of the most powerful structural devices employed to articulate female subjectivity. This is amply demonstrated in earlier films such as Carlos Saura's *Cría cuervos* (through the adult Ana's direct address to camera and the flashback/flashforward structure) or Víctor Erice's *El sur* (through Estrella's first-person voice-over). This strategy is employed in a variety of ways in contemporary films as diverse as Ventura Pons's *Actrices*, where the film characters' autobiographical reminiscences are recounted by veteran actresses in their own extra-diegetic right. It also appears in Chus Gutiérrez's documentary *Sexo oral* (1994), which involves interviewees of both genders talking directly to camera about their sexual experiences and attitudes. It is perhaps not surprising that many of the most moving films by female directors draw directly on their own personal experiences, thus offering autobiographical discourse in an intertextual sense. *Los años oscuros* and *Entre rojas* exemplify this aspect, as do some of Pilar Miró's most powerful feminist films.

Formal techniques such as camerawork, framing, editing, lighting, etc. are crucial to the construction of point of view and emotional empathy with the female protagonist. It is perhaps not surprising that many of the most powerful and striking representations of female subjectivity are generated by narratives focusing on situations of conflict and tension which produce extreme emotional responses. It is the striking camera angles and tight framing which visually convey the limitations of Gloria's marital, domestic, working and social life in *¿Qué he hecho yo para merecer esto?*. This is seen, for example, in the high angle shot of Gloria in the sitting room in a rare moment of repose, sticking together the broken fragments of a gaudy ornament and alleviating her trampled spirits with a sniff of glue; or the symbolic shot from inside the washing machine which frames her strained efforts to carry out her domestic chores; and the frequent shots of action in the tight-framed cramped passages of her flat. Editing techniques can be used to introduce critical comment on the action as is demonstrated between the TV pastiche of the song *La bien pagá* (The Well-Paid Woman) and the bedroom where Antonio refuses to give Gloria money for the children's busfares and when they have sex falls asleep as soon as he reaches orgasm, leaving her both physically and emotionally unsatisfied. In *Cosas que nunca te dije*, the end of a love affair is harrowingly represented as the camera focuses relentlessly on the protagonist in full-length and medium shots as she conducts the painful telephone conversation with the lover who is jilting her. The film's steadfast refusal to switch to alternating shots of the person at the other end of the phone and the confinement of the soundtrack to Ann's end of the conversation formally mirror her frustration. They also reflect her relentless inner pain as she grapples with this emotional bombshell, unable to see her boyfriend or make sense of his change of feelings.

A number of other contemporary films centre on the female body as the physical, psychological and symbolic focus of their protagonists' sense of self to establish female subjectivity. The spectator is thus confronted, through identification with these characters, with the problematic area of gender difference as a determining factor in existential experience. *El pájaro de la felicidad* (1993) rehearses Pilar Miró's recurrent preoccupation with social and psychological alienation, existential frustration, and the difficulties of communication from a particularly female perspective. The film's critical narrative crux centres on the specificity of the main protagonist's womanhood: Carmen is attacked in the street at night by strangers and raped. Her sense of disempowerment and alienation is reflected in the predominant imaging of the sequence in long shot, creating a distancing effect and followed by distorting, dehumanising close-ups of her own and her assailant's faces. This traumatic experience launches her into a process of existential self-questioning, specifically centred on her position as a woman. The paucity of dialogue, a shot structure dominated by the long shot and long take, and the predominantly blue colour coding, reinforce Carmen's sense of dissatisfaction, isolation and alienation from herself and establish a slow pace and contemplative mood. The recovery of her female identity and subjectivity, compromised in the process of integration into a male social, professional and symbolic order, becomes the focus of a healing process. She reviews past relationships, undertakes a period of self-imposed isolation in the South, and opts for the experience of motherhood again by adopting her grandchild. This restorative process is mirrored in the intimate sequences of her professional artwork restoration, the sensual relationship she establishes with her daughter-in-law and the warm hues which dominate the second half of the film.

Female subjectivity is represented through the symbolic focus on the female body in a number of other contemporary films. As in *El pájaro de la felicidad*, Carlos Saura's *Dispara* (1993) also focuses on a rape which identifies the spectator with the protagonist's quest for revenge. In Josefina Molina's *Lo más natural* (1990), childbirth and motherhood acquire liberatory connotations of independence rarely associated with that specifically female experience when protagonist Clara' (Charo López) reassessment and revamping of her life finds its ultimate expression in a new relationship with with a younger, socially-reconstructed man and the birth of their child (imaged with striking intimacy in a swimming pool). In a much lighter comic vein, male football coach Díaz Conde (Toni Cantó) temporarily experiences the physical manifestations of womanhood in Eva Lesmes body-swap film *Pon un hombre en tu vida* (1996) and learns a few useful lessons about female approaches to life and work.

The desiring subject

One of the most significant and indicative signs of a shift in the perception of women in contemporary Spanish society must surely lie in the representation of female sexuality in the cinema. The representation of women as desiring sexual subjects constitutes a major departure from the Francoist-Catholic desexualisation or sublimination of female sexuality. In Francoist cinema this contradiction was consistently negotiated by visual celebration (objectifying specularisation) but narrative condemnation of the sexualised woman, epitomised in the *femme fatale*. Whilst the *femme fatale* continues to appear in contemporary Spanish cinema and frequently comes to a sticky end, the moral force of her elimination or punishment is now usually tempered in some way. In *El maestro de esgrima* (Pedro Olea 1992), for example, Astarloa, the victim of Adela's machinations, articulates his admiration for her skill and intelligence as he deals the final sword stroke which kills her, thus privileging the pleasures offered by her deviance over and above the formality of the resolution. Vicente Aranda's *Amantes* ends with the apparent triumph of Luisa (Victoria Abril) as her young lover presses his bloody hands against the train window having despatched his fiance at her behest. It is only in the afterword that the spectator reads that the lovers were later arrested and convicted, thereby minimising narrative condemnation. In Carlos Saura's *Carmen* (1983), the contemporary reworking of the Carmen theme shifts the burden of responsibility for the climactic violence away from the transgressive female and onto the obsessive male figure. The ambiguity of the narrative and destabilisation of the boundaries between the film's internal reality and fantasy make it unclear in the first instance whether Carmen is unfaithful or whether it is Antonio's imagination, and secondly whether he really kills her or whether that too is his fantasy. In *Matador*, the death of both male and female serial killers becomes their triumph – the culmination of their own death-wish – rather than a narrative condemnation of their actions. Perhaps one of the most ironic reversals of the *femme fatale* tradition in contemporary Spanish cinema is in the conversion of the infamous icon Gilda into a mother and Republican underground heroine in *Madregilda* (Franciso Regueiro 1993).

Not only are women now shown to be sexually active, but their desire and awareness of their entitlement to sexual satisfaction is clearly articulated on screen. They freely discuss orgasms or lack of them in *Salsa rosa*, refer nonchalantly to masturbation fantasies in *Puede ser divertido* and refuse to accept sexual dissatisfaction. In *Función de noche* (Josefina Molina 1981), Lola Herrera delivers a stunning blow to her soon-to-be-divorced husband's ego and foregrounds women's sexual expectations when she speaks the unspeakable and informs him that her orgasms have always been faked. In films such as *¡Hola! ¿Estás sola?*, the traditional need to locate sexual desire within the context of romance is absent as Trini demonstrates a matter-of-fact attitude to sex in her nonchalant proposal that the two women take turns to sleep with Nina's Russian conquest. However, when it becomes clear that the relationship developing between the other two is more than a merely physical one, she demonstrates a similarly uncomplicated sensitivity to their intimacy, relinquishing her claims to the shared bed and tactfully bedding down in the kitchen. As in *Amo tu cama rica*, women may be presented as more independent and progressive than their male counterparts. Sara's uncomplicatedly liberal lifestyle, her multiple partners and disinterest in commitment are presented as a kind of *nouveau* common sense which contrasts with the more traditional feelings of jealousy and desire for commitment which her would-be suitor is unsuccessful in denying.

Screen recognition of women's sexuality clearly indicates a positive achievement, but its modes of representation can also pose a number of difficulties. *¡Átame!*, probably Almodóvar's most controversial film, provides an eloquent illustration of the dangerous ambiguities which can arise. The film contains a sex scene in which Marina (Victoria Abril) literally and symbolically takes charge, physically assuming the dominant position over her battered lover Ricky, and proceeds to orchestrate the proceedings to maximise her own pleasure, instructing him when to move, when not to move, to delay his orgasm, and so on. In the USA *¡Átame!* attracted an X certificate on the strength of this scene and a sequence suggesting, though not explicitly showing, Marina's masturbation with a wind-up bathtoy in the shape of a frogman. Although the sequence may offer a positive image of female sexual assertion, its narrative context suggests an apparent condonement of violence as an effective means of securing both sex and romance, since this scene occurs after Marina has been held captive by Ricky for most of the film.

Explicit sex scenes also negotiate the ambiguous borderland

between the progressive representation of sexual identities and subjectivities, and the danger of objectification and exploitation. A number of films tackle the issue of looking by making explicit the voyeuristic qualities of the cinema and position the spectator to recognise her or his own complicity. Voyeurism thus becomes the subject of the film in Bigas Luna's *Bilbao* (1978), Aranda's *Si te dicen que caí* (1989) and Almodóvar's *Kika* (1993). Other films attempt to address this problem by self-consciously avoiding exploitative camerawork or seeking other representational strategies. In *Cosas que nunca te dije*, for example, Ann and Dan's lovemaking is symbolically represented through a close-up shot of the legs of the chair on which they are sitting and the position of their feet, moving to a full shot of the (still-clothed) lovers in intimate post-coital immobility. The effectiveness of the sequence stems precisely from its contrast with the usual treatment of sex scenes. Other films opt for establishing a more equitable balance between the focus on male and female bodies.

A small number of contemporary Spanish films self-consciously reverse traditional representations of women as the *object* of heterosexual male desire, so that the *male* figure becomes the object of the desiring *female* gaze. This occurs in a simple, but pointed fashion in *Puede ser divertido* when Carmen and Alicia first spot Ángel and, in a medium close-up two-shot, agree that 'está como para mojar pan' (he's good enough to eat), followed by a point-of-view long shot of a clearly specularised Ángel gliding around the icerink. In *Belle Epoque*, specularisation of the male is given a highly comic and challengingly disruptive twist by initiating the female gaze from a character whose own sexuality is ambiguous and directing it at a Fernando (Jorge Sanz), who is cross-dressed for the carnival party. More conventional reversals of traditional looking occur, for example, in *La Lola se va a los puertos* (1993), where the camera, in a point-of-view shot initiated by the mature Lola, meanders sensuously over the naked contours of her young lover's body, thus presenting a double challenge to gender conventions in the cinema: Lola's affair flies in the face of the older man/younger woman convention as well as making the man the object of the erotic spectacle. Female erotic gazing is stressed narratively in *Las edades de Lulú* (Bigas Luna 1990) where the female protagonist actively seeks out a male couple to provide the erotic spectacle for her contemplation, and in *Pon un hombre en tu vida* (Eva Lesmes 1996), it receives comic treatment when the female protagonists attend a male stripper club. The homoerotic look directed at the male body in such sequences as the mock bullfighting in *Jamón Jamón*, the bullfighting school scenes in *Matador* or Mario's semi-naked bedroom scene with the *marqués* in *Las cosas del querer* (1989) may also offer specular pleasures for the female gaze.

Representing lesbianism

If the above instances of the sexualised female gaze represent rare but ground-breaking departures from the specular norm in the cinema, rarer still is the representation of the lesbian gaze. Its most effective and striking instance in Spanish cinema probably remains the characterisation and structuring of the looks in a much-commented sequence from Almodóvar's *Entre tinieblas*. The impact of the sequence is magnified by the cultural connotations of the two women's identities – cabaret singer and nun – as the Mother Superior mimes a sensual serenade to her female idol, thus reappropriating and recasting erotic specularisation of the female icon in lesbian terms.

The marginal representation of lesbianism in film reflects its generally low profile in contemporary Spain as a whole. John Hooper points out that only 1.4 per cent of Spanish women describe themselves as lesbian and the first evidence of an organised movement did not appear until the late 1970s and has had a low level of activity (Hooper 1995: 162–3). This, of course, mirrors the universal phenomenon of lesbian invisibility which, as Annamarie Jagose observes, is most commonly attributed to the fact that lesbianism so radically disrupts dominant patriarchal concepts of gender and sexuality that 'the lesbian is not able to be thought' (Jagose 1994: 1–2). Jagose also argues that lesbianism's outsider status endows it with a powerful transgressive potential and, as Paul Smith points out, the complicity which Almodóvar establishes between the spectator and the drug-taking lesbian nuns of *Entre tinieblas* introduces a political dimension: 'a libertarian ethic typical of post-Franco Spain, an ethic in which the audience must acquiesce lest it be accused of authoritarianism' (Smith 1996: 28–9).

Secondary characters in some of Almodóvar's other films, such as *Pepi, Luci, Bom y otras chicas del montón* also introduce lesbian issues into the text. Bom, a singer with a punk rock band and Luci, the masochistic wife of a policeman, strike up a sadomasochistic lesbian relationship in a knitting class when Bom arrives and delights Luci by peeing on her. This follows the typical pattern in Almodóvar's earlier films of confronting the spectator with an unexpectedly explicit sequence at the beginning of the film to disrupt spectatorial complacency and signal the film's departure from the thematics typically associated with its generic packaging. A similar tactic is employed in *La ley del deseo* with the opening sequence of male masturbation. Subsequent sequences then rely on a reversal of this distancing process to draw the spectator in to identify with potentially unfamiliar characters and identities such as lesbian subjectivity. Towards the end of *Pepi, Luci, Bom y otras chicas del montón*, shock tactics are replaced with an intimate sequence in which Pepi and Bom are seen cooking together. The increasing bond between them

Gender and sexuality

and their gentle exchanges are shot through the kitchen window which frames the image of their intimacy. More recent images of lesbianism in Almodóvar's work include the remarkable character-isation of the maid Juana in *Kika*, played by the striking Rossy de Palma, who offers one of the most originally-crafted and endearing characters of the film: a love-struck lesbian who fiercely defends her right to sport facial hair, claiming that moustaches are not the sole prerogative of men, and dreams of working in a women's prison so that she can be surrounded by women all day.

Marta Balletbó-Coll's film *Costa Brava (Family Album)* (1995) has recently secured the unprecedented achievement of a foreign release for a Spanish lesbian film. Paul Smith points out that this film also breaks new ground in Catalan and Spanish cinema by placing a les-bian romance at the centre of the narrative and treating it 'as some-thing taken for granted (no longer a social problem or a psychic anomaly)' (Smith 1997: 43). As with many male gay movies, *Costa Brava (Family Album)* draws upon the popular generic traditions of humour and romance with an upbeat, utopian, happy ending. Nar-rative and visual strategies encourage the spectator to empathise with both women's emotional anticipation, anguish and pleasures from a lesbian perspective as the relationship develops. The film cir-cumnavigates the difficulties posed by the representation of lesbian sex on screen and its potential appropriation as titillation by male. heterosexual audiences by avoiding such scenes, apparently against the wishes of the distributors (Smith 1997: 4).

A lesbian theme is also tangentially introduced in Pilar Miró's *El pájaro de la felicidad*. The increasing intimacy of Carmen's relation-ship with her daughter-in-law is most sensitively represented in the sequence in which she tends a burn on Nani's arm. Tight framing in close-up on their hands and Carmen's gentle healing touch and the structure of looks established through a series of close-up, shot-reverse-shots, create an atmosphere of sensual intimacy. However, as the narrative motivation for the sequence demonstrates, the rela-tionship is presented as part of Carmen's process of self-rediscovery and emotional experimentation rather than as a significant assser-tion of lesbian identity.

Framing men

The assault on traditional notions of masculinity constitutes a sig-nificant trend in contemporary Spanish cinema. Critical images of the patriarchal order and traditional formulations of masculinity are not only concerned with revealing their repressive conse-quences for women. They also indicate the restrictive and destruc-tive implications for men and demonstrate that male identity is fragile, provisional and constantly under threat. Such preoccupa-tions in the cinema testify to a Spanish inflection of what some have

Costa Brava, Marta Balletbó-Coll, 1995   **19**

called a 'crisis in masculinity' in contemporary Western society (Cook 1982: 38–46).

Constructing masculinity

The status and validity of traditional concepts of masculinity are repeatedly undermined by the consistent – and usually comic – failure of a range of male characters to live up to the impossible masculine ideals of bravery, superiority, virility, etc. In *Demonios en el jardín* (Gutiérrez Aragón 1982), Juan's initially commanding position is progressively eroded as his weakness, financial dependence on and submission to his mother (as well as his delusions of importance and professional status by association with Franco) are gradually revealed. This culminates in the revelation that he is merely a waiter to the *caudillo*, the irony of which is articulated by his son's disillusionment and rejection. In *Bwana* (Imanol Uribe 1996), Antonio's pretence of fearlessness for the benefit of his wife and children is shattered when he turns tail and runs away from the large (harmless, as the spectator knows) African holding his cigarette lighter.

Martínez Lázaro's *Los peores años de nuestra vida* (1994) explicitly addresses the impossibility of fulfilling traditional expectations of the male. In the film, the musician (Gabino Diego) has a brother (Jorge Sanz) who seems to be everything that he is not: good-looking, self-confident and successful, both professionally and with women. Diego's gift of the gab, however, enables him to articulate his frustration and anger at the unrealistic expectations raised by society and the media. He rails against the mismatch between impossible utopian images of love and romance promoted on all sides and the disappointments of real life. Cinematic constructions of romance in particular are self-reflexively parodied into transparency as the lovers in the film-within-the film 'float' in each others arms. The young musician, Woody-Allen-style, harangues the on-screen characters for promoting a false, romantic notion of life, love and relationships and raising unattainable romantic expectations in their audiences. As the camera zooms out to reveal the artifice, we see they are actually standing, not lying. His demystification of models of masculinity and romance is partially undermined by his final success with María (Ariadna Gil), the girl of his dreams, once he lands a job as a cabaret artist. Their romantic tryst takes place in his father's bed shop ironically named 'El país de los sueños' (Land of Dreams). Again, reminiscent of Allen's *Play It Again Sam*, the more inept brother makes the ultimate sacrifice for his 'smarter' sibling (and his attachment to María), and in recognition of their 'true love', gives him his train ticket to Paris to accompany María on her three-month study visit. Unable to assume successfully the masculine role so deftly modelled by his brother, the male lead finally reproduces an alternative model based on emotional restraint and paternalistic largesse.

Bigas Luna's recent trilogy of films specifically addresses questions of masculinity and their relationship to national and regional stereotypes. The first of these, *Jamón Jamón* (1992), produced the garlic-chewing, ball-scratching, muscle-flexing Raúl in a conflation of stereotypical Spanishness and *machismo* based on images of food. bullfighting and sex. *Jamón Jamón* may fall foul of its own comic excess by permitting Raúl to redeem his absurdly stereotypical masculinity through seductive manipulations of wit and humour, and thus threaten to reinforce the very notions it sets out to criticise. Nevertheless, narrative location in the world of advertising and consumerism conflates the images and stereotypes of Iberian masculinity with the more obviously constructed images of publicity. The film thus draws attention to the socially and culturally constructed origins of male identity by focusing on the images through which it is reproduced and the processes by which role models are promoted.

By privileging the child's point of view in his later *La teta y la luna* (1994), Bigas Luna introduces a critical distance into its focus on the socialisation of the male child into the adult symbolic order, founded on absurdly exaggerated models of masculinity based on physical strength, virility, pride and denial of fear. The young Tete struggles with his obsession with women's breasts, jealousy and hatred of his baby brother, fear of his father and the demands of the *castellet* (Catalan tradition of building human towers) and male rivalry (from his Andalusian friend and her French husband) for the object of his affections and fantasies (Estrellita). The combination of

Jamón Jamón, José Juan Bigas Luna, 1992   **20**

Tete's awakening sexuality with his innocence and candour produce a perceptive and highly amusing critique of the posturing, pretence and performance which inform adult male behaviour.

Critical images

Contemporary Spanish cinema also offers a series of strong critical images of the pernicious effects of traditional gender binaries and the power relations of patriarchy in operation. In the comic genre, this critique is primarily articulated through exaggeration and parody where the field has clearly been led by the films of Pedro Almodóvar. Almodóvar's films are more noted for the strength and interest of their female characters than their male counterparts. His heterosexual male characters tend towards caricatures and stereotypes, but these are placed under the magnifying glass of black humour to produce a critical 'discourse of the absurd' (Morgan 1992b: 399–40). Typical examples of this are the gross insensitivity and chauvinism of Gloria's taxi-driver husband in *¿Qué he hecho yo para merecer esto?*, or the misogynistic sadism of Luci's policeman husband in *Pepi, Luci, Bom y otras chicas del montón*, whose battered masochistic wife smiles in unmistakably parodic adoration from her hospital bed as he twists her broken arm.

Manuel Gómez Pereira creates similarly exaggerated chauvinists in *Todos los hombres sois iguales* (1994) where three divorced men share a flat which becomes a haven of *machismo*. The film measures their retrograde attitudes and behaviour against the critical perspective of their ex-wives and girlfriends and, above all, the steadfastly commonsensical and emotionally-detached perspective of

Gender and sexuality

their housekeeper Yoli (Cristina Marcos). *Huevos de oro* (Bigas Luna 1993) again locates its critique of masculinity within the context of consumer society and the pursuit of wealth and success. Benito González's (Javier Bardem) chauvinism is unequivocally represented as greedy megalomania – epitomised in his ambition to become the King of Benidorm and erect a giant phallic skyscraper in his own honour – and violent misogyny – as he humiliates and abuses the women in his life. A series of self-inflicted disasters, however, ensure that Benito gets his comeuppance and the end of the film sees him broke, crippled and obliged by his American partner to accept the kind of *ménage à trois* which he had previously forced on others. Although this harsher critique of masculinity attracted considerable critical recognition, it failed to achieve the popular success both at home and abroad of Bigas Luna's first film of the series.

More controversially in *Matador* and *¡Átame!*, Almodóvar establishes a causal link between the fear of failing to achieve the impossible goals of traditional masculinity and violence towards women. Women, as the necessarily submissive element of the patriarchal power balance, pose a constant threat – not just to male superiority and power position – but to male identity itself. The very essence of traditional formulations of male identity hinges on men's ability to reproduce themselves in the light of these role models and reproduce the patriarchal order. In *Matador*, when his heterosexuality is questioned, Antonio sets out to prove himself by raping his neighbour Eva; and serial killer Montes can only achieve sexual satisfaction through the total domination of women – either by killing them or by getting his girlfriend Eva to 'play dead' while they make love. *¡Átame!* attracted a great deal of controversy for its apparent condonement of violence to women as a means to a romantic end. After holding Marina bound and gagged for days, Ricky finally wins the affections of his victim, leaving the film vulnerable to accusations of producing an apologia for misogyny. Also, as with the Raúl character in *Jamón Jamón*, Ricky's wit in *¡Átame!* is confusingly attractive. However, Ricky is one of Almodóvar's few heterosexual male protagonists to receive sustained narrative scrutiny and, despite its dangerous ambiguities, the film clearly attempts a serious critical study of the mechanics of masculinity. Ricky is obsessed with the idea of marriage and fatherhood as a ratification of his dubious sanity and normality when he leaves the psychiatric institution. Pressure to conform to the codes and conventions of the traditional patriarchal social order are posited as the root causes and rationale for Ricky's behaviour. The film's one weakness is less an irresponsible condonement of misogyny (as some have suggested) than a failure to place its critique of patriarchy beyond the dangers of misinterpretation (Morgan 1995: 126–7).

Social and family pressures to reproduce the paradigms of traditional male and female role models and the patriarchal order they underpin are examined in films ranging from Saura's *Cría cuervos* (1976) to *Alas de mariposa* (Bajo Ulloa 1991) and *¡Átame!*. In their dramatic extremes, these films posit a range of symptoms of violence as the result of the institutionalised reproduction of the patriarchal order's fundamental power imbalance. The exploitation of women by men can also lead to female violence as defence or revenge. In Almodóvar's *¿Qué he hecho yo para merecer esto?* this is treated comically, but Gloria's murder of her husband with a hambone is not merely condoned by the narrative but also positively celebrated as a symbol of her self-esteem and emancipation. Gómez Pereira's *Todos los hombres sois iguales* (1994) similarly features the poisoning of retrograde Manolo by his ex-wife who is narratively exonerated. Violent female revenge is more darkly represented in Carlos Saura's *Dispara* (1993) where Anna sets out to find and punish her rapist and in *La pasión turca* where Desideria shoots Yaman in revenge for his sexual promiscuity.

Power relations of patriarchy and violence

Critical representations of gender relations in period films frequently focus on the operation of an underground sexual economy, particularly in those set in the 1940s. Men in powerful economic positions sexually exploit women for whom their protection represents the sole means of survival in the postwar years of hunger, or to whom social or professional improvement by any other means seems impossible. On the hungry streets of wartorn Madrid, Pepita's (Angela Molina) ardour is easily aroused when she spots a loaf of fresh bread in Antonio's coat in *Las cosas del querer* (Chávarri, 1989); Julia (Ana Belén) desperately needs money for her fiancé's hospital treatment in *La colmena* (Camus 1982); Paca's resistance is finally broken down by the prospect of a proper home for her sick father in *Pim, pam, pum ... ¡fuego!* (Olea 1975); Java (Jorge Sanz) and the heavily pregnant Victoria Abril both perform for the repressed voyeur of *Si te dicen que caí* (Aranda 1989) in order to make a scant living. The collusion of women in their own exploitation becomes more problematic when sexual compliance represents one of the few opportunities other than a good marriage to secure social or professional advancement. In *La mitad del cielo*, Rosa's (Angela Molina) hard work and entrepreneurial spirit are of no use without the financial backing of her benign protector Pedro (Fernando Fernán Gómez). *Retrato de familia* (Giménez Rico 1976) presents a critical representation of the abuse of class and gender power in the way in which both Cecilio and later his son Cécil make use of their mistress Paulina. However, Cecilio's wife Adela is also negatively represented. Her willing ignorance of the affair not only indicates her hypocrisy, but the dubious terms of her own marriage. Marriage in this social context is presented as institutionalised prostitution where marital protection for the wife is exchanged for the husband's right to sexual relations. Since Adela does not want to engage in sex, she willingly and hypocritically colludes in turning a blind eye to Cecilio's relationship with Paulina in order to free herself from sexual obligations. The continuing sexual economy of patriarchy in the contemporary context is also articulated critically in films such as *¿Qué he hecho yo para merecer esto?* where parallels are drawn by the constant movement between scenes with Gloria and her chauvinist husband, the activities of the prostitute next door, and the occupants of the middle-class flat where she is paid to do the cleaning.

Return of the repressed; threat of 'the Other'

Democratic Spain's confident rhetoric of liberalism and equality is destabilised in several recent films in which violence and misogyny are shown to lurk threateningly beneath the surface of the contemporary culture of tolerance. *El techo del mundo* (Felipe Vega 1995) warns of the fragility of that cultural control when, after a bump on the head Tomás (Santiago Ramos) reverts to an almost primitive state, displaying the most obnoxious features of *machismo*, egotism and racist attitudes. This dark side to human nature surfaces in both *Mi nombre es sombra* (Gonzálo Suárez 1995), inspired by the Jekyll and Hyde myth, where Doctor Beiral has a sinister alter ego, El Otro (The Other), who indulges his darker instincts to the full, and *Mi hermano del alma* (Mariano Barroso 1993) where Charlie's (Carlos Hipólito) irrepressible brother Toni (Juanjo Puigcorbé) another sinister kind of *alter ego* – comes back from the past to disrupt the conventional life he has established with his girlfriend (Toni's ex who ran away with Charlie to escape his violence). Charlie's attachment to his brother goes beyond fraternal loyalty and Toni's unrestrained emotional responses and behaviour clearly rehearse the desires and emotions which Charlie must keep in check. Living on borrowed time with a terminal illness, Toni drinks and gambles continually, attacks and later kills Charlie's rival in the insurance stakes and, when a potential client refuses to sign up after Toni's inappropriate intervention, he takes revenge by breaking up his campsite at night.

These films are thematically linked to a small group of recent films featuring women revisited by men from their past. In both of these movies, the returning man physically invades the traditionally female sphere of the home and introduces violence or emotional disruption into the harmonious status quo of their stable, middle-class family lives. As with Toni in *Mi hermano del alma*, in all of the films, the returning male protagonists have been abandoned in the past by the women they now seek out, and their violent characters contrast with the gentler – sometimes more overtly 'feminine' – men who now partner the women. In Bigas Luna's *Lola* (1986), her lover from the past comes back to stalk her and destabilise her life with her French husband and daughter. In Vicente Aranda's *Intruso* (1993), Luisa's (Victoria Abril) ex-husband Ángel (Imanol Arias) reappears and introduces sickness and tension into the household. In *La ardilla roja* (1993), Lisa's psychopathic husband's appearance introduces a structurally, narratively and thematically violent twist into the final section of the film. The violence and disruption these men introduce is represented as threatening and excessive. Lisa's husband is presented as almost parodically manic in distorting close-ups which contrast him starkly with her new lover, the gentle, laid-back new man Jota; Lola's sadistic lover from the past is presented as threateningly obsessive through the visual conventions of the thriller; and Ángel's mysterious sickness and vindictive parasitism cast him as an increasingly sinister threat, reflected in the film's dark images. Despite their negative representation, however, the female protagonists often display an almost obsessive attraction towards these threatening men. Despite the comfort and apparent satisfaction of her marriage, Lola is haunted by a contradictory, ill-advised and ultimately fatal attraction to the lover from the sadomasochistic relationship from her past, and in *Intruso*, as Ángel becomes more and more dangerous, so Luisa becomes more obsessively attached to him. Mary, in *Mi nombre es sombra*, displays a similarly inexplicable attraction towards El Otro and willingly submits to his perverse demands. As was the case with Almodóvar's *¡Átame!*, such representations are problematic in that they seem to reinforce discredited myths of female masochism.

Women, as the Other, and strong women in particular, have traditionally been seen as a potential threat. In psychoanalytical terms, they have represented the threat of castration, and in social terms they pose the ever-present threat of rebelling against their subordination to male dominance and ultimately usurping the male's dominant position. In cinematic terms, this threat has been minimised through a series of narrative and representational strategies such as punishment and violence, mystification, fetishisation and reification, all fully-exploited in the Spanish cinema of the dictatorship. Marsha Kinder has perceptively observed the eroticisation of violence in films of the late Francoist period and traces its origins back to the Counter-Reformation (Kinder 1993: 136–98). In contemporary Spain, the changing role of women may explain the emergence of particularly extreme screen images of violence towards women. Such representations of gender relations might also be considered symptomatic of the contemporary destabilisation of traditional notions of masculinity.

Representing homosexuality

As we have already observed, homosexuality in Francoist cinema was limited largely to images of comic ridicule. Its representation in oppositional cinema also tended to reinforce its association with perversion, frequently cast as the perverse result of repression – particularly at the hands of the matriarchs of the seventies, as in *Ana y los lobos* and *Mamá cumple cien años*. This unfortunate association also persists in contemporary cinema. Even in the work of Almodóvar, homosexuality is sometimes attributed to the castrating influence of overbearing mothers.

The psychological effects of the exclusion of gay subjectivities under Franco is the specific focus of Vicente Aranda's *Cambio de sexo* (1976), which introduced Victoria Abril as an effeminate adolescent whose traditionalist father attempts to masculinise him by a cathartic trip to a Barcelona brothel. The boy finally has a sex change operation at the end of the film. Although Aranda regrets the imposition of a 'happy ending' on this film, a 1990s re-reading of this resolution is perhaps more tragic and illustrative of the pernicious effects of the imposition of rigid models of gender and sexuality. The film identifies the choice of equally pernicious options for those who are able to conform to the required sexual orientation of the gender paradigm. Both options imply a denial of self and identity. Aranda suggests that the choice is limited to changing personality or changing sex.

Despite the decriminalisation of homosexuality in 1979 and the existence of the gay liberal oasis of Sitges, attitudes towards homosexuality in Spain in general have changed very little. As Chris Perriam observes, although there has been some recent evidence of a slightly higher media profile for gay and lesbian issues, 'There is as yet very little cultural production about, by or for ordinary lesbians and gay men' (Perriam 1995: 394). Despite the caveats expressed above, the films by Eloy de la Iglesia, Montxo Armendáriz and Pedro Almodóvar represent a crucially important contribution to the dedemonisation of homosexuality.

It was not until the seventies that cinema began to address the question of homosexuality more directly. Ventura Pons's subversive realist documentary *Ocaña, retrato intermitente* (1978) broke new ground in its focus on the well-known Barcelona transvestite artist. Consistent with the desire for 'unmediated' realism and authenticity which characterised the documentary revival of the transition period, the film took the form of an interview in which Ocaña discussed the impact of homosexuality on his personal life and painting. As Jo Labanyi points out, the images of Ocaña and the 'contrived nature of her/his pose also makes the point that gender is a construction which perhaps cannot be escaped, but can at least be manipulated at will' (Labanyi 1995: 401). What characterises the representation of homosexuality in post-Franco cinema is its celebration of a kind of aesthetic transvestism. Styles and genres are freely cannibalised as Ocaña's appropriation of all the traditional folkloric accoutrements exemplifies. Contemporary cinema displays a range of generic and stylistic appropriations for the expression of gay identity – ranging from de la Iglesia's location of his homosexual narratives within the framework of melodrama to the visual flamboyance of Almodóvar's kitsch.

Initially banned by the Francoist censor, Eloy de la Iglesia's *Los placeres ocultos* first placed homosexuality at the centre of its melodramatic narrative as early as 1976. Although de la Iglesia has later become well-known for his voyeuristic imaging and Eduardo's homosexuality is the thematic focus of *Los placeres ocultos* (1976), despite the film's release at the height of the *destape* trend, Spanish cinema was not yet ready for explicit images of gay sex. The film offers a discrete but nevertheless critical denunciation of homosexual discrimination and marginalisation. It is perhaps in its open-ended final shot that the film articulates its most significant statement, as Eduardo opens the door to a caller we never see, hoping it will be Miguel. If it is not Miguel then his hopes will be shattered, but equally his presence cannot provide the desired narrative, emotional and sexual satisfaction. Miguel is a confirmed heterosexual and this is respected by Eduardo. This final conundrum reflects the impossibility of the open expression of homosexual identity within the hostile and restrictive context of a patriarchal society, still in the cultural grip of Francoism (Smith 1992: 142–3).

Whereas *Los placeres ocultos* mainly focused on the discriminatory attitudes of conservatism (particularly represented by Eduardo's dismissal by the bank where he worked), both de la Iglesia's *El diputado* (1978) and Imanol Uribe's *La muerte de Mikel* (1984) address leftist hostility towards homosexuality. *El diputado* concerns Roberto, a politician belonging to an imaginary Socialist Party who first denies then conceals his own homosexual orientation believing it to be a deviant manifestation of bourgeois indulgence. A contrast is drawn between the continuing clandestinity of homosexuality and the new political freedoms in the immediate post dictatorship period and Roberto is eventually forced by the strength of his sexuality to recognise both its inevitability and the political right to live consistently with his identity. Another melodramatic open-ended finale focuses on Roberto as he prepares to come out to his colleagues at a public meeting and a freeze-frame enigmatically captures his mixed emotions of anger and distress as he is about to speak. We never discover how the party reacts. On similar terrain, *La muerte de Mikel* concerns a homosexual pharmacist who is dropped from the list of candidates for the Basque Parliament by the left-wing party to which he belongs. After an illegal police interrogation (including torture) about his ETA involvement under Francoism, Mikel commits suicide and his death is hypocritically exploited as a political martyrdom by the party. The film both denounces the continuation of repressive practices by the authorities, despite their official banning in the democratic era, and questions the willingness of left-wing politics to come to terms with the new challenges being presented by changing sexual politics.

Paul Julian Smith discusses at length the way in which the films of Pedro Almodóvar appropriate popular genres and narratives such as melodrama and romance for the gay imagination (Smith 1992: 163–215). Striking examples occur in the homosexual melodrama-thriller *La ley del deseo*, particularly in the use of music (nostalgic Latin American themes) and camerawork, to induce the spectator to empathise with the on-screen homosexual romance. This is so, particularly in emotional sequences such as the moment when Antonio and Pablo are reunited in the latter's besieged flat, and the final tableau in which Pablo cradles his dead lover in a gay appropriation of the Pietá. The striking formal features and iconography of certain genres – such as the musical and *film noir* – reflect the camp aesthetic which characterises so much of contemporary gay cultural production. As Susan Sontag observed in 1964, 'Homosexuals have pinned their integration into society on promoting the aesthetic sense. Camp is a solvent of morality. It neutralises moral indignation, sponsors playfulness' (Sontag 1964: 118). Perhaps the way in which the potentially subversive subtexts of these genres in their original forms also offered themselves up for readings between the lines makes them all the more attractive now for subversive redirection. If Almodóvar is often described as a woman's director because of the predominantly female world his films create, this profile must also be partially attributed to the melodramatic content of his films and their proximity to the tradition of the Hollywood Woman's Film. Like these films, but in a much more obvious way, the visual and emotional excess of the film subverts the norms of patriarchal roles and behaviour. Unlike their classic precursors which tried to restore the patriarchal status quo through a frequently unconvincing narrative closure which was unable to contain the excess of the subtext, these films encourage alternatives to the paradigms of social and sexual convention.

La ley del deseo is Almodóvar's only film with a central focus on a male homosexual relationship. Other gay males in his films tend to be secondary characters, for example Ángel in *Matador*, and smaller roles in early films such as *Laberinto de pasiones* (1982) and *Pepi, Luci, Bom y otras chicas del montón* (1980). As Paul Julian Smith points out, 'while earlier interviews (with Almodóvar) reveal an open pleasure in kitsch, camp and homoerotic fantasy, later pieces display an increasing disavowal of homosexuality, whether it is understood as a cultural identity, a recognisable sensibility, or a specific film tradition' (Smith 1992: 164). Rather than indicating a radical *volte face* in his defence of homosexuality, this paradoxical refusal to parade his personal or artistic homosexual identity is consistent with the 'liberal' discourses of his films where homosexuality is merely another possibility in the collage of identities his

21

La ley del deseo, Pedro Almodóvar, 1986

characters assume. Whilst this attitude is, on the one hand, an admirable defence of equality and freedom of choice, it can also be problematic. As with other articulations of this philosophy (as in the previously discussed *¡Átame!*, for example, where the director defends Marina's freedom to fall in love with a violent kidnapper if she so chooses) freedom of choice might work within the filmic world Almodóvar seeks to construct – a world free from dominant ideological concepts and discrimination – but it fails to engage with the realities of the world his audiences inhabit where discrimination and misogyny remain deeply entrenched within social and psychological consciousness. The positive aspect of such unproblematised representations is that they may in turn promote a similar level of tolerance outside the film world.

As with lesbian themes, the comedy and the thriller remain the preferred location for gay narratives in recent Spanish films. These popular genres represent a symbolic appropriation of cultural forms previously colonised by heterosexuality and their conventions

Gender and sexuality

permit the operation of processes which promote strong identification with their protagonists and facilitate the effective representation of their particular perspective and subjectivity. Recent examples include a movie with the defiantly camp title *Perdona bonita, pero Lucas me quería a mí* (1996), directed by newcomers Félix Sabroso and Dunia Ayaso. The narrative hinges on the discovery of Lucas's dead body in the flat he shared with three gay men, all enraptured by him and fighting amongst themselves for his attentions. Rather than positing the characters' homosexuality as the film's subject for scrutiny, its main thematic concern is the subjective delusions and illusions of the individual in love as each character reveals a totally different picture of the deceased Lucas. This film again avoids turning homosexuality into an issue, representing gay identity as just another option in the contemporary social collage. In other films, the problems facing homosexuals in a hostile social environment are addressed. The significance and difficulty of coming out, for example, are broached in *Boca a boca* (Gómez Pereira 1995), where a secondary narrative thread traces the painful process of a high-profile plastic surgeon accepting himself and coming out publicly.

New Spanish man

If the role and perspective of women in contemporary Spain has changed quite radically, traditional constructions of heterosexual male identity have also been radically disturbed. What is also perhaps surprising is the increasing visibility of a new male identity predicated on the recognition and acceptance of the fluid movement across gender divisions of both 'feminine' and 'masculine' characteristics. A number of films demonstrate the existence of a contemporary cultural impetus to break down such traditional gender binaries. As traditional notions of masculine and feminine identity are being challenged and redefined by such notions as the reconstructed 'new man' and the independent 'new woman', the very concept of such separate gender categories is being destabilised in a number of ways.

Films by Pedro Almodóvar have been particularly instrumental in introducing and promoting the fluidity of traditional gender attributes in particularly challenging ways. In *La ley del deseo*, as noted earlier, transsexual Tina (Carmen Maura) displays far more maternalism than Ada's 'natural' mother, ironically played by real-life transvestite Bibi Andersson. Other films challenging fixed gender categories include *Matador*, where gender fluidity is inscribed within the ambiguity of the film's bullfighting context and the central characters' rejection of gender binaries as they recognise one another as members of the same species, beyond gender difference. More recent films illustrate the fluidity of traditional gender attributes in similarly challenging ways.

The stronger female protagonists of a number of contemporary Spanish films are registering their rejection of the traditional *macho* male and a preference for the socially and emotionally reconstructed 'new' Spanish man who displays gentleness, sensitivity, tolerance, etc. A number of films focus particularly on their female protagonists' rejection of violent men in favour of male characters who are constructed in various ways as more 'feminine'. In *Tierra* (Julio Medem 1995), the gentle, internally-divided, pest-control expert Angel (Carmelo Gómez) communes with nature; his symbiotic relationship with the elements sets him apart from Angela's (Emma Suárez) violent husband (Karra Elejalde). In *La ardilla roja*, a film which is essentially concerned with identity, Lisa (Emma Suárez) constructs an entirely new past and present identity for herself to exclude and erase the husband from her past who appears at the end of the film as an almost cartoon caricature of violence and evil. Her new companion Jota (Nacho Novo), in stark contrast to their fellow camper, the *macho* taxi-driver from Madrid and Lisa's husband, self-consciously constructs himself as a gentle, non-competitive figure. It is also interesting to note that in *¡Átame!*, it is ironically only when Ricky, beaten and wounded by drug-dealing thugs, displays the kind of weakness traditionally associated with the 'feminine' that Marina falls for him. However, the preference for the gentler, reconstructed man is not only a reactive alternative to the experience of violent misogyny. In *Mujeres al borde de un ataque de nervios*, Pepa finally realises the limited attraction of middle-aged philanderer Iván and in *Tacones lejanos*, Rebecca (Victoria Abril) opts sexually and emotionally for the judge/transvestite Letal (also played by Miguel Bosé, who has been associated both on and off-screen with sexual ambiguity); Clara in *Lo más natural* (Josefina Molina 1990) ditches her conservative and traditional husband for a younger, more liberal and relaxed lover (Miguel Bosé). However, as Peter Evans observes, Clara is still susceptible to the continuing allure of the more traditional male figure (Evans 1995: 328).

The more 'feminine' characteristics attaching to contemporary constructions of male identity are positively promoted in a range of characters played by young actors such as Jorge Sanz in whom such 'unmasculine' traits as innocence and inexperience become associated with desirability in films such as *Orquesta Club Virginia* (Manuel Iborra 1991), *Amantes* (1991) and *Belle Epoque* (1992) where he is successively manipulated and feminised by the women of the house. Similar characteristics are displayed by other young male actors such as Pere Ponce in *Amo tu cama rica*, Coque Malla in *Todo es mentira* (Alvaro Fernández Armero (1994) and the appeal of the inexperienced young man portrayed by Gabino Diego – inept but deserving – in *Tierno verano de lujurias y azoteas* (Jaime Chávarri 1993), *Los peores años de nuestra vida* (Emilio Martínez Lázaro 1994) and *El rey pasmado* (Imanol Uribe 1991). Even Javier Bardem, in serious danger of becoming permanently cast as the stereotypical *macho ibérico* following his performances in *Jamón, jamón, El amante bilingüe*, etc., has adopted a different masculine identity in *Boca a boca* (Gómez Pereira 1995). The psychological and behavioural characteristics of these new male identities are also translated into new physical models: the fresh-faced appearance of the younger actors, or the androgenous features of actors like Antonio Banderas, emphasised by the range of sexual identities he has assumed particuarly in Almodóvar's films – from the homosexual obsessive of *La ley del deseo* to the hen-pecked fiancé of *Mujeres al borde de un ataque de nervios*, or Ricky in *¡Átame!*.

These more progressive constructions of male identity rely heavily on a recognition of both the social construction of the characteristics traditionally ascribed to the respective gender categories and the actual fluidity of the psychological and behavioural concepts of the 'feminine' and the 'masculine'. In *Pon un hombre en tu vida* (Eva Lesmes 1996), traditional masculine approaches are comically but effectively undermined when football coach Díaz Conde (Toni Cantó) finds himself trapped in Belinda's (Cristina Marcos) female body and discovers that her gentler approach proves to be more persuasive and effective. Both characters have something to learn from the psychological and behavioural make-up of the opposite gender, demonstrating the positive benefits of a receptive attitude to the fluidity of the 'masculine' and the 'feminine'. Belinda becomes more independent, more concerned with real emotions than finding husband, forming family and conforming to social patterns, and Díaz Conde learns to recognise his dependence on other human beings (admitting he needs her in the final resolution). As Eva Lesmes explains, the film was trying to

hablar de los hombres y de las mujeres, de si son tan distintos como parece, con la premisa de que lo ideal es tener un equilibrio entre la parte femenina y la masculina, reconocer ambas y utilizar las dos (speak about men and women, about whether they are as different as they seem, with the premise that the ideal is a balance between the feminine and the masculine). (*Fotogramas* 1996: 75)

References

Barañano, M. (1992), *Mujer.Trabajo. Salud*, Editorial Trotta, Madrid, Fundación Primero de Mayo 14.

Brooksbank Jones, A. (1995) Work, Women and the Family: A Critical Perspective, in Graham, H., and Labanyi, J. (eds), *Spanish Cultural Studies. An Introduction*, Oxford, Oxford University Press, 386–93.

Cook, P. (1982), Masculinity in Crisis, *Screen*, 23: 3–46.

Evans, P. (1995), Back to the Future: Cinema and Democracy, in Graham, H. and Labanyi, J. (eds), *Spanish Cultural Studies. An Introduction*, Oxford, Oxford University Press, 326–31.

Fotogramas (1995), La nueva ola, 1825, 36.

Fotogramas (1996), Pon un hombre en tu vida: La ópera prima de Eva Lesmes, 1834, 75.

Graham, H. (1995), Women and Social Change, in Graham, H., and Labanyi, J. (eds), *Spanish Cultural Studies. An Introduction*, Oxford, Oxford University Press, 99–116.

Holden, A. (1992), Almodóvar: the man who loves women, *Cosmopolitan*, 141: 99–100.

Hooper, J. (1995), *The New Spaniards*, London, Penguin, 162–3.

Jagose, A. (1994), *Lesbian Utopics*, London, Routledg, 1–2.

Kaplan, A. (1988), Is the gaze male?, *Women and Film*, London, Routledge, 22–35.

Kinder, M. (1993), *Blood Cinema. The Reconstruction of National Identity in Spain*, Berkeley, Los Angeles and London, University of California, 136–423.

Kuhn, A. (1982), *Women's Pictures. Feminism and Cinema*, London, Pandora Press, 3–18.

Labanyi, J. (1995), Postmodernism and the Problem of Cultural Identity in Graham, H., and Labanyi, J. (eds) (1995), *Spanish Cultural Studies. An Introduction*, Oxford, Oxford University Press, 396–406.

Monaco, J. (1977), *How to Read Film*, Oxford, Oxford University Pres, 121–42.

Monterde, J. E. (1993), *Veinte años de cine español (1973–1992). Un cine bajo la paradoja*, Barcelona, Ediciones Paidós, 165–6.

Montero, R. (1995), The Silent Revolution: The Social and Cultural Advances of Women in Democratic Spain, in Graham, H., and Labanyi, J. (eds), *Spanish Cultural Studies. An Introduction*, Oxford, Oxford University Press, 381–5.

Morgan, R. (1992a), Dressed to Kill, *Sight and Sound*, 1: 12, 28–9.

Morgan, R. (1992b), Pedro Almodóvar's *Matador*: Degenderising Gender?, *Journal of Gender Studies*, 1: 3, 399–404.

Morgan, R. (1995), Pedro Almodóvar's Tie Me Up! Tie Me Down!: The Mechanics of Masculinity, in Kirkham, P., and Thumim, J. (eds),), *Me Jane. Masculinity, Movies and Women*, London, Lawrence & Wishart, 113–27.

Mulvey, L. (1989), Visual Pleasures and narrative Cinema, in *Visual and Other Pleasures*, London, Macmillan, 14–26.

Perriam, C. (1995), Gay and Lesbian Culture, in Graham, H., and Labanyi, J. (eds), *Spanish Cultural Studies. An Introduction*, Oxford, Oxford University Press, 393–5.

Ponga, P. (1996), "Tu nombre envenena mis sueños" La venganza según Pilar Miró, *Fotogramas*, 1835, 109–10.

Rabalska, C. (1996), Women in Spanish Cinema in Transition, *International Journal of Iberian Studies*, 9: 3, 166–79.

Smith, P. J. (1992), *Laws of Desire. Questions of Homosexuality in Spanish Writing and Film 1960–1990*, Oxford, Clarendon Press, 28–215.

Smith, P. J. (1996), *Vision Machines. Cinema, Literature and Sexuality in Spain and Cuba, 1983–1993*, London, Verso, 28–9.

Smith, P. J. (1997) Review of *Costa Brava (Family Album)*, *Sight and Sound*, 7: 3, 43–4.

Sontag, S. (1964), Notes on Camp, in Sontag, S. (1983), *Extracts from Susan Sontag's Work. A Susan Sontag Reader*, London, Penguin, 105–19.

Trashorras, A. (1996), Los jóvenes directores toman las riendas, *Fotogramas*, 1835, 57–63.

Vernon, K. M., and Morris, B. (1995), *Post-Franco, Postmodern. The Films of Pedro Almodóvar*, Westport, Connecticut and London, Greenwood Press, 10.

Yráyzoz, F. (1996) Mónica Laguna, directora de *Tengo una casa*, *Cinemanía*, 12, 18.

Gender and sexuality

4 Recuperating nationalist identities: film in the autonomous regions

Introduction

Under Franco, especially in the early years, as the regime attempted to 'rehispanicise' the Spanish nation, regional languages, cultures and identities other than Castilian were effectively outlawed and forced underground. As we have seen, cultural life in Franco's Spain would be conducted virtually exclusively in Castilian. In both practical and symbolic terms, this was the language of Civil War victory and the new central state, the idiom of internal colonisation as well as that of a 'glorious' imperial past (Labanyi 1995a: 208). With one or two isolated exceptions (Molina-Foix 1977: 26; Caparrós Lera 1992: 121 and 127–8), filmmaking in vernacular tongues other than the 'language of empire' was almost totally absent. Moreover, filmic representations of regional cultures and peoples in officially-sponsored film output (whether in *No-Do* news-reels or commercial features) tended to reinforce crude, folksy stereotypes and, by eliding regional differences, create an illusory sense of national homogeneity (Evans 1995: 216–17). Only in the 1960s, in a context in which the cultural sphere began to provide limited spaces for dissident activity, did conditions allow for the rise of a small independent film culture in Spain, located mainly in Madrid and Barcelona, out of which the so-called Escuela de Barcelona (Barcelona School) emerged (Molina-Foix 1977: 22–7). This was not so much a clearly defined film movement as a set of young directors, aspiring *auteurs* and producers including Jacinto Esteva, Pere Portabella, Antoni Padrós, Joaquín Jordá, Vicente Aranda, Josep María Forn, Gonzalo Suárez, Antoni Ribas; etc. They were anxious to use film in more imaginative, challenging ways in order to deal with social and political issues; issues relevant to the realities of specific regions, something that was totally absent in the institutional cinema under Franco (Hopewell 1986: 116–17). Their output was not large or widely viewed, indeed many productions failed to see the light of day. Yet a few films, for example, dealt with problems specific to Catalonia in the 1960s, such as generational conflict, emigration and industrial relations, as in Aranda's *Brillante porvenir* (1964), Forn's *La piel quemada* (1964) and Ribas's *Medias y calcetines* (1969) (Hopewell 1986: 116). Significantly, at that time, among members of the Escuela de Barcelona, there existed no explicit commitment (neither theoretical nor political) to filming in Catalan. Because of obvious constraints, all their features were shot in Castilian, a few of which were later dubbed into Catalan (Molina-Foix 1977: 22–7). The so-called Escuela fell apart in 1970/71; some of the pioneers moved into the commercial cinema, though making mainly up-market, arthouse movies (Aranda, Suárez), others maintained their position as independents (Portabella) and, until very recently, some simply abandoned the business altogether (Esteva and Jordá – who has returned to filmmaking with the thriller *Un cos al bosc/Un cuerpo en el bosque* (1996)).

As Hopewell points out (1986: 114), the death of Franco and the sustained popular pressure for political and cultural liberalisation in Spain in the mid- and late 1970s created the climate for a resurgence of nationalist cinema in the regions. However, the re-emergence of filmmaking in the Spanish regions since 1975 has been consistently problematic. Film output has been highly variable and irregular, both in quantity and quality. This has been a function not only of adverse economic conditions and changing policies at national level but of the many different cultural and political agendas to which film production has had to adjust since the death of Franco (Monterde 1993: 90).

We find most cinematic activity in those regions which had the strongest film cultures and nationalist movements before these were suppressed by Franco, i.e. Catalonia, the Basque Country and, to a much lesser extent, Galicia. In these so-called 'historic nationalities', alongside other cultural activities, filmmaking would play an important though uneven role in the the recovery of national identities through the reconstruction of nationalist consciousness and the affirmation of political and cultural difference.

For obvious reasons, given its long tradition of film production and its considerable industrial infrastructure (though this was severely run down by the end of the dictatorship), the Catalan cinema possessed major advantages over other national cinemas. After 1975, it was the first to re-emerge, followed by some cinema activity in the Basque Country and then later by a number of different cinematic intitatives and projects in other regions such as Galicia, Valencia, Andalusia and the Canaries, etc. However, apart from Catalonia and the Basque Country, film production in these other regions has been fairly modest. Here, despite financial support from regional governments, television stations and some public funding for individual projects and ideas, such initiatives as have emerged have not generated significant industrial investment or created serious and sustained bodies of work. Our consideration of cinema in the regions is thus concerned mainly, though not exlusively, with developments in Catalonia and the Basque Country.

As Monterde suggests (1993: 90), it might be useful if we divide up the post-Franco development of cinema in the autonomous regions into two main phases, that is, before and after the transfer of powers from central government to the autonomous regional governments, starting in the 1980/81 period. Not surprisingly, the first *autonomía* (autonomy) to recover its 'competencias' (powers) in the cultural and cinematic arenas was Catalonia. This did not take place, however, without a bitter political struggle during the 1975–81 period, a phase during which filmmaking in the region formed part of a wider political process aimed at recovering a distinct cultural and national Catalan identity.

Catalan cinema

Taking stock

By 1976, if Francoist repression had managed to galvanize Catalan nationalist political resistance to centralist Spain, it had also managed to reduce the number of film production companies in Barcelona, the level of industrial infrastructure and the total number of films made in the region to alarmingly small porportions (Hopewell 1986: 116). The industrial basis for relaunching a Catalan film culture, as yet unsupported by public money, was thus highly precarious. The tapping of alternative sources of finance was equally problematic. Indeed, in the face of decades of centralist discrimination and neglect, sections of the Catalan bourgeoisie who might have been persuaded to support filmmaking with private finance, were understandably reluctant to invest serious money in a risky, run-down business, especially in a period of political uncertainty. Moreover, the few existing commercial film production companies based in Barcelona (e.g. Balcázar, Ifisa, Profilmes) tended to specialise in the making of 'subgeneric' features (mainly comedies) for the national Spanish market (Monterde 1993: 91). At the other end of the production spectrum, among certain Catalan filmmakers unwilling to compromise with the demands of the commercial sector, a certain, marginal, independent *cine de autor* (*auteur* cinema) just about survived, having had its origins in the Escuela de Barcelona of the 1960s (Molina-Foix 1977: 22–3). Unfortunately, between the low-budget, popular genre film and the art-house movie, destined for an elite audience, there was little or nothing in the way of middle-of-the-road, commercial cinema for a wider Catalan public. This crucial lack, and thereby the failure to rebuild an audience base for Catalan film, would constitute major challenges to those engaged in the reconstruction of an indigenous film industry in Catalonia and in the re-establishment of local means of distribution and exhibition of film products spoken in Catalan.

Reasserting difference: a new Catalan cinema

In December 1975, almost immediately following Franco's death, more than seventy film professionals joined forces and set up the Institut de Cinema Catalá (ICC) (Molina-Foix 1977: 26–7). It offered a new forum for debate and inaugurated the first of a number of attempts to define what Catalan film and a Catalan film industry ought to be doing and how Catalan professionals should develop their sector. Taking the form of a limited company, the ICC established a number of committees in order to develop strategies to meet its two main aims: a) the use of film as a vehicle to promote the culture of all Catalan peoples; b) the engagement of film in the struggle for democracy and political autonomy. These aims were further underpinned by one overriding linguistic objective: to promote a cinema, spoken in catalan, which would 'reflejar la realidad del país, basándose en sus problemas humanos, políticos y culturales' (reflect the realities of the country, in terms of its political, cultural and human problems) (Caparrós Lera 1992: 129). In this, the ICC coincided fully with the aims of the Congrès de Cultura Catalana (1976), a major national conference which helped establish the Catalan cultural agenda for the coming years and in particular, emphasised the importance of linguistic normalisation, a process in which film was seen as playing a key role.

If the definition of Catalan cinema was closely linked to the defence and normalisation of the Catalan language in these early years, adjustments and revisions to the meanings of 'Catalan cinema' would be proposed by film professionals and intellectuals in a series of conferences and public meetings in the later 1970s and early 1980s, reflecting the always lively but conflictive evolution of the pre-autonomy debates on national culture and cinema in Catalonia. Such debates had their beginnings in the Congrès de Cultura Catalana (1976), as noted above, in whose conclusions the emphasis on linguistic exclusivity was complemented by the desirability of producing a Catalan cinema which better reflected and critically explored the realities of the nation. Also, by the time of the major conferences specifically devoted to Catalan film, such as the Jornades de Cinema Català (1979) and the Converses de Cinema de Catalunya (1981), a rather more technical, production-oriented definition of Catalan cinema began to emerge, taking into account not only earlier linguistic and political priorities but also questions of film aesthetics and infrastuctural aspects, i.e. the use of Catalan technicians, laboratories, dubbing, sound and post-production studios and the need for support from Televisión Española (Monterde

1993: 93–4; Caparrós Lera 1992: 199). So, in the run up to the transfer of powers, at the turn of the 1980s, definitions of what constituted Catalan cinema varied between an understandable early emphasis on linguistic and political priorities and those which focused on the somewhat more practical aspects of funding, investment and film production, including the editing, distribution and exhibition process. Of course, well before the various interest groups could all agree on their definitions of Catalan cinema, certain examples of Catalan filmmaking had already emerged.

Rebuilding a nationalist consciousness

Reflecting trends and developments at national level, the first examples of Catalan language films to be screened after the death of Franco in Catalonia took two main forms: on the one hand, Catalan filmmakers exploited various aspects of the realist documentary genre; on the other, a certain 'high-culture', Catalan, political cinema re-emerged in the form of the historical fiction film. The trend in realist documentaries was arguably anticipated in the important archival work of Jaime Camino and his detailed focus on the region in *La vieja memoria* (1977). However, it has been convincingly argued that Camino's mode of presentation of his material was rather more oblique than directly testimonial (Hopewell 1986: 173). The adoption of the documentary form responded to several obvious critical requirements of the time: the need to focus on specifically Catalan realities; the requirement to chronicle but also to valorise positively the ways in which Catalan cultural activities had been in the vanguard of an anti-Francoist political resistance; the pressing need to recover and rebuild a nationalist consciousness in the ongoing struggle for political autonomy and pluralist democracy in the run-up to the establishment of the Autonomous Government.

Initially, certain filmmakers adopted a mainly realist, objectivist documentary form, as represented by Francesc Bellmunt's *Canet Rock* (1976) and *La nova cançó* (1976). These pioneering pieces attempted to record and to some extent celebrate (without resorting to crude triumphalism) the popular music and the songwriters' protest movements in Catalonia of the 1960s and 1970s. They combined examples of the 'nova cançó' (of Raimón and Lluís Llach, for example) with interviews involving a spectrum of people (songwriters, politicans, intellectuals) linked to the movement. These films succeeded in capturing not only the background to a cultural phenomenon but also the euphoric mood of the times. They chronicled a crucial historical conjuncture, showing Catalans revelling in their freedom after forty years of Francoist oppression and confidently facing the ensuing struggle for political autonomy.

In June 1977, following a Setmana de Cine dels paisos catalans (Catalan Film Week), held in Madrid, and adopting a more critical, inquiring, investigative attitude, we find the first of a series of home-grown Catalan newsreels, the *Noticiaris de Barcelona*. Arising from an initiative originally supported by the ICC and based on a planned series of twelve films (the first of which was shot by Josep María Forn), these fortnightly newsreels were clearly conceived as a Catalan riposte to the official Francoist *No-Do* newsreels and also to the very limited coverage of topical Catalan issues on national television. Polemical, highly critical of Madrid and focusing on serious social and political issues (health, education, regional policies, land speculation), the longer term viability of these newsreels was not secured because of disagreements between the ICC and the provisional regional government (Hopewell 1986: 121).

In contrast to the above, other Catalan filmmakers tried to exploit the documentary form in rather different ways, eschewing its testimonial function and 'reality effect' in search of a more obviously staged, stylised 'documentary as performance' look. In this vein, we can locate Ventura Pons's sympathetic, subversive portrait of Barcelona's transvestite community in *Ocaña, retrat intermitent* (1978). By staging as well as attempting to chronicle the activities of his subjects, Pons managed to blur the boundaries between reality and performance and indirectly brought into question the ability of the realist documentary genre to deliver 'the real' at all. His film succeeded in capturing changes occurring in the expression of sexual identites in the late 1970s in Spain, particularly in the gay and transvestite communities. It also represented the city of Barcelona as a welcoming metropolis (compared to the repressive provinces), where new styles and different sexual orientations could be absorbed and publicly displayed (Labanyi 1995b: 399). Also reacting to the frequent mystifications of Francoist *No-Do* newsreels, other documentalists sought to *épater le bourgeois*, determined to shock and disturb audiences with particularly unsavoury topics and graphic accounts of unwholeseome professions, as in *Cada ver es*, (1981) by Ángel del Val, dealing with the daily routines of a mortuary worker or tales of murder and mayhem, as in *El asesino de Pedralbes* (1978) by Gonzalo Herralde. What is clear is that the testimonial function of Catalan documentary, initially dominant in the late 1970s, was gradually overtaken by films which challenged their 'reportage effect', either by exploiting the conventions of the fiction film (as in Camino's *La vieja memoria*) or by passing off obviously staged actions, events and scenes as direct reporting.

Antoni Ribas's epic portrayal and critique of the *fin de siècle* Catalan bourgeoisie in *La ciutat cremada* (first screened in September 1976) was a prime example of the historical fiction film, which was the other form of Catalan cinema to emerge. A sprawling period piece, overly derivative, of but not quite equal to, Visconti's *Il Gatopardo* (1963), Ribas nonetheless offered a biting critique of the passivity and lack of nationalist consciousness of the Catalan middle classes towards the radical social movements they had initially supported at the turn of the century. In terms of its historical focus, the film was in many ways a manifesto for Catalan rights and culture. It also illustrated particularly well the striking obsession of some of the more ambitious and radical Catalan filmmakers with the region's modern history and the development of the late nineteenth-century bourgeois nationalism up to the present, to the exclusion of virtually all other historical periods (Monterde 1989: 52). The historical feature film continued to attract interest in the shape of Josep María Forn's hagiographic, though politically 'consensual' biopic of the Catalan president of 1933–40 Lluís Companys in *Companys, procés a Catalunya/proceso a Cataluña* (1979). In similar historical vein, though treating an earlier period, we find Jacinto Grau's more commercial, sentimental *El timbaler del bruc/La leyenda del tambor* (1981), a Hispano-Mexican co-production dealing with a popular legend concerning the defence of Spain (read Catalan nationalist identity) against the French during the Peninsular War. The modern focus of the Catalan historical feature was no doubt attributable in part to a perceived need to promote and galvanise Catalan nationalist feeling by drawing on modern examples, especially during the difficult transition years as the provisional Catalan government wrestled with Madrid over the return to full political autonomy. But, as we shall see, in terms of historical periodisation and ideological focus, some of the cinema produced in the Basque country offers an illustrative and challenging contrast.

Despite these few signs of life, as well as the emergence of the occasional production company in the late 1970s prepared to support Catalan film production (such as Pepón Coromina's Figaró Films, which incidentally helped launch the careers of Bigas Luna and Almodóvar), filmmaking in Catalonia remained very problematic until the creation of the Departament de Cultura in 1980 and the transfer of powers to the Generalitat or regional government in 1981. Moreover, a few documentaries and one or two historical features hardly constituted a clear-cut, firmly based renaissance for Catalan language films.

And so it remained, with few features being produced in Catalan. Indeed, only if we count the output of a more commercial nature, made by Catalan-born directors, on Catalan territory, but in Castilian for a national audience, do we find any significant level of production taking place at all, in this pre-autonomy hiatus. This is the case with Francesc Bellmunt's outrageous depiction of youth culture and sexual experimentation during the transition years in *L'orgia* (1978). And in similar 'pasota' (i.e. drop-out, nonconformist) fashion, following the success of Bellmunt's anti-militarist *La quinta del porro* (1980), Catalan director Joan Minguell made the sequel *La batalla del porro* (1981). Also, within the comedy area, and in equally vulgar but more sarcastic fashion, Valencian filmmaker Carles Mira was developing a certain iconoclastic, revisionist historical cinema, not so much politically Catalanist in sensibility as southern Mediterranean and filtered through the gags and conventions of choral black comedy, as in *La portentosa vida del padre Vicent* (1978), *Con el culo al aire* (1980), *Jalea Real* (1981) and *¡Que nos quiten lo bailao!* (1983). And at the margins, though initially screened in cinerama and in Catalan, we find Eugeni Anglada's *La ràbia* (1977). Projected through the difficult rural upbringing of the child of an ex-Republican prisoner of war, Anglada presents a searing critique of how Catalan language, education and culture were repressed during early Francoism (Caparrós Lera 1992: 159). The film's bitter, vengeful tone and its implicit demand for a 'settling of accounts' reflected widespread political concerns and in certain aspects evoked a militant, radical nationalist consciousness.

Despite the above titles, it is clear that before 1981/82, not enough Catalan cinema was being made and certainly not enough of a certain type or style to signal the effective rebirth of a 'new Catalan cinema'. Leaving aside those film features with dialogue in Castilian for the commercial market, made by Catalans such as Grau and Minguell, there was simply not enough diversification of output of films in the regional vernacular. Perhaps more alarmingly, not enough people in the Catalan-speaking areas wished to spend money in order to see Catalan films. In short, given the power of American film products dubbed into Castilian at national level and the dominance of Castilian over Catalan in the same geographical/cultural territory, Catalan films were unable to attract audiences in sufficient numbers and were invariably uncompetitive. Also, with commercial distributors seeing films shot in Catalan as a potential marketing handicap (Fernández 1995: 345), it was perhaps unrealistic to expect significant numbers of private financiers to begin to move into the market, willing to invest in Catalan film production with little prospect of a real return.

New powers: new policies

In February 1981, Catalonia's regional government, the Generalitat, began the always conflictive process of assuming responsibilities and powers relevant to the cultural field, including those relating to the cinema. Not unexpectedly, the Ministry of Culture in Madrid refused to transfer two major areas of responsibility and funding: On the one hand, Madrid stalled on giving the Generalitat control over its share of monies from the Fondo Nacional de Protección al Cine (National Protection Fund), monies used for subsidising national film production. On the other, it refused to hand over control of the relevant Catalan holdings in the Madrid-based Filmoteca (National Film Archive). As regards the main issue, that of funding, the non-transfer of film subsidies was not totally unforeseen. Indeed, any clear-cut devolution of the fund to the relevant regional authorities (and these were still being created in the 1981 period) was probably impractical. Were it to happen, it would have effectively fragmented the funding mechanism for Spanish film-making as a whole, transforming Spanish cinema into a 'reino de taifas' (kingdom of outlaw gangs) as Monterde argues (1993: 118). For their part, the Catalan authorities saw Madrid's retention of central control over funding as a manouevre to prevent the fuller development of an autonomously funded protection policy for Catalan film. Of course, if it wished (and as Madrid made clear), the Generalitat could redirect towards the cinema sector a proportion of the funding contained in the general budget of the region's Consellería de Cultura. In April 1981, Miquel Porter Moix, cinema historian, was appointed Director General of the Servei de Cinema de la Generalitat, charged with managing and disbursing the film budget. However, when compared with the amount of money devoted to Catalan theatre or the visual arts or to the Department of Culture's own budget, Porter's fund was, on balance, derisory (Gubern, et al. 1994: 415).

From the start, after 1981, the Generalitat's official policy towards the public funding of Catalan cinema tended to eschew large production subsidies for feature films (as was the case at national level and for which Catalan filmmakers could also apply) in favour of other, less risky forms of public support including: a) the dubbing of films into Catalan (including those shot in Catalonia as well as those emanating from outside the region, i.e. Spanish and foreign films) in accordance with the policies of linguistic normalisation, including the broadcasting of dubbed films on Catalan television, (i.e. on TV3 (established 1983) and Canal 33 (established 1989)); b) the provision of grants for writing screenplays; c) the availability of small amounts of advance credits for certain production projects; d) the creation of film prizes; e) the promotion of newsreels; f) the development of co-financing deals with television companies for the production and eventual screening of Catalan film on the small screen and co-production arrangements; g) subsidies for making copies of films. (Gubern 1994: 415; García Fernández 1985: 301; Monterde 1993: 118–20).

Unfortunately, during the 1980s, such measures did not create a strong, stable, filmmaking base in Catalonia. Moreover, none of the main Catalan producers could afford to make 'Catalan-only' films (Hopewell 1986: 122–3). Most importantly, films made in Catalan for a Catalan audience had virtually no commercial potential beyond the region's linguistic frontiers, despite being dubbed into Castilian and made available for distribution further afield (Fernández 1995: 345). Indeed, between 1981 and 1985, the number of features produced in Catalonia plumeted from forty-one (in 1981) to thirteen (in 1985) (Gubern, et al. 1994: 415). And given that on one crucial occasion (1983), the Generalitat felt obliged to withhold its main annual film prize for the best full-length feature, it appears that the overall quality of Catalan output was variable, to say the least. With the industry approaching a crisis situation in 1985, and at the margins of official channels, film professionals themselves (as in the mid-1970s) banded together and supported the creation of a Colegi de Directors i Directoras de Cinema de Catalunya. The latter was responsible for sponsoring several important initiatives, including: support for new, young Catalan directors; the creation of a Sub-comisió de Valoració (Assessment Panel), to disburse Catalonia's share of the national film-funding budget and to assign production subsidies to the most deserving film projects; and in 1986, it supported the creation of the Oficina Catalana de Cinema, a rather short-lived agency charged with stimulating the development of Catalan cinema in Europe and promoting its products overseas. These developments coincided with the departure of Miquel Porter Moix and the appointment of Josep María Forn to head up the Servei de Cinema. Unlike Porter Moix, Forn had wide professional experience as a film producer and director. The combination of these developments, according to Gubern, allowed for a stabilisation of film output in Catalonia at approximately fifteen features per year up to the early 1990s, as a result of increased production subsidies and the crucial role of TV3 in injecting money into the business through the acquisition of television rights for Catalan films (Gubern, *et al.* 1994: 416).

Catalan film during the 1980s and 1990s

Celebrating *el poble catalá*: the historical feature
Apart from Luis José Comerón's unique 'ecological' musical *La revolta dels ocells/La rebelión de los pájaros* (1982), starring a very young Jorge Sanz, the early to mid-1980s were characterised by the continuing dominance of the historical fiction film, as in veteran Jordi Grau's nationalist, period piece *El timbaler del Bruc/La leyenda del tambor* (1981) and Francesc Betriu's adaptation of Mercè Rodoreda's acclaimed novel, *La plaça del diamant/La plaza del diamante* (1982). The latter was made for national television by Figaró Films in conjunction with TVE (under the 1979 agreement) but released for the big screen simultaneously. Running times varied, with a two-hour version made for the cinema compared to the four-hour package for television, screened in one-hour instalments. In the feature film, Betriu captured particularly well the evolution and frustrations of family life and class relations from the 1920s to the early 1950s in the Barcelona suburb of Gràcia. For Catalan audiences especially, the traumatic impact of the Civil War on the heroine Colometa (especially the loss of her husband) and her transformation into an alienated, introverted, shadowy creature, dispossessed

of family and personal identity, offered a poignant metaphor for the fate of Catalonia under the Franco regime. (Hopewell 1986: 123–4).

The mission to explain Catalonia's modern history arguably reached its peak with Antoni Ribas's *Victòria* (1983/84). In this huge, sprawling, three-part historical fresco, set in Barcelona in 1917 during three days in June, Ribas sought to evoke the conditions and issues surrounding the development of anarcho-syndicalism in Catalonia within the context of the class struggle. The piece was financed largely from private sources (though linked to a significant contribution from the Catalan Protection Fund), had a strong international cast (including Helmut Berger) and cost a massive (by Spanish standards) 450 million pesetas. Once again, it appeared that Ribas had succumbed to the dreaded 'imitation effect' and had attempted to do for Catalan filmmaking what Bertolucci had managed to achieve in his acclaimed *Novecento* (1976). Unfortunately, as in his previous attempt at the historical epic and at a colossal 417 minutes running time, Ribas was unable to create a well-constructed, smooth-flowing epic feature. Relying on overlong set pieces and over-simplisitic dialogue, he was arguably unable to impose sufficient control and editorial coherence on a mass of variegated filmed material. For Monterde, Ribas's epic stood as a 'monumento al despilfarro y la incompetencia' (a monument to waste and incompetence) (1993: 52). Caparrós Lera's view was that the film:

hace un triste servicio a Cataluña ... deja a la autonomía y al *cinema català* en un mal lugar, no sólo en el resto del país sino allende las fronteras (does a disservice to Catalonia ... puts the region and Catalan cinema in a difficult position, not only in the rest of country but also abroad) (1992: 251).

After the critical and commercial failure of *Victòria*, Ribas's career seemed to lack any clear or coherent direction and did not prosper. Subsequently, apart from working in television, he made two strikingly different features, the first *El primer torero porno* (1985), a dire sex comedy and curious throwback to the subgeneric cinema of 1970s. The second, *Dalí* (1990), coproduced with TV3 and the champagne company Freixenet, marked yet another return to the ambitious big-budget project and concerned various aspects of the life of the controversial Catalan artist. For example, the film efficiently recreated the *première* of Buñuel's *Un chien andalou* (1929), Dalí's visit to New York in 1940 and his break with his parents. In other ways, however, the film's level of historical accuracy was questionable (the controversial events surrounding Lorca's death) and perhaps Ribas's portrait of Gala could have been rather more searching. Whether as a maker of sex comedies or biopics, Ribas's fortunes remained problematic since both films were successive box-office flops. A further corollary of the financial aftershock of *Victòria* was that it led to a major rethink in the allocation of production credits offered by the Catalan Servei de Cinema and an end to supporting over-ambitious single projects.

With major names in Catalan cinema such as Ribas unable to repeat earlier sucesses and consolidate their careers, during the mid- to late 1980s the film industry in the region tended to shift its attention towards more tractable and commercially more marketable projects. The documentary and the historical feature thus tended to recede somewhat and the business was sustained mainly by commercial directors, working within two main areas: genre movies and literary adaptations. As a consequence, the more politicised and consciously nationalist cinema of the transition and the early 1980s began to give way to a politically more neutral, middle-of-the-road type of output.

Genre cinema

The thriller, *novela negra*, melodrama

As noted in Chapter 2, among certain types of genre cinema such as the thriller, the crime novel provided a prominent filmic source over the period: Manuel Vázquez Montalbán was adapted by Vicente Aranda in *Asesinato en el comité central* (1982) and by Manuel Estéban in *Els mars del sud/Los mares del sur* (1991). Unfortunately neither version did justice to Spain's leading crime novelist nor did they manage to capture on screen the rich texture of temperament and values embodied in the Carvalho character. Andreu Martín, another specialist in the crime genre, inspired Vicente Aranda's *Fanny 'Pelopaja'* (1984), an ironic tale of the conflictive relationship between a cop and his underworld lover. Raúl Nuñez's *Sinatra* (1988) was adapted for film and television by Francesc Betriu as was Ferrán Torrent's *Un negre amb un saxo/Un negro con un saxo* (1988) by Francesc Bellmunt, neither of which had significant commercial success.

Within the broad categories of the thriller and the melodrama, a number of features appeared, including: Carlos Balagué's *Adela* (1986) and *L'amor es estrany/El amor es extraño* (1988) as well as Bigas Luna's provocative *Angoixa/Angustia* (1987). Set in Los Angeles, with the dialogue in English (from an international cast), but shot entirely in Catalan studios, Bigas's dark and disturbing tale of oppressive, manipulative mothers and murderous sons (who specialise in gouging out eyes) deals in a macabre and playful manner with the issue of screen violence. The 'frame' story, we soon learn, is simply another film, a B movie screened in a Hollywood cinema, but which inspires another serial killer to embark on a spree of murder and mayhem. A similar level of self-conscious, ludic awareness regarding the fuzzy boundaries between film and reality can be found in Luis José Comerón's *Puzzle* (1986), a competent thriller, containing classic ingredients, whose complex narrative structure forms an integral part of the criminal 'puzzle' to be unravelled. Combining thriller elements but also (and unusually) radical, left-wing Catalan politics is Francesc Bellmunt's polemical and ambitious *El complot dels anells/El complot de los anillos* (1988). Set within the context of the 1992 Olympic games, and against a vaguely futuristic/science-fiction background, it deals with a terrorist threat to the games from an extreme nationalist group (strongly reminiscent of *Terra Lliure*) and seems to endorse their radical separatism as the way forward for Catalonia.

More recent thrillers, while exploiting Catalan settings, have tended to play down Catalan issues in favour of a more commercial, more widely acceptable, linguistically non-exclusivist product. These include the prize-winning (Premi Ciutat de Barcelona) *Un cos al bosc/Un cuerpo en el bosque* (1996), which marks the return to filmmaking of veteran Catalan *cinéaste* of the 1960s, Joaquín Jordá. Combining classic thriller conventions with light humour (and, in an apparent spirit of co-operation and non-separatism, offering dialogues in both Catalan and Castilian), Jordá's piece employs erstwhile 'chica Almodóvar', Rossy de Palma, as Lt. Cifuentes whose task it is to investigate the murder. At the stronger, more truculent end of the spectrum is Carlos Pérez Ferré's *Best-seller (El premio)* (1996), in which a husband is pressurised into killing his wife in order to settle a debt. Also, as noted elsewhere and in similar violent but also highly erotic territory, is Antonio Chavarrías's *Susana* (1996). Told in flashback, after she has been found murdered, the film follows the tragic, emotional life of a middle-class woman whose affair with Alex returns to haunt her when she appears to have found love and stability with Said, her Moroccan lover. Interestingly, the film coincides to some extent with Aranda's *La pasión turca* (1994) in its exploration (in emotional and sexual terms) of the cultural 'other' and the extent to which different cultural traditions are compatible. And as well as Jesús Garay's more conventional generic pieces *Mès allá de la passió/ Más allá de la pasión* (1987), *La banyera* (1990) and *Els de davant/Los de enfrente* (1994), we must include under this rubric Aranda's *Amantes* (1991). *Amantes* was arguably one of the most significant movies of the early 1990s, as much for its subject matter as its highly charged and explicit treatment of sexual desire and *amour fou*. As Marsha Kinder has correctly argued, the film is particularly important for the forceful way in which it exposes the threatening and subversive power of female sexuality in a repressive context, characterised by a brutal Francoist patriarchy (1993: 206–13). Also, what is intriguing, as noted elsewhere, is the fact that where the male protagonist Paco is slow, dull and inept, the mature female lead Luisa is portrayed as strong, passionate, determined and devouring.

Amantes, Vincente Aranda, 1991   22

Reflecting the above growing emphasis on 'empowered' female figures, in adjacent territory though in a contemporary setting, is Mar Targarona's *Muere, mi vida* (1996), a tale which shows how four women attempt to deal with male deception and betrayal by teaming up to murder the same lover. In a rather different vein and generic register, but still exploring how women cope with and overcome emotional damage and betrayal, is Isabel Coixet's memorable *Cosas que nunca te dije* (1996). Her second feature, winner of several awards, shot in English in the USA with American actors, Coixet's story of solitude and the need for affection is reminiscent of a long American independent film tradition, represented in particular by Robert Altman or Woody Allen. Beginning with a phonecall, the film sensitively explores the emotional responses of a young woman to being abandoned by her lover and how, through friendship and affection, she gradually adjusts to her new situation. Finally, in the area of the 'fantastic/science-fantasy/fiction' genre, Catalan filmmaking has not been well-known for its support for such projects, but it did make possible Oscar Aíbar's futuristic western hybrid *Atolladero* (1996), a promising first outing which is to be followed by another spoof hybrid *Yo también fui alienígena adolescente* (1997).

The literary connnection

As regards the field of the literary adaptation, we find a number of features over the period drawing upon both classic and modern Catalan texts including: Llorenç Villalonga's *Béarn o la sala de las muñecas* (Jaime Chávarri 1983), Narcís Oller's *La febre d'or/La fiebre del oro* (Gonzalo Herralde 1993), Víctor Catalá's *Solitut* (Romá Guardiet 1990) as well as Antoni Mus's *La senyora* (Jordi Cadena 1987), Mariá Vayreda's *La punyalada* (Jordi Grau 1989), Miquel Llor's *Laura a la ciutat dels sants/Laura en la ciudad de los santos* (Gonzalo Herralde 1987) and Jordi Cabré's *La teranyina/La telaraña* (Antoni Verdaguer 1990). Most prolific among (nominally) Catalan directors, however, has been Vicente Aranda who, apart from adapting Antonio Gala's *La pasión turca* (1994), has developed something of a specialism in making screen versions of novels by Juan Marsé. Of course, Aranda in not alone in adapting Marsé, given Gonzalo Herralde's version of *Últimas tardes con Teresa* (1986) and Betriu's *Un día volveré* (1994). But with *La muchacha de las bragas de oro* (1980), *Si te dicen que caí* (1989) and *El amante bilingüe* (1993), Aranda has the more sustained and developed track record. Perhaps his most accomplished version is that of *El amante bilingüe*, a tragi-comic tale of the sado-erotic relations between a high-society Catalan woman (Norma) and a *charnego* (non-Catalan Spaniard) from Murcia (Marés) who marry then split up. Cuckolded by his wife, horribly disfigured in an explosion (an anti-Catalan bombing incident), Marés develops an alternative identity or alter ego as Faneca and seeks to recapture the sexual favours of his wife. The film takes up topical issues of sexual desire, gender identity and regional/national differences. In particular, the movie explores the split personality of Marés/Faneca, the 'double' of classic pyscho-analysis, and how his own masculine identity is progressively stripped away through the clash with Catalan 'difference', the linguistic and cultural 'other'. Here, Norma embodies the threatening, castrating power of cultural difference. And in her own search for 'otherness', through the seduction of 'charnegos', she stands as a powerful symbol of an independent, even marauding female sexuality, determined to assert control over her lovers. As we have seen, in a less extreme fashion, this is also a theme developed by Aranda in *La pasión turca* (1994), though in this case, the assertion of female sexual passion has its price. Here, initially, Desideria's obsessive quest for sensual pleasure is a powerful affirmation of a self in revolt against traditional notions of marriage, children and family, which have failed her. However, her fateful obsession with her bisexual Turkish lover Yaman will lead to degradation and humiliation. Desi becomes a slave to the senses, a being destined solely for the bedroom, until the dramatic scene in the restaurant, in which she recovers some semblance of self-esteem and shoots her lover. Here, she reasserts a rather different self, based on shame, exploitation and self-respect, a finale which arguably makes better sense in Aranda's 'open ending' to the film, rather than in Gala's literary ending, in which Desi finds the solution to shame and humiliation in suicide – an alternative ending which Aranda also shot.

Comedia catalana

Reflecting developments and production preferences at national level, Catalan film has devoted most of its energy and resources to the exploitation and heavy recycling of the film comedy and its subsidiary forms. And for a number of years, it has been developing its own home-grown *comedia catalana*. This has taken various forms, principally the exploitation of the 'esperpento'/black comedy style seen in the work of two of Catalonia's major directors in this area, Francesc Bellmunt and Ventura Pons.

After a degree of success at the end of 1970s with his anti-establishment 'hippy/pasota' comedies, as noted above, Bellmunt continued to exploit this particular vein, especially in such features as *Pà d'Angel/Pan de Angel* (1983), *Un parell d'ous/Un par de huevos* (1984), *La ràdio folla/La radio folla/Radio Speed* (1986) and *Rateta rateta/Ratita ratita* (1990), this latter, a curious, contemporary version of a traditional Catalan 'popular' story, incorporating both human and animal characters, in which a woman wins a large amount of money on the lottery. More recently, Bellmunt has directed *Escenas de una orgía en Formentera* (1995), a feature with a limited release, which clearly recycles the idea of 'orgy' from his 1978 feature of the same name. *L'orgia* (1978) arguably stands as the paradigm film of Bellmunt's output: a manic, sarcastic celebration of sexual and political freedoms, projected through the vehicle of hippy students, determined to have fun. By contrast, in the more sober, politically correct 1990s, *Escenas* bears little relation to the earlier film. It exploits a very different story line (a professional couple who love each other but cannot communicate) and appears to contain none of the *joie de vivre*, the reckless but joyous sense of fun and frivolity epitomised by the student drop-outs of the transition years.

Occupying similar territory, targeting the regional audience and enjoying a degree of success in the late 1980s after capitalising on the vulgar toilet humour of *Puta miseria* (1988), Ventura Pons has tended to specialise in the youth comedy subgenre with such titles as *¿Qué t'hi jugues Mari Pili?/¿Qué te juegas Mari Pili?* (1990), *Aquesta nit o mai/Esta noche o jamás* (1991) and *Rosita Please* (1993). However, such examples of the typically salacious, down-market Catalan comedy have had little or no resonance outside of the region. With *El perquè de tot plegat/El porqué de todas las cosas* (1994), however, this situation changed radically. Pons appeared to have discovered a new seam and direction within the youth comedy subtype and a new set of concerns, of interest to most young filmgoers, all of which have attracted major critical and commercial recognition. Unlike previous efforts, *El perquè ...* has impeccable credentials, being based on the sketches of Catalan literary megastar Quim Monzó, whose name/logo is a virtual guarantee of artistic quality and credibility as well as commercial success. Monzó's fifteen vignettes are taken from two of his collections and revolve around the eternal questions which form part of *la condition humaine*, though protagonised by Spain's younger generations. They thus include stories of love, jealousy, desire, passion, and pain, sharply observed from an ironic, demystificatory, deflationary perspective. In the filmic adaptation, Pons has given each story a name, as in the original, but has varied the point of view and treatment, freely exploiting first- and third-person narration (voices off), as well as the means of delivery, such as the monologue, dialogue or the use of the telephone. Inevitably uneven, given the large number of short and heterogenous sketches, Pons has nonetheless created a fascinating mosaic of the emotional issues which trouble contemporary Spaniards, underpinned by a healthy sarcasm and self-awareness.

Redefining the *comedia catalana*

Pons has consolidated the shift in direction of his output and the success arising from *El perquè ...* by making *Actrices* (1996), based on the stage play by Josep María Benet i Jornet and capitalising on his own long association with the Catalan theatre. The film concerns three jobbing actresses, one (Anna Lizaran) employed by a dubbing studio, another (Rosa María Sardá) working as a television presenter and a third (Núria Espert) living the life of the theatrical diva. Enter a research student (Mercè Pons), who is studying the career of the mythical actress Ribera, who taught all three of the working actresses and from whom the student receives three very different versions of the mega-diva's colourful life. A celebration of the theatrical profession as well as a homage to the American 'women's' film of the 1940s, particularly Cukor, Pons allows his actresses to re-evaluate the great Ribera as well as reflect on their own careers, on what they have sacrificed in order to work and on what they might have achieved had conditions been different. All in all, and again in large measure because of the quality of his source material, Pons presents a cleverly-scripted, elegant and highly engaging female comedy which transcends the more parochial, scatological forms of the Catalan Comedy and appeals to a wide, commercial audience.

Still within the area of the *comedia catalana* but, like Pons, attempting to move beyond its thematic and stylistic boundaries, we find Rosa Vergès's timely *Boom Boom* (1990), whose title refers to the 'heartbeat' of the film's closing song. Very different to the kind of smutty, sensationalist subproducts of the early Bellmunt or Pons, Vergès's story of love and frustration between Doctora Dalmau and the Argentine dentist is a cleverly contrived, though intelligent and absorbing tale, set against a background of certain thriller elements. According to Marsha Kinder, the film attempted to 'woo international audiences by presenting Barcelona in the way Almodóvar has presented Madrid' (1993: 422). Unfortunately, Vergès's rather derivative, formula-driven, screwball comedy was unable to deliver anticipated success, partly because of the 'over-rootedness' of its female leads in Catalan culture, but more importantly because of the unfortunate timing of its release (high summer, in competition with the World Cup) (Kinder 1993: 427). Vergès had better luck with *Souvenir* (1994), another comedy, this time enjoying a more appropriate Christmas release. Like Medem's *La ardilla roja* (1993) and Felipe Vega's *El techo del mundo* (1995), Vergès's tale relied on the device of amnesia to bring together but also to compare and contrast the cultural identities of a hapless Japanese tourist and a kind-hearted Catalan air hostess. Apart from the rather obvious clichés of cultural differences (West/East, Catalan/Japanese) being overcome by love and mutual understanding, we see the city of Barcelona again presented as a more cosmopolitan, polyglot arena than before, where problems of language and communication are more tractable and can be solved with mutual respect and sensitivity.

Within the comedy remit, but with a more pronounced parodic, sarcastic, historical focus, we must include here Valencian Carles Mira's *Daniya, el jardí de l'harém* (1988), best film of the Generalitat for 1988, and also Carlos Pérez Ferré's *Tramontana* (1991), a vicious skit on the Reconquest. In a rather different vein, we find a collective piece, developed by a trio of Catalan actors, El Tricicle, who have teamed up as directors in their very first picture entitled *Palace* (1995). In the manner of Chaplin and Keaton, this is a silent movie, slapstick comedy, dealing with the restoration of an old hotel and the fraught relations between the new owners and the ever-interfering moneylenders. In its shooting style and acting, the piece clearly reveals its roots in and indebtedness to a theatrical tradition and previous incarnation on the small screen. Also, returning to the comedy scene in the 1990s was Jordi Grau, with his *Mangas Verdes* (1994), a big-budget vehicle for Carmen Maura in another 'woman on the verge' situation. Interestingly, Grau's more recent *Tiempos mejores* (1995) is reminiscent of Aranda's *El amante bilingüe* and echoes Vergés's plea for dialogue and cross-cultural sensitivity but on a micro rather than macro regional scale. The film deals with the relationship (and cultural clashes) between an ageing *charnego* bullfighter (i.e. an Andalusian resident in Catalonia) a Catalan prostitute/exotic dancer and young female black dancer, a competitive, triangular relationship in which mutual respect and affection seem to triumph over cultural barriers. Continuing the theme of the eternal triangle, Antoni Verdaguer's *Parell de tres/Pareja de tres* (1995) has two mature female protagonists settle their differences and in order to achieve their romantic and emotional objectives, they team up with the same man, in a supportive *ménage à trois*. The comic possibilities of cultural difference also lie at the heart of Felipe Vega's *El techo del mundo* (1995), in which amnesia turns a liberal, left-wing Spanish migrant in Switzerland into a raging xenophobe.

Questions of cultural identity and the play of similarity and difference are also fundamental to Bigas Luna's recent feature *La teta y la luna* (1994), final part of his Iberian trilogy, which includes *Jamón Jamón* (1992) and *Huevos de oro* (1993). Clearly indebted to Fellini and with dialogues in Catalan, French and English, the film appears to propose a much less-exclusivist, more 'Euro-friendly' attitude towards national identity. Indeed, the film takes for granted the notion that a *charnego* (Miquel) who sings flamenco is just as Catalan as the young protagonist Tete. Like the other two features in the series, *La teta y la luna* revisits the world of national stereotypes, this time with respect to Catalonia, where *castells* (human towers), *pà tomacet*, classical architecture and local heritage groups – Tete's father works as a late night petrol pump attendant but asserts his cultural roots by dressing up as a Roman legionary – are sentimentally recycled and reaffirmed. There is also a strong connection made between the reverence for Catalan cultural roots and masculine identity. But if the film is a 'rites of passage' tale in which the young Tete apparently reaches manhood (he finally climbs the castle and shows he has balls), it is also a celebration of the 'pre-oedipal', of Tete's breast and anal fixation, his confusion of his (fantasy) lover Estrellita (who is happy with the impotent *pétomane* Maurice) with his own mother and his inability to separate himself from the maternal breast and thus completely grow up. The film is an affectionate, child-centred evocation of oedipal and sibling rivalries (exiled by his baby brother, Tete vies with Maurice and Miquel for Estrellita's attentions) and of national and sexual obsessions (while Tete believes she needs a sexual athlete, Estrellita melts at the sound of Miquel's plaintive song and lovingly accepts Maurice's bread stick in place of an erect penis). In the end, the film seems to suggest that boys do not grow up at all but tend to remain obsessed with and fixated upon the maternal bosom.

Bigas Luna followed *La teta y la luna* with his eleventh feature, the first of a new trilogy on women and the sort of obsessions and desires they supposedly engender. Entitled *Bambola* (1996) – after the song by Patty Bravo – (to be followed by *Marie, la camarera del Titanic* – dedicated to the French *femme fatale* and *Carmen* – symbol of Spanish womanhood), this initial foray is devoted to the Italian female, embodied in the owner of a *trattoria-pizzeria* (played by Valeria Marini). As in previous outings, Bigas Luna explores the libidinal excesses of his national stereotypes, their passions and uncontrollable, irrational urges for sex, food and emotional security. All this is projected through the character of Bambola, an apparent victim of the very violent male sexual urges she is incapable of restraining. The film very obviously raises the issue, though indi-

23

La teta y la luna, José Juan Bigas Luna, 1994

rectly, of the extent to which sexual desire, like gender, is socially constructed and responsive to the dominant assumptions which commonly define and differentiate notions of masculinity and femininity.

Passion not persuasion: the reprise of the historical feature

Curiously, in the 1990s, there appears to have been a significant revival of interest in the Catalan historical feature. Of course, the period picture is no longer being used as a vehicle to promote a radical, left-wing, Catalan nationalism as in the late 1970s and early 1980s. Rather, and perhaps inevitably, we find a much stronger emphasis on the commercial and 'entertainment' value of the product. Unfortunately, this has led in some cases to treatments of major historical events, especially events in the twentieth century and the Civil War, which have sacrificed complexity and nuance for passion and production values. On a more positive note, Catalan historical features are no longer fixated on the modern period and now range much more widely, taking into account, for example, the medieval period as in Manolo Matji's medieval 'rites of passage' tale *Mar de luna* (1995), Antoni Verdaguer's *California* (1996) and Lluís María Güell's television super-production *El comte Arnau* (1995), costing 725 million pesetas and dealing with the eleventh century Catalan count and the historical origins of Catalonia. Corresponding to the early modern period, we also find Gerardo Gormezano's *Sombras paralelas* (1994), set in the seventeenth century and Santiago Lapeira's *1714* (1995), concerned with the siege of Barcelona.

Of more recent historical interest is Carlos Benpar's *Capitán Escalaborns* (1990), classic adventure tale of pirates, smugglers and buried treasure, set in the early eighteenth century and very much a generic product, inspired by the Hollywood 'swashbucklers' of the 1940s. Far more instructive and appealing is Francesc Bellmunt's attractive, precise and emotionally-charged homage to the obsessive inventor of the submarine and icon of Catalan scientific idealism, *Monturiol, el señor del mar* (1993). Much less celebratory is Antoni Verdaguer's ambitious, big-budget (500 million pesetas), international copro *Havanera* (1993), at bottom, another genre movie mixing period features and aspects of the high-seas adventure/melodrama, though also incorporating elements of political critique. Set in the 1820s, and wrapped within a narrative framework involving hatred, betrayal, revenge and political intrigue, the film explores the relations and business dealings between slave traders and shipping magnates. Unusually, in taking up a type of film topic normally produced only by Americans, Verdaguer has bravely and tellingly relocated the origins of slavery to Europe and the Third World. And though working very much within the adventure format, he nonetheless presents a highly critical, indeed damning image of a Catalan mercantile class, obsessed by profit and individualist ambitions and ego, highlighted by the many scenes involving explicit and exploitative eroticism. In similar territory, but adopting a very different outlook is Gonzalo Herralde's television/film adaptation of Narcís Oller's classic novel *La febre d'or/La fiebre del oro* (1993), tale of the rise and fall of the Catalan banker Gil Foix at the end of the nineteenth century. Lasting 160 minutes in its film version, the piece effectively captures the lavish period detail as well as the greed and ambition underlying the Foix dynasty. Interestingly, in contrast to Verdaguer's critical vision of the Catalan bourgeoisie, Herralde presents his model banking family as a positive example of a self-confident class, fired by great idealism and a strong faith in progress and modern ideas.

As regards the twentieth century, in *La moños* (1995), and through the eyes of two nine-year-old children, newcomer Mireia Ros recreates the life of Barcelona's imaginary, colourful and popular female street character of the same name at the turn of the century. In chronological proximity, we also find Antoni Verdaguer's *La teranyina/La telaraña* (1990), prize-winning, super-production (600 million pesetas) concerned with Catalonia's 'Setmana trágica'

(Tragic week). Based on the novel by Jaume Cabré, set in 1909, on the eve of the general strike, the film reconstructs the conflictive relations between the bourgeoise and the working classes in textile town Terrassa. Overdependent on its source text (which shows in the rather 'literary' nature of the dialogue), the film presents a rather sentimental, manichaean view of the class struggle, contrasting the corrupt bourgeoisie (bad) with the poor, noble working classes (good). A similar tendency towards simplification is visible in Jaime Camino's *El llarg hivern* (1991), dealing with the winter of 1939 and the fall of Barcelona. Again, we have another ambitious historical reconstruction and a convincingly accurate evocation of the end of the Civil War. Unfortunately, the contending sides are represented in rather too schematic a fashion, with the Republicans invariably shown as heroic and noble and the Nationalists irretrievably fanatical and cruel. Finally, and apart from Paco Betriu's admirable recent portrait of the Communist Duchess of Medina Sidonia in *La duquesa roja* (1995), responsible for foiling land speculators, we must include Aranda's highly successful, though controversial, *Libertarias* (1996).

Very much in the tradition of Malraux's *Sierra de Teruel* (1939) and Loach's more recent *Land and Freedom* (1995), *Libertarias* is set in the period July–October 1936, around the Aragon front, in the early months of the Spanish Civil War. The film deals with a heterogeneous group of women (including nuns and ex-prostitutes) who decide to join the anarchist-inspired 'Mujeres Libres' (Free Women), in order to take a direct, active, fighting role in the war. In doing so, and at a time in which revolutionary social change seems to be on the agenda, they rebel against social convention and prejudice and actively seek to discharge their own moral and political responsibilities. Aranda's film traces their political idealism and their temerity in seeking direct involvement in the struggle; he also graphically portrays their 'heroic' slaughter at the hands of Moorish troops, who cut their throats. By no means an action film, more a film concerned with issues, *Libertarias* is an attractive mix of spectacle laced with a strong dose of historical and political debate. And here, Aranda explores the revolutionary dream that vanishes, a period of unparalleled desire for political change which collapses into disillusionment and defeat. However, his incursion into the Civil War via the story of his female fighters begs certain questions. With its insistence on strong characters, rapid-fire dialogue and above all its desire to celebrate the iron resolve and commitment of his female protagonists to their cause, *Libertarias* seeks the spectator's complete emotional identification with the passionate idealism of the female struggle (which comes up against various forms of 'male authority'). Thus, more difficult questions to do with gender roles and the differences between men and women in wartime tend to be elided. There is also the difficulty that Aranda's celebration of his women's indomitable spirit, his defense of their utopianism and blind commitment, become an emotional glorification of the losing side in the Civil War, a clichéd, sentimental expression of solidarity with a noble, heroic defeat. As noted above, such schematic approaches arguably obscure rather than seriously elucidate the female contribution to the Republican cause and, more widely, their role in the Civil War as a whole. At the same time, in reopening issues arising from the Civil War, *Libertarias* has no doubt contributed positively to a fresh filmic re-examination of the war, which will lead to other such films being made.

Independents, new directors, new directions

In terms of Catalan filmmaking by independent directors not overly driven by political or nationalist concerns or by commercial pressures, and by younger people anxious to enter the business, several trends have emerged in the late 1980s and 1990s.

Pere Portabella, pioneer of independent Catalan cinema, stalwart of the legendary Escuela de Barcelona of the 1960s and 1970s and absent from filmmaking in the 1980s because of political duties in Gerona, returned to filmmaking in 1989 with *Pont de Varsòvia/ Puente de Varsovia*. Reminiscent of Godard and reflecting the style and content of the vanguard films of the old Escuela, this dense, complex, unfriendly feature confirmed that Portabella's film style had not evolved significantly since the 1970s (Torres 1994: 384).

As regards the literary connection, after his commercial feature *La senyora* (1987), Jordi Cadena produced an unusual, experimental, homage in black and white to the poet J. V. Foix, *Es quan dormo que hi veig clar/Lo veo más claro cuando me duermo* (1988), screened at the 1988 Barcelona International Film Festival, but followed by a very limited release in *Arte y Ensayo*. Manuel Cussó Ferrer's *Entracte* (1988) also offered a detailed, absorbing study of the visual poetry of Joan Brossa, though it played only a few days in the cinema (Caparrós Lera 1992: 342). It was followed by his *L'ultima estació/La última estación* (1992). After his uniquely harrowing *Tras el cristal* (1986), which explored the eroticisation and strangely purifying nature of physical violence and has now become a cult movie (Kinder 1993: 183–96), young Mallorquín Agustí Villaronga went on to produce a reasonably successful second feature *El niño de la luna* (1989) and later a thriller, *El pasajero clandestino* (1995): a big-budget feature, set in Tahiti, with international stars including Simon Callow. His gradual shift towards mainstream commercial cinema is perhaps indicative of the pressures filmmakers have been under to show a financial return on their work. Among younger directors working within a commercial framework but trying to extend established genres, we find the well-received 'lesbian comedy' from Marta Balletbó-Coll, whose *Costa Brava (Family Album)* (1995) recounts (in English) the love story between an aspiring actress and an English teacher working in Barcelona. Dealing with urban alienation and the difficulties of artistic creation, plus at the same time containing a critique of the Generalitat 's cultural policy, are Juan Carlos Bonete's first two features: *Nunca estás en casa* (1991) and *Un único deseo* (1993). Also worthy of note is the 'ópera prima' of Lluis Zayas *Bufones y reyes* (1994), a self-referential, film within a film, dealing with the interminable problems and crises during script rehearsals for a new film.

Among the younger school of Catalan directors who have been making a major impact at national and international film festivals (San Sebastian, Valladolid, Barcelona, Sitges, Berlin, Venice, etc.) we must include: Pablo Llorca, whose *Jardines colgantes* (1994) and *La espalda de Dios* (1995) have gained significant critical plaudits. Indeed, *Jardines colgantes* is a remarkable film, a mix of fairy-tale/gothic fantasy and nightmare, involving voyeurism, sadism and sexual perversion, which follows the fortunes of a tailor who makes a suit for a landlord and is attracted to his young, female assistant (Icíar Bollaín). Also attracting critical acclaim has been Teresa de Pelegrí's *Roig* (1994) and the more abstract, rather soporific visual style of Marc Recha's *El cielo sube* (1992) as well as his more recent *Es tard/Es tarde* (1994).

Finally, we have in Alejandro Amenábar's *Tesis* (1996) what appears to be the first anti-snuff movie to be made not only in Catalonia but in the whole of Spain. Winner of seven out of the eight Goyas for which it competed in the 1996 classifications, including those for best film, best new director and best script, *Tesis* has become one of the major successes of the decade. It also joins a series of recent features by young directors such as de la Iglesia and Bajo Ulloa which have explored, in part or in whole, the complex relations between screen violence and the spectator. The film concerns a graduate student (Ana Torrent) whose doctoral thesis deals with the effects of visual violence, particularly in the rarefied, degenerate genre of the snuff movie (comprising images of autopsies and real killings, accidental as well as staged). Her supervisor is suddenly found dead after viewing such material himself. With a replacement mentor in the background, the film explores the young woman's relationship to her unsavoury thesis subject and to the act of murder on and off screen, in a bizarre twilight world in which she is kidnapped and threatened with the same fate as befell those in the movies she has witnessed.

Amenábar's excursion into the marginal, specialist world of the snuff movie was a major challenge given that it could have easily been an excuse to make an exploitative subproduct, concerned solely with titillating the spectator and avoiding any serious engagement with the conventional wisdoms and film clichés associated with male screen violence. In fact, Amenábar has managed to resist the lure of the exploitation movie and the sickening sensationalism that goes with it for a thoughtful though harrowing journey into a virtually unknown filmic world. Though making a distinction between soft and hard versions of the snuff subgenre (and acknowledging the criminality obviously associated with the hard material under consideration), the thesis of Amenábar's film is that, besides its illegal and criminal nature, such material is fundamentally sick and degenerate, though no less fascinating. Those involved in its production and those who, by association, defend its legitimacy as a product serving a social need in a commercial market, are exposed as just as degenerate and subhuman. Interestingly, while acknowledging the issue of the spectator's fascinated gaze, the film draws back from analysing more deeply the reasons why viewers may be captured by screen violence, the nature of the fascinations and fantasies of power and control implicit in viewing acts of violent dismemberment and ultimately the troubling addictiveness such repulsive acts might induce in the unwary and unguarded.

Conclusion

During the transition period and well into the 1980s, Catalan cinema was caught up in the struggle over political autonomy, linguistic and cultural normalisation and the recuperation of a nationalist identity. Whether it was effective in helping to promote those struggles and to reaffirm Catalonia's political and cultural uniqueness remains a matter of debate. What is clear is that while the Generalitat and the Servei de Cinema used large amounts of the regional film budget to support the dubbing of foreign television and film productions (in line with the programme of linguistic normalisation), this and other policies diverted valuable resources from supporting indigneous filmmaking. As a result of such political imperatives, the authorities failed to re-establish a healthy, sustainable Catalan film industry in the 1980s (Kinder 1993: 396).

The difficulties faced by the Catalan cinema have been further compounded by the fact that since the early 1980s, films shot in Catalan have made a relatively small impact on the six million Catalan speakers of the *paisos catalans* and even less impact beyond the region. The fact is that very few films made in Catalan manage to cover costs through ticket sales. And even when we take into account television transmission rights as well as potential international sales, income is rarely sufficient to amortise costs. Moreover, significant numbers of completed films are simply left to gather dust on distributors shelves. In short, most films shot in Catalan are uneconomic. This may go some way to explaining the 'fuga de talentos' (loss of talent) mentioned by Gubern (1994: 417) and exemplified by filmmakers of the stature of Aranda and Bigas Luna who work in Madrid, the USA and beyond, as well as in Barcelona, though less frequently.

Catalan cinema is arguably a microcosm of how Catalan culture as a whole has had to come to terms with the realities, i.e the limitations, of its geographical and political territory and its status as a minority language and culture. There is no escaping the fact that the territory covered by the *paisos catalans* is occupied by two cultural markets, with the Spanish/Castilian one in a position of some dominance. As the communications revolution continues to grow and the two national and three private Spanish television channels, as well as satellite and cable services, compete for viewers' attention, not to mention a growing market in international audio-visual services, the space left for Catalan language and cultural activities, film and television services (including TV3 and Canal 33, which broadcast in Catalan) is bound to be squeezed. These are the inevitable consequences of globalisation, which appear not to bode well for the Catalan film industry. Indeed, in a more competitive, globalised economic environment, Catalan filmmaking may only be truly viable if it can attract a much wider, international audience and respond to a much broader set of cultural and linguistic concerns. As a result of such cultural hybridisation, this may inevitably lead to a de-emphasising of those signs of a particular Catalan identity and thus a blurring of cultural differences. (Kinder 1993: 399–400).

On the other hand, the situation may create new opportunities for filmmakers in which local/regional identities can be reimagined, not in a narrow sense, but in a more internationalist, inclusive, Euro-friendly manner. In fact, this is already happening, as illustrated by Bigas Luna's *La teta y la luna* (1994), a Spanish-French copro, which parades a wide-angled, inclusive form of nationalism, using three languages (Spanish, French and Catalan) and takes for granted that a 'charnego' (Miquel, son of immigrants) who sings flamenco is just as Catalan as the young Tete.

Finally, there are signs that the regional government is responding positively to the issues raised above. At the beginning of 1997, in order to stimulate the Catalan film industry and attract more filmmaking to the region, the Generalitat decided to modify its definition of 'Catalan film'. Belatedly falling into line with what the Basque regional government had been doing for the last fifteen years (and extending a policy reluctantly adopted in 1990), the Generalitat now appears to regard as Catalan productions all those films made in Catalonia, irrespective of the language in which they are shot. In other words, if film producers wish to qualify for public subsidies, the authorities have finally dropped the requirement of linguistic exclusivity. Also significant (and comprising additional incentives to shoot films in Catalonia) is a series of measures, announced by TV3, which will inject more funding into the filmmaking process in Catalonia through a programme of pre-production purchases of films and higher fees for transmission rights. It remains to be seen whether such initiatives will help to regenerate the film industry in Catalonia, but the signs are certainly more hopeful then they were (*Fotogramas* 1840, February 1997, 129).

Basque cinema

As already noted in the last chapter, Catalan cinema was able to rely on a significant historical tradition in filmmaking and a linguistic identity based on a common vernacular language understood, if not spoken, by most of the six million inhabitants (incuding the immigrant population) of the *paisos catalans*. However, a post-Franco Basque cinema would enjoy neither of these apparent advantages. Indeed, in the Basque Country, there was much less of a tangible cinematic tradition on which to draw, virtually no industrial infrastructure for film production and most importantly, out of a population of less than 2.5 million, only one in five people even claimed to speak the national vernacular *euskera* or Basque (Zunzunegui 1989: 68). Moreover, until recently and unlike Catalan, the Basque language was regarded as low status, linked with rural backwardness and traditionalism, and seen as relatively inaccessible, especially to a large non-Basque immigrant population, most of whom were unwilling to learn a difficult, non-romance language (Mar-Molinero 1997: 35–40).

Yet, unlike Catalan cinema, which has difficulty in travelling beyond its natural frontiers (even in dubbed versions), recent examples of Basque cinema have gained significant national and international exposure. Arthouse and minority television audiences in France, Germany and the UK, as well as in Latin America, have had opportunities to see the work of young Basque directors such as Juanma Bajo Ulloa, (*Alas de mariposa*, 1991, *La madre muerta*, 1993, and *Airbag*, 1997), Julio Medem (*Vacas*, 1992, *La ardilla roja*, 1993 and *Tierra*, 1995) and Alex de la Iglesia (*Acción mutante*, 1992, *El día de la bestia*, 1995 and *Perdita Durango*, 1997). Interested spectators will have seen these movies promoted as examples of a burgeoning trend in Basque cinema, but this may be somewhat misleading. While Basque in origin, most Basque directors tend to live and work outside the region. Moreover, even if they have been asked to produce versions in *euskera* (in order to secure regional film funding), their films nearly all tend to be shot, distributed and exhibited in Castilian. But as Lasagabaster indicates, this has not stopped filmgoers and critics using the term Basque cinema, though it might be more accurate to describe these products simply as films made by Basque directors (Lasagabaster 1995: 353). The notion of 'Basque cinema' has become a broadly accepted category, even though (for obvious reasons of commercial viability), the vast majority of films do not exploit the Basque language, *euskera*. In other words, the concept of Basque cinema does not rely fundamentally on a linguistic imperative for its identity and standing.

Thus, representations of national identity and culture in the Basque cinema have tended to be constructed not so much around a defence of the indigenous language as according to elements drawn from fields such as folklore, regional customs, popular culture, history and politics. Paradoxically, compared to its Catalan counterpart, far from being a handicap, a Basque cinema spoken in Castilian has proved to be highly advantageous in creating a wider awareness of Basque film culture, the Basque region and the variability of cultural identities within Spain as a whole.

Reconstructing a regional film culture

Under Franco, only a very small amount of film activity relating to the Basque Country took place. Comprising mainly shorts and newsreels, and one main documentary feature (*Ama Lur* 1968, by Fernando Larruquert and Néstor Basterretxea), filmic images of Basque life and culture tended to emphasise a very traditional, folkloric, *costumbrista*, touristy identity. An essential, unchanging Basque spirit was to be found in its traditional sporting activities (rowing, wood cutting, *frontón*), popular song, its religiosity and its impressive rural scenery. After Franco's death, and as in the case of Catalonia, Basque intellectuals and film professionals moved quickly to rebuild the sector. By means of conferences, new mediating organisations and rapidly prepared political agendas, they sought to recapture and reconstruct a regional film culture and connect this with wider cultural and political concerns. At the first of many conferences (Las Primeras Jornadas de Cine Vasco, held in February 1976), debates inevitably turned on the definition of Basque cinema and a corresponding film aesthetics appropriate to such a project (Zunzunegui 1985: 385–6). In these early, highly charged sessions, Basque cinema was defined as one made by and for Basques, made in *euskera*, which dealt with Basque issues and demonstrated 'una estética vasca' (a Basque aesthetic), still to be developed. Moreover, reflecting the conflictive political atmosphere of the early reform period (1976–80), the above definition included the demand that Basque cinema should be not only radical and independent but untainted by commercial considerations or capitalist exploitation (Zunzunegui 1985: 386). The naivety of some of these early maximalist positions gradually gave way to a more realistic appraisal of what it would take to develop a sustainable Basque cinema. The latter would clearly require government support, which would only become available after the transfer of powers in 1980. Between 1976 and 1980, then, during a period in which politically radical voices in the Basque cinema arena were obliged to accept some measure of capitalist involvement in film production, a developing Basque cinema took several forms.

As in the Catalan case, radical Basque nationalism found an outlet in a series of newsreels or *ikuska* (1977–85), shot by many established Basque directors (Olea, Uribe, Eceiza, Armendáriz). According to Monterde, however, these early efforts were 'aquejados de un cierto anacronismo en su visión anclada en un Euskadi rural y tradicionalista' (marred by a certain anachronistic vision anchored in a rural, traditionalist Euskadi) (1993: 95). The creation of an Association of Basque Directors helped promote a modest level of output of shorts and bring forward fresh, younger talents. We also find a small number of very different features, of variable quality and interest, little noticed in the region itself and virtually ignored in the rest of Spain, such as Fernando Larruquert's documentary panegyric to popular music *Euskal Herri Musika* (1978) and Pedro de la Sota's hagiography of the founder of Basque nationalism *Sabino Arana* (1980). Understandably, perhaps, at the height of nationalist radicalism during the reform period, some filmmakers tended to emphasise the folkoric, traditional, idyllically rural version of Basque life, disconnected from the outside world, a view which was largely out of step with political and social change in the region. Also, more widely, a politically radical Basque nationalism appeared to be somewhat in thrall to an essentialist vision of Basque culture and identity, predicated on just such a version of the Basque Country as an unchanging rural arcadia.

Film representations thus appeared somewhat detached from and failed to account for the real changes to Basque life wrought by modernisation, urbanisation and capitalist development. However, before 1980, one film did bring current Basque issues and Basque filmmaking to national prominence, because of its highly polemical subject matter and treatment: *El proceso de Burgos* (1979). Directed by Imanol Uribe (born, incidentally, in El Salvador, though immigrant to the Basque Country in early childhood), shot in Castilian and with no public subsidy, this pioneering documentary was the first of a trilogy of films by Uribe on ETA, dealing specifically with the trial of sixteen ETA suspects held in Burgos jail in 1970. Criticised in the rest of Spain for its biased, uncritical and unapologetically pro-ETA outlook (Caparrós Lera 1992: 185), but defiantly intercutting samples of traditional Basque song and clips of rural scenery into its record of the trial, this account offered a view totally in keeping with a radical Basque nationalism anxious to reassert its political credibility. Despite suffering official interference and a restricted circulation, Uribe's film captured national attention and gave rise to a number of other features which confidently focused on political issues and relations between the Basque Country and the central state.

Transfer of powers: developing a macro-regional film policy
The relevant powers over film production and promotion were transferred to the Autonomous Basque Government in September 1980 and delegated to the Consejería de Cultura. Even before the

drafting and formal approval of a regional film policy, the autonomous government demonstrated its political commitment to promoting an indigenous film industry as a crucial instrument in the process of nation building by quickly subsidising two major features: Uribe's second ETA film *La fuga de Segovia* (1981) and the comedy *Siete calles* (1981) by Javier Rebollo and Juanma Ortuosti. In particular, Uribe's second feature on ETA attracted a generous, one-off subsidy of 10 million pesetas from the Basque government, allowing him to complete the fictionalised dramatisation of the escape of thirty *etarras* from Segovia prison. The film was based on a first-hand book account (*Operación Poncho*), written by *etarra* and ex-prisoner Ángel Amigo, close collaborator of Uribe, who would quickly become a major figure in scriptwriting and film production in the Basque Country through the production company *Igeldo Zine Produkzioak*. Located within the thriller remit and adopting the coventional format of the prison escape story, *La fuga de Segovia* easily managed to evoke the spectator's sympathies for the escapees (none of whom, in the end, evaded recapture), although the film's well-crafted drama documentary style was undercut somewhat by Uribe's undisguised support for ETA's politico-military activities.

As Monterde argues (1993: 122), the politically motivated decision taken by the Basque Administration to finance Uribe's second project was surprisingly farsighted, even prescient. It was a move which demonstrated that a viable Basque cinema, as a matter of public and commercial policy, could not be realistically based on the use of *euskera* or rely a small local/regional market. Rather, for it to survive and prosper, a re-emerging Basque cinema had to come to terms with macro-regional as well as international competition right from the start. This meant not only shooting in Castilian but making conditions as financially advantageous as possible in order to attract film business and filmmakers to the region. In particular, this meant doing everything possible to persuade established Basque directors resident in Madrid and elsewhere to return to Euskadi to shoot film as well as support and encourage the development of local talent. And in many ways, the Basque government's new policy paid off handsomely.

The funding rules for the award of government production subsidies in the Basque Country were deliberately undemanding. Indeed, in return for shooting in 35mm, depositing a copy of the subsidised film dubbed in Basque (assuming it had been made in Castilian), using 70 per cent Basque actors and technicians and filming in the region, the Consejería provided 25 per cent of the film budget 'a fondo perdido' (i.e. no need to pay it back). Such subsidies could also be added to other forms of financial support (deriving from state funding via the ICAA, private sponsors, television/video contracts or international distribution contracts) with no penalties or claw-backs. As Zunzunegui points out (1989: 70), such generous funding rules made film production in Euskadi particularly attractive, turning the region into 'una especie de paraíso' (a sort of paradise) and certainly helped to ensure the return of numerous, well-established Basque directors to the region, such as Pedro Olea, Alfonso Ungría, José Antonio Zorrilla and Eloy de la Iglesia.

Main trends: political/historical features

During the 1980s, Basque film policy (which soon included transmission contracts with the new regional public television stations *Euskal Telebista* 1 and 2) produced startling results. As many as thirty-five major film features were able to benefit from official government support (Gubern 1994: 417). As Monterde remarks, though not massive by comparison with national figures in Spain and not all having the same degree of national impact, this significant level of output 'dio la sensación de una pequeña avalancha de cine vasco, convertido en una de las puntas de lanza del cine español' (gave the impression of a small avalanche of Basque cinema, which became one of the spearheads of Spanish cinema) (1993: 123).

Over the period, two main trends in Basque filmmaking were observable: a political cinema, concerned broadly with centre-periphery conflicts, the contradictions of democratic politics and specifically with the position and role of ETA; and the historical fiction film. This political trend was represented mainly by the work of Imanol Uribe, whose third feature, *La muerte de Mikel* (1984), transformed him into a major national as well as leading Basque director. Uribe's film demonstrated a tangible line of development from the politicised documentary to the political fiction film, allowing the exploration of narrative, character, and spectacle to overcome gradually an earlier over-reliance on *cinéma verité* techniques and a certain *revanchismo* or the settling of old ideological scores. Also, if *La muerte de Mikel* shows a certain maturity in filmmaking terms, it also reveals a concern to convey a more modern, complex, urban vision of the Basque Country. This is made clear in the way the film explores the relations between Basque democratic politics and sexual identities, focusing on the conflict between the protagonist's aspirations to become a left-wing, democratic, parliamentary candidate and his homosexuality. The latter becomes a source of considerable difficulty for his mother and wife and creates controversy for his political ambitions leading to betrayal by his erstwhile political allies. His subsequent suicide is cynically exploited by those same political colleagues, who then declare him a martyr of state repression and police torture.

Unfortunately, Uribe was unable to build upon these considerable early successes, which culminated with *La muerte de Mikel*.

Later forays into commercial genre cinema, such as the crime thriller *Adiós pequeña* (1986) and the horror shocker *La luna negra* (1989) were largely failures, though his careful adaptation of Torrente Ballester's humorous period piece *El rey pasmado* (1991) was more successful, commercially and artistically. Even more emphatic in its sucess was Uribe's *Días contados* (1994). Winner of the *Concha de Oro* at the San Sebastian Film Festival of 1994, the film follows a clear line of development already evidenced in the work of Ana Díez (*Ander eta Yul*, 1988) and Antxón Eceiza (*Días de humo*, 1989). It is set against the contemporary background of national politics and ETA terror activity in Madrid, where an ETA 'comando' is setting up a terror bombing. The film concerns the passionate, strange, intimate relationship between two apparently very different though 'marginal' young people: a Basque terrorist (member of the Madrid 'comando') and a junkie prostitute, surviving in an underworld of drugs, prostitution and delinquency. Uribe successfully blends and explores a number of contemporary social and political issues, including youth culture, drug addiction, sexual hangups, urban alienation as well as ETA politics. Yet he does so by focusing on the romantic love story between the two youngsters, both of whom are trapped in a forbidding, hostile urban environment represented by Madrid. The more awkward, political issues concerning ETA, the use of terrorist violence and the legitimacy of the armed struggle are significantly played down, offering a relatively unobtrusive backdrop to the couple's evolving relationship. In his more recent and very successful *Bwana* (1996), a black comedy with a serious underlying humanitarian message, Uribe adopts a similar narrative arrangement. Here, he again foregrounds the relationship between a husband and wife, using it as a filter through which to observe contemporary middle-class Spanish prejudices towards race and cultural difference.

As already noted, Uribe's pro-ETA trilogy inspired a number of other features concerned with the political situation in Euskadi (the Basque Country) and which tended to focus on the political resistance to the central authority undertaken either directly by ETA militants or indirectly by other nationalist sympathisers. In this category, we can include: José L. Madrid's *Comando Txikia* (1977) and of course (Italian) Gillo Pontecorvo's sober, non-sensationalist interpretation of Carrero Blanco's assassination, *Operación Ogro* (1980). In many ways, the latter emerged as a relatively detached, quasi-documentary reconstruction of events, while also exploiting the action/thriller format of the 'special mission'. However, with the benefit of hindsight, in the light of events and developments in ETA politics in the 1990s, the film has been seen more recently as being too superficial. And while it acknowledges alternatives to the armed struggle within the frame of democratic politics, for Caparrós Lera, it remains 'en buena parte mitificadora del terrorismo, o al menos, justificadora de ETA' (in large part a mythification of terrorism or at the very least a legitimation of ETA) (1992: 189). Films noted for their engagement with other forms of political protest and nationalist struggle include Iñaki Aizpuru's *Los reporteros* (1983), Javier Rebollo's *Golfo de Vizcaya* (1985), Ernesto del Río's *El amor de ahora* (1987), Antxón Eceiza's *Días de humo* (1989), Ana Díez's *Ander eta Yul* (1988) and Manuel Macia's *Proceso a ETA* (1988). In different ways, all of the above tried to grapple with the contradictory relations between ETA militants, their role in the armed struggle and the status of democratic politics. But in particular, they focused increasingly on the tensions arising between the armed struggle and the hitherto unexplored worlds of personal relationships and the heavy toll imposed by social marginalisation.

The historical fiction film has been the other major trend in Basque cinema. As mentioned previously, whereas Catalan cinema has tended to concentrate on events occurring in the last 100 years or so, emphasising the origins, development and betrayals of modern bourgeois, Catalan nationalism, the most significant movies to emerge from recent Basque cinema, which have also enjoyed reasonable success nationally, tend to be set in pre-modern times, particularly in the Middle Ages or the Age of Discovery (Monterde 1993: 51–3). Clearly, in their exploration of the more remote past, Basque filmmakers have gone in search of parables, metaphors and analogues for the condition, problems and cleavages of contemporary Basque society. They have also looked to historical events and wars as well as myths and legends as appropriate sources for the recuperation of a national cultural memory and a redefinition of a modern nationalist consciousness. In particular, and not without ambiguities and contradictions, they have been engaged in representing Euskadi in terms of its wild, rugged, romantic lansdscapes and its noble, austere, heroic inhabitants, defending a unique, traditional way of life from the outside world.

Signalling his return to filmmaking in Euskadi after a five-year gap spent working in advertising, a return prompted by the attractive subsidies avalailable via the Ley Miró and the Basque government's new film policy, Pedro Olea's *Akelarre* (1983) is a case in point. The film explored the themes of witch-hunting and torture in the Middle Ages, focusing on the bloody and repressive activities of the Spanish Inquisition in the region. Despite some dramatic license in the depiction of inquisitorial method and procedure (which reinforced many of the clichés associated with Spain's enduring 'black legend'), the piece effectively offered an obvious model for the conflict between the central authorities and Basque traditions and culture. In *La conquista de Albania* (1983), Alfonso Ungría (with Ángel Amigo as producer), presented a striking historical parable of the region. Set in the fourteenth century, the film followed the obsessive attempts of a Navarrese warrior (disturbingly reminiscent of the deranged figure of Lope de Aguirre, explored in Werner Herzog's *Aguirre, der Zorn Gottes/La cólera de Dios* (1972) and Carlos Saura's *El Dorado* (1988) to achieve imperial conquest by invading Albania. Very much a panegyric to the obstinate character and determined spirit of the Basque race in the face of impossible odds, the film rather worryingly seemed to endorse a medieval notion of *führerprinzip*, a blind faith in the qualities of a Basque *caudillo* (leader), seen as spiritual core of the Basque nation (Zunzunegui 1989: 71; Monterde 1989: 54). Set in the sixteenth century, Pedro de la Sota's *Viento de cólera* (1988), in similar fashion to *Akelarre*, is very much a homage to a settled rural lifestyle and as Monterde argues is 'legible como una clara parábola sobre la defensa de la tierra ancestral' (readable as a parable concerning the defence of the homeland) (1993: 54). Other representative films within this subcategory of historical fiction include: José Ángel Rebolledo's *Fuego eterno* (1985), set in the seventeenth century, José María Tuduri's *Crónicas de las guerras carlistas* (1988) and his *Santa Cruz, el cura guerrillero* (1991), Pedro de la Sota's *Sabino Arana* (1980), and also José Antonio Zorrilla's *A los cuatro vientos* (1987), biopic of Basque poet Lauaxeta, marred somewhat by its over-emphatic reference to contemporary politics.

Genre cinema: melodrama/comedy/thriller

During the reform period (1976–80), Basque filmmakers tended not to exploit the genre film to any great extent. But where they did so, their films focused on a range of social, moral and political issues which had been buried under Francoism only to be excavated during the transition. This was arguably the case with the work of Eloy de la Iglesia, a commercial director, but one who made a series of provocative, iconoclastic and lurid features from the mid-1970s to the mid-1980s mainly to do with sexuality and its discontents. Conflating but also subverting disparate generic formats (including *cine negro*, melodrama, thriller, as well as pornography), de la Iglesia took up the stories of different marginalised groups in Spanish society, particularly homosexuals, drug addicts, delinquents and prostitutes. In features such as *Los placeres ocultos* (1976), *El diputado* (1978) and *Otra vuelta de tuerca* (1985) – based on the novel by Henry James – he attacked the hypocrisy of Spain's new, democratic civil society towards sexual freedoms by exploring the difficult position of the gay community during the transition and after. In later features, and anxious to raise public awareness of socially marginalised groupings and their problems, he used the family melodrama format to explore the worlds of delinquency, drug subcultures, homosexuality, radical Basque politics and the forces of order, particularly in *Navajeros* (1980), *Colegas* (1982), *El pico* (1983) and *El pico II* (1984) (Smith 1992: 129–62; Kinder 1993: 430). While his political motives and his support for the alternative sexualities and the class underdog were generally applauded, critical opinion tended to deride de la Iglesia for his film style, i.e. his lurid *tremendista* images, his lack of realism and his pamphleteering tone. Indeed, he was heavily criticised for making sensationalist, exploitation 'B' movies around more serious social issues (Smith 1992: 161). Subsequently, and again exploiting a literary source, he made a further foray into the sordid world of juvenile crime in *La estanquera de Vallecas* (1987), the film version of the stage play by Alonso de Santos.

More recently, Basque cinema has diversified significantly into most of the accepted generic categories. After one or two mediocre attempts at the 'crazy comedy' subtrend, as in *Siete calles* (1981) by Javier Rebollo and Juanma Ortuosti and *Tu novia está loca* (1987), by Enrique Urbizu, Urbizu realigned the gender balance and developed the woman-centred high comedy, achieving considerable success with *Cómo ser infeliz y disfrutarlo* (1994) and *Cuernos de mujer* (1995). Like Ana Belén's *Cómo ser mujer y no morir en el intento* (1991), both of these films are adaptations of novels by journalist Carmen Rico Godoy and deal with the difficulties and frustrations facing professional women who seek independence from traditional patriarchal power structures. More recently, Urbizu has adapted the novel by Arturo Pérez Reverte *Un asunto de amor* and made *Cachito* (1996), a solid, unpretentious, sentimental 'road movie' in which an orphan girl is helped to find her mother by a rootless lorry driver. Joaquín Trincado, Urbizu's producer on earlier films, made his directorial debut with *Sálvate si puedes* (1994), a 1990s version of Berlanga's classic black comedy *Bienvenido, Mr Marshall*. The film's modest success depended in part on its recycling of the established *esperpento* style of Berlanga and others; it also benefitted from a cast of attractive, bankable Spanish 'stars', including the versatile Antonio Resines as well as Fernando Guillén, Imanol Arias and María Barranco. Also exploring the social-*costumbrista* comedy was Antxón Eceiza, responsible for the political, 'return-of-the-exile' movie *Días de humo* (1989) and author of *Felicidades Tovarich* (1995), another sentimental combination of road movie and *comedia de enredos* (comedy of intrigue).

In the early 1980s, José Antonio Zorilla began his film career with the crime thriller *El arreglo* (1983). The film was well received and seemed to mark a turning point in the development of Spanish *noir*, auguring well for other projects from other commercial Basque directors. During the 1980s, however, results were not particularly encouraging in this area, as evidenced perhaps by Imanol Uribe's unconvincing oedipal drama *Adiós pequeña* (1986). By contrast, in the 1990s, the output of genre cinema, including the crime thriller, has been striking, especially from a new generation of younger directors. Indeed, as noted elsewhere, within the area of the crime movie, Enrique Urbizu's *Todo por la pasta* (1991) has made a significant impact. The film offers a well-structured, rapid-paced, visually striking account of the consequences of armed robbery, set against the sordid, marginal urban underworld of drug dealing, sexual perversion and police corruption. What perhaps distinguishes the film, apart from its indictment of a corrupt police and justice system, is the way it places the stories of two very different women, from contrasting backgrounds, at the heart of the narrative. Initially vulnerable figures, open to threats and betrayal and competing against each other for the proceeds of the robbery, they gradually develop an understanding and solidarity which helps them overcome their hostile masculine counterparts and, as sisters in arms, retrieve the money. Moreover, Urbizu's treatment of his material is particularly truculent and, in line with other recent examples of the genre (e.g. Javier Elorrieta's *Cautivos en la sombra* (1994)), indulges in frequent and remarkably graphic images of physical violence.

Excess and the cult of violence
Violence in contemporary Spanish genre film is nothing new. Indeed, Spanish audiences tend to expect strong, explicit, lurid, *tremendista* images of brutality in their crime thrillers and action movies as well as their 'social issue' films. However, among some of the younger Basque directors of recent times, we find a certain fascination with the excesses of screen violence and what might appear to be a knowing, self-conscious indulgence in physical injury and cruelty. In some cases, such truculence forms part of a wider parodic intent, the impact of which is lessened by its very explicitness, exaggeration and excess, all of which tends to distance the spectator. In other cases however, the violence sometimes becomes transformed into a sensationalist visual spectacle. Blood and gore are fully and explicitly displayed for the specular delight and delectation of the audience, the horrors of aggression and physical injury are given a deliberately graphic, shocking treatment. Needless to say, the boundaries between the filmically warranted portrayal of the terrible effects of violent behaviour and screen violence as an aestheticised visual spectacle in itself tend to become seriously blurred. This filmic tension has arguably been a key feature of the work of rising Basque star director Juanma Bajo Ulloa.

Bajo Ulloa came to prominence with *Alas de mariposa* (1991), a collaborative first feature, written with his brother Eduardo, which won several Goya awards as well as the San Sebastian *Concha de Oro* Prize for 1991. The film deals with a dysfunctional working class family living in Vitoria in which the young daughter murders her younger brother out of jealousy. In her turn, she is raped by her father's friend and becomes pregnant. Through his anguished child protagonists, Bajo Ulloa relates an austere, tragic and violent tale of family relations and how these degenerate into jealousy, revenge, sexual perversion and pyschological breakdown. Up to a point, the conflictive family unit of the film might be readable as a metaphor for the social cleavages and tensions in the Basque region. However, Bajo Ulloa seems more concerned to predicate the disintegration of the family unit on a Freudian psychologism, involving childhood trauma, repression and the violent sublimation of infantile sexuality. Moreover, the director does not spare the sensibilities of the audience with his hard-hitting and detailed depiction of domestic strife and violence.

Alas de mariposa was followed by *La madre muerta* (1993), again set against a sordid, marginalised, but grotesquely realist background. The film concerns the disturbed and bizarre relations between a thief-turned-psychopath (Ismael), his girlfriend (Maite) and a subnormal girl (Leire), who never smiles and is obsessed with eating chocolate (a correlative for human faeces?), whom Ismael kidnaps. The film title is intriguing if only because after the 'murder' of the *madre* at the beginning of the film, her character/persona disappears, becoming a detached, almost vacant container to be filled with meanings. The 'mothering' function then appears to be taken over by Ismael who, while verbally abusing his captive Leire is gradually drawn towards her emotionally. Indeed, Leire becomes a crucial object in Ismael's fantasies of power and control as well as his possible redemption since she elicits sympathy and compassion from him and provides him with a possible vehicle for overcoming his cruelty. These aspects remain highly conjectural however. Bajo Ulloa was clearly concerned with exploring the nature of psychological disturbances leading to violence and the fluid boundaries between normal and abnormal human behaviour. Hence, the focus on the weird, pathological conduct of the main protagonist and also his partial redemption through his master–slave relationship with the disturbed kidnap victim. But, the director refuses to provide the spectator with much in the way of behavioural background or motivation; thus, our understanding of Ismael's behaviour is left intriguingly incomplete. At the same time, the film's dark, disturbing narrative is punctuated by scenes of sickening, graphically realistic violence (in which the bar owner is brutally slain). Though not widespread, rather than enrich our understanding of the protagonist's motivations for his appalling aggression, such violent images run the risk of lapsing into lurid spectacle whilst dulling the emotional sensibilities of the bashed and battered spectator. In his most recent venture, *Airbag* (1997), Bajo Ulloa abandons his lower-class misfits for the upper echelons of the Basque bourgeoisie. And, in this much lighter, action/comedy/road movie, centring on the pursuit and recovery of a stolen wedding ring, a group of young Basque scions seek revenge and sublimation by taking on drugs barons and international organised crime in a spree of violence and mayhem.

Another young Basque filmmaker who has had major success in

24

Alas de mariposa, Juanma Bajo Ulloa, 1991

the genre movie, specialising in the trash feature and satirical spoof, is Alex de la Iglesia. With only one short film behind him (*Las Mirindas asesinas*) and at the age of only twenty-six, de la Iglesia managed to convince Almodóvar and *El Deseo S.A.* to finance his first major, full-length feature *Acción mutante* (1992). At light years distance from Spain's low-grade, low-budget *cine fantástico y de terror* of the 1980s, *Acción mutante* broke new ground in Spanish filmmaking. Indeed, it represented the country's first internationally credible and commercially viable sci-fi 'effects' movie, albeit in the form of a surrealist comedy-pastiche of the genre. In the film, a gang of comically grotesque freaks and disabled retards calling themselves *Acción mutante* kidnap the daughter of an industrial tycoon. They then fly to the exhausted mining Planet Axturias to collect their ransom money. Readable at any number of levels, the film can obviously be regarded as a metaphor for and satire on the situation of unrest and violence in the Basque Country and the struggle of terrorist organisation ETA with the central Spanish state. But the film also offers a biting critique of 1980s yuppies and designer Socialists, their tastes, values and styles, which are mercilessly mocked and subverted by the outrageously trashy, 'grungy' gang members. At the same time, *Acción mutante* is a veritable anthology of references, homages, nods and winks to a host of other films and their particular stylistic peculiarities, including *Blade Runner*, *Alien*, *Mad Max*, *Dune* and *The Texas Chainsaw Massacre*, to name but a few. Also, echoing a theme developed in several films by his patron Almodóvar (particularly in *Kika*), de la Iglesia offers a sharp satire of the intrusiveness and manipulative nature of the visual media of television and video, which wilfully confuse presentation and representation, exploit the bizarre and the banal and tend to desensitise the spectator towards the horrifying realities of violence and destruction. Above all, de la Iglesia seeks to outdo the trash movie, in an orgy of blood, gore, killing, deplorable visual gags in utter bad taste and an all round emphasis on filmic excess. However, while he plays his moments of ultra violence and mayhem for laughs (e.g. the massacre of the wedding guests, Yarritu's murder of his colleagues), the parodic presentation of these acts of slaughter detaches them from their real and devastating effects. This leads to an emotional draining of the spectator and finally to a situation in which another fist in the face is greeted with mildly amused indifference.

De la Iglesia followed *Acción mutante* with another generic spoof, this time plundering the resources of the horror movie (*cine de terror*) in the remarkably successful *El día de la bestia* (1995). (After Fernando Trueba's *Two Much* (1995), *El día de la bestia* was Spain's highest grossing film in 1996). Cruelly parodying earlier 'demonic possession' movies such as *The Exorcist* and *The Omen*, *El día de la bestia* throws together a quiet, unassuming but redoubtable Basque priest, a heavy-metal freak and a fraudulent television satanist/ evangelist. The perilous mission of these unlikely Three Kings is to save the world by preventing the birth of the anti-Christ on Christmas Eve, a birth scheduled to occur not in a stable but in the environs of two unfinished, ultra-modern, skyscraper towers, ironically designated as the 'Gate to Europe'. Here, de la Iglesia sets up without perhaps fully developing one of the enduring thematic threads of the movie: the contrast and interconnections between traditional and (post)modern Spain, represented by Madrid's crumbling *hostales*, its heavy-metal nightclubs and futuristic architectural symbols of (euro-)capitalism, also parodically embodied in such characters as the naked, drug-taking grandfather and the absurdly monstrous, M16-toting landlady (Terele Pávez). At the same time, de la Iglesia pays mischievous homage to a host of source materials including, not only a citation from Almodovar's *Kika* (Mina ironing in front of the television), but also a finale involving a vicious recreation of the 'ultraviolence' displayed in Kubrick's *A Clockwork Orange*. Also, returning to the manipulative role of the media, the film's lurid recreation of a television 'exorcism' presents a witty, shrewd and savage critique of media prophets, evangelists and hucksters. And by actually recreating the birth of the anti-Christ

El día de la bestia, Alex de la Iglesia, 1995   **25**

(with expensive and visually striking special effects, courtesy of mega-producer Andrés Vicente Gómez), the film mocks all those con artists and charlatans on the inside and outside of the visual media who thrive on popular ignorance and wish fulfilment to peddle their predictive nonsense.

Also intriguing and enjoyable is the perverse juxtaposition of the heavy-metal maniac and the Basque priest, who are drawn together through the medium of 'heavy' music, supposedly laden with secret meanings if played backwards. More intriguing (if not disturbing for its subversive effects) is the role reversal of the priest who, in order to propitiate the devil, has to engage in all manner of evil acts including indiscriminate violent behaviour. This device gives rise to scenes of unparalelled violence and cruelty, including the kidnap and torture of the television satanist and his girlfriend and especially the gruesomely funny murder of the psychopathic landlady. After his success with *El día de la bestia*, and still only in his early thirties, de la Iglesia was given his first opportunity to work in the USA by substituting Bigas Luna in the production of the road movie *Perdita Durango* (which began shooting in August 1996, for release in 1997). It was even rumoured that de la Iglesia had been offered *Alien 4* or *Zorro* – a remarkable offer in many ways, given his brief track record and especially when compared to figures such as Trueba who took years to achieve their Hollywood debuts as directors.

Genre film, metaphysics and a new *auteurism*?

Taking a rather different approach towards the genre movie, though clearly engaged in its parodic recycling and subversion, Julio Medem is another young Basque director who has already gained significant national and international recognition. He has made three critically – acclaimed full-length features: *Vacas* (1992), *La ardilla roja* (1993) and *Tierra* (1995), broadly commercial films which have tended to appeal, however, more to film *cognoscenti* and *aficionados* than a wider, popular audience. Given their commercial and critical reception as well as their unusual, if not unique, filmic style, not suprisingly Medem has been dubbed as a budding *auteur*. Noted for its visual flamboyance (the stunning subjective, optical point of view shot through the animal's 'eye') but derided for the improbabilities of its script, its complex temporal structure and its technical ambition, Medem's rural saga *Vacas* was nonetheless an unusual, indeed remarkable, first feature. On the surface, it sought to excavate the historical roots of Basque national identity using the steady, unflinching perspective of the silent witnesses (the 'vacas' of the title), who contemplate the bitter rivalries between two Basque families over a fifty-year cycle of war and aggression. However, the film also displays a clear awareness of its status as a textual production; it presents itself as a text which is both a clarification as well as another mystification of Basque history and identity. In short, it stands as another version of events to be questioned rather than be unquestioningly accepted.

In *La ardilla roja* (1993), a hybrid mix of thriller, comedy, melodrama and kidnap movie/love story, Medem takes an even more playful, ludic approach to questions of masculine/feminine as well as regional identity. Again revealing a virtuoso shooting style, the film explores the relationship between a young man (Jota) and a female amnesiac, whom he proceeds to refashion as his lover. Set against the background of the Red Squirrel campsite in La Rioja, Jota sets out to reinvent the identity of the woman he has 'found' according to his own needs and desires. Yet, in a love game of appearances and deceptions, seductions and rejections, this 'found' woman remains a mystery (as do her underlying motivations and the veracity of her feelings) and is finally unamenable to male control and possession. If *La ardilla roja* raised issues of life and death, mortality and transcendence, Medem's next movie *Tierra* (1995) developed them even further. In a nominally realist, rural setting, Medem creates an atmosphere of fantasy, poetry and hyperreality, in which wild boars are attracted by female smells and widowers search for their dead, departed lovers among the stars. Against this magical background, through Ángel, (whose job it is to fumigate a vineyard, destroy the cochineal beatle and rid the grapes of the taste of 'tierra'), Medem explores an unusual man's quest for transcen-

La ardilla roja, Julio Medem, 1993   **26**

dence, his search for an elusive state of calm and inner peace. Ángel (an 'angel', whose name is illustrative of his divided condition) is a complex, disturbed figure who seeks simplicity. Portrayed as a split personality, with a strong *alter ego* and inner 'voice', he is capable of experiencing death and nothingness; he also engages in debates concerning the metaphysical and philosophical virtues of spiritual and earthly desires. The film explores this bizarre dualism through his love relationships with two different women (Ángela and Mari), the first a mature housewife, whom he will reject; the second an attractive adolescent, with whom he will stay. Through the interplay of these contrasting love stories and some intriguing positions adopted towards sexual orgasm (by Mari), Ángel is swayed into relinquishing his metaphysical quest for serenity by settling for a life in the real world. But where does happiness lie? What is the nature of Ángel's desire and longing? Is his dilemma a genuine one or a somewhat self-indulgent, rhetorical exercise? Medem's convoluted but fascinating meditation raises more questions than it answers.

In Medem's work as a whole, we find something of a regional postmodern response to the creation of identities, a set of doubts creeping in regarding the status and value of 'Basqueness' and Basque traditions. As Jo Labanyi succinctly points out, Medem helps to 'expose the constructed nature of all identities' (1995b: 403). This gives rise to a satire of the Basque heritage industry and all the cultural 'work' involved in constructing the materials for a certain timeless nationalist foundationalism. Medem thus offers a critique of those cultural and textual processes which help to reinforce and reproduce a bogus essentialist consciousness. Such scepticism is also seen in the way Medem lovingly exploits but also subverts generic formats such as the rural saga. This questioning of the essentialisms of Basque identity is bound to be further developed in his latest venture *Los amantes del Círculo Polar* (1998).

Icons of (Basque?) filmmaking

It would be impossible to round off a review of contemporary Basque cinema without mentioning several major figures whose direct contribution to Basque filmmaking may be debatable but whose importance as film professionals at national and international level is unquestionable.

Firstly, Montxo Armendáriz, protegé of producer Elías Querejeta. His early short *Carboneros de Navarra* (1980) provided the thematic basis for his *Tasio* (1984), one of the most important films of the 1980s, even though it deals with rural life in Navarre. Concerned with the life cycle of the charcoal burner, the film offers a careful exploration of the intimate relations between the individual and the environment, providing a positive, non-escapist portrayal of rural Navarrese life, one which was arguably emblematic of the best of Basque 'rural' cinema up to the mid-1980s. Exploring social issues in the highly successful *27 horas* (1986), concerned with drug abuse in San Sebastian, Armendáriz's later feature *Las cartas de Alou* (1990), focused on illegal immigration by poor Africans and issues of racism. (Interestingly, very few directors have dealt with the topics of xenophobia and racial prejudice and of those who have – Saura, Uribe and Armendáriz – two are Basque by birth or adoption). Armendáriz's *Historias del Kronen* (1995) shifts geographically to the alienating, urban, nocturnal wasteland of low-life Madrid, in a series of mini-stories which chronicle the antisocial behaviour of the capital's 'niños pijos' (posh kids). In the film, gangs of middle-class youngsters, in revolt against their elders, overcome their adolescent tribalisms and learn the iron laws of adult life, according to which some people are destined to lead and others to be enslaved. Interestingly, the film deals sympathetically with the issue of male bonding and male friendship compared with relations with the opposite sex, thereby opening up opportunities for a certain youthful, male (homoerotic?) identity. In other words, girls are fine for occasional sex, but male friends are for life and for dealing with life's priorities, such as conjuring up the money for the next fix. In his feature *Secretos del corazón* (1997), Armendáriz continues to explore the emotional hang-ups of adolescents and their troubled transition to adulthood in a period, 'rites of passage' movie, this time set in the 1960s in a rural context.

Armendáriz has arguably played a major role in giving Basque cinema a national profile and standing, achievements which have opened doors for a number of new talents in the late 1980s and 1990s, including Ana Díez's *Ander eta Yul* (1988) and *Todo está oscuro* (1995), Gracia Querejeta's *El último viaje de Robert Rylands* (1996), Arantxa Lazkano's *Los años oscuros* (1994), Carlos Zabala &

Eneko Olasagasti's *Maité* (1994), (a big screen version of an ETB1 series *Bi eta Bat*) as well as Daniel Calparsoro's promising *Salto al vacío* (1995) and his *Pasajes* (1996), made with the backing of Almodóvar's production company *El Deseo S.A.*

Before closing this section, and in order to illustrate once again the difficulty of defining Basque cinema in any meaningful, coherent fashion, we must mention briefly the careers of two major figures who, though Basque in origin, show little of any definable 'Basqueness' in their work. Indeed, they are more properly thought of as being synonymous with the national film industry as a whole. This has partly to do with their longevity in the film business, the fact that they learnt their trade under Francoism, at the Escuela Oficial de Cine (National Film School) in Madrid and settled in the capital in order to pursue their careers. They thus developed during a period in which the construction of a Basque cinema and a Basque national consciousness were illegal as well as filmically almost impossible. This perhaps accounts in some ways for their own apparent lack of specific concern for Basque issues. We refer to Elías Querejeta and of course to the enigmatic and still hugely influential Víctor Erice, whose limited film output remains as allusive and mysterious as the director himself.

With over forty movies to his credit as a producer, one time footballer Elías Querejeta has had a massive influence on Spain's national cinema and is one of the few leading figures in the field who still command international recognition and respect. In the 1960s and 1970s, he produced as many as eighteen features, most of them made by Carlos Saura, from *La caza* (1965) right through to *Deprisa, deprisa* (1980). But he has also produced Erice's three features to date as well as work by Chávarri, Martínez Lázaro, Regueiro, Gutiérrez Aragón, Armendáriz, Franco, the virtually unknown newcomer Fernando León de Aranoa and his own daughter Gracia, including *Una estación de paso* (1992), *Todas las almas* (1994) and *El último viaje de Robert Rylands* (1996). Perhaps one might identify his trade marks as a producer through his support for stories and scripts which focus on the inner world of dreams and personal desires, rites of passage, generational conflicts and the more contemplative life. It still remains the case, however, that compared to his national standing, he has made far less impact on the post-Franco Basque film renaissance.

As for Víctor Erice, it is arguable that, alongside Saura and Suárez, his work came to symbolise both nationally and internationally, almost the only serious, searching, demanding and formally sophisticated Spanish cinema of the 1970s and early 1980s, despite making only one feature per decade. Creator as well as analyst of cinematic mythologies, indefatigable student of the limitations of the medium, committed to the narrative enigma as the basis for the hermeneutic process, Erice made two films which remain landmarks in contemporary Spanish film history: *El espíritu de la colmena* (1973) and *El sur* (1983). Both are fascinating, evocative, richly textured studies of family life on the losing side under Francoism in the 1940s and 1950s, as seen through the innocent though confused eyes of children. And they appealed to a liberal, intellectual, educated, mainly international audience, anxious to find in some corner of Spanish cinema the sort of complex, subtle, allusive texts of the kind associated with great European *auteurs* such as Bergman and Godard. Erice thus became a prism through which arthouse audiences and academic specialists abroad tended to approach Spanish cinema and through whom they constructed their views of what a quality Spanish cinema ought to look like. And from a liberal, European, anti-Francoist perspective, Erice became appropriated as a figure with intellectual credibility and gravitas, a filmmaker who had deliberately rejected the commercial mainstream for the upper end of the 'high culture' film market.

In 1992, almost a decade after his last film, Erice broke with his previous focus on fictional narrative and made a quasi-documentary feature *El sol del membrillo* (1992). As always, though adopting a documentary style using both film and video, Erice's third feature was a multi-layered master-class on the nature of representation in different media. It followed the ultimately futile and ritualised attempts by celebrated national painter Antonio López to capture on canvas and in drawings the 'reality' of the light hitting the 'membrillo' or quince tree growing in the painter's garden. The film also hit many more buttons, including the nature of time and space, reality and dream, the artist and her or his work, the relations between different media, visual and graphic, as well as a more mundane though revealing awareness of conflict in the world (war in the Gulf), of the daily routines of immigrant workers as well as a sceptical attitude towards the cultural value of television output (Morgan 1994: 40–1). Above all, perhaps, this third film exemplified a confidently marginal, non-commercial elitist cinema, one which had deliberately rejected a wider public for an appreciative, select audience. Yet this was also an important, richly suggestive and demanding cinema which would enhance Erice's already unassailable position and status rather than detract from it. Confounding his admirers as well as his detractors and refusing to wait out a full ten years until embarking on his next feature, it appears that Erice has agreed to undertake the film adaptation of the novel by Juan Marsé's *El embrujo de Shanghai*. Whether his status as Spain's most enigmatic and mercurial *auteur* survives this excursion into the genre film remains to be seen.

Other regions, other voices

On the whole, other autonomous regions in Spain have had neither

El sol del membrillo, Victor Erice, 1992

the infrastructure, finance, planning nor talent to develop their own separate film cultures, at least on the scale of the Basque Country or Catalonia. Nor has there been the sort of political pay-off in terms of building a regional consciousness by putting money into film. Film production has thus been fairly modest, although in certain areas (Galicia, Valencia, the Canaries, Andalusia) several projects have managed to prosper. The point must be made, however, that film projects have been somewhat erratic, one-off events, rather than part of a clear policy or plan of campaign. Moreover, they have been totally dependent on public funding since they have made little or no impact beyond the confines of their own autonomous communities. In Andalusia, if we can properly talk of a *cine andaluz*, then this has been represented by Gonzalo Garciapelayo whose *Corrida de alegría* (1980) and *Rocío y José* (1982), explored local culture and customs and in the latter case, used the cult of the Virgin and the *romería* (pilgrimage) as a backdrop to a rather banal, conventional love story. In the 'País Valenciá', apart from Carles Mira and to some extent, but only indirectly, Berlanga and José Luis García Sánchez in *Tranvía a la Malvarrosa* (1996), a Valencian/Mediterranean cinema has been represented by Carlos Pérez Farré in *Quimera* (1987) and *Tramontana* (1991), which came and went without any public or critical acknowledgement. A similar indifference awaited *Guarapo* (1988), a solitary attempt at a commercial film made in the Canaries until María Miró's tale of the exile of Saharan people and racism in *Los baúles del retorno* (1995).

In Galicia, the situation was rather different in that the regional government, through the Conselleira de Educación y Cultura in 1989, decided to launch a cinema initiative by inviting several well-known independent media names to make Galician films. Several features emerged including *Urxa* (1989) by Alfredo García Piñal, *Continental* (1989) by Javier Villaverde and (having made the well-received *Mamasunción* in 1985), Chano Piñeiro with *Sempre Xonxa* (1989). Unfortunately, despite the effort, the initiative to launch a Galician cinema had too little public exposure. Moroever, throwing money at two competent directors was arguably not the way forward. As Monterde points out, what was needed was 'una operación mucho más compleja de promoción y difusión que, en el marco de la permanente y general crisis cinemátografica, se hace poco menos que inviable' (a more complex publicity and distribution operation which, in the context of the generalised crisis in the film industry, is virtually impossible) (1993: 127). In other respects, of course, Galicia has figured prominently as a dramatic setting and narrative source for a number of features since the late 1980s including Antonio Giménez Rico's *Jarapellejos* (1987), Pedro Carvajal's *Martes de carnaval* (1991) and *El baile de las ánimas* (1993), Juan Pinzás's *La leyenda de la doncella* (1996) and Gerardo Herrero's forthcoming *Frontera sur* (1997), which concerns 'gallegos' who emigrated to Argentina at the end of the ninteenth century.

Internationalisation and diversification of funding

To conclude this section, it is clear that, by and large, the support policies of the Autonomous Basque Government towards filmmaking in the Basque Country have been highly successful. They have helped to generate a strong, varied body of work, across a number of genres, which in some cases, has achieved national and international prominence. Of course, in order to bring a film project to fruition, money from the Consejería de Cultura has usually constituted only one element in a more complex financial package, but nonetheless a crucial one. The Basque authorities have also managed to attract numerous established producers and directors to return to work in the region and have helped to promote new, promising talents, especially the young and highly promising Daniel Calparsoro. On the downside, as Pedro Olea once noted, the system of panels for adjudicating subsidies and grants for various projects tended to be subject to manipulation and favoritism, leading to accusations of insider dealing and fraud (Caparrós Lera 1992: 347). This and the fact that, until recently, public support was not in any way related to box office success (Monterde 1993: 126), meant that Basque cinema remained fully dependent on public money and producers and directors showed litle sign of wishing to explore alternative sources of finance. The growing cost of public subsidies however, reflecting developments at national level, has forced the

Autonomous Basque Government to investigate other forms of financing film production. As Gubern notes (1994: 417), the very generous subsidy system has been replaced by the creation of an agency, Euskal Media, which handles public money destined for subsidies but also seeks to promote much greater levels of co-operation with other sources of funding, including state funding, television contracts and advances from private production companies. Such financial diversification and resorting to multiple coproduction arrangements can be seen in the case of the film *Maité* (1994), by Carlos Zabala and Eneko Olasagasti. A love story, set in Cuba, the film was financed partly through regional subsidies and partly through central funding; it also benefited from a small injection of Cuban investment and monies from international distributors. This project may be a unique development, representing the first Basque/Cuban copro ever to be made, financed on a wide front, shot in Castilian and later dubbed into Basque. Another trend, of course, equally vital to the health of Basque filmmaking is a need for the continuing support of independent Spanish producers such as Almodóvar's *El Deseo S.A.* which launched the career of Alex de la Iglesia and recently produced Daniel Calparsoro's female love story *Pasajes* (1996).

References:

Caparrós Lera, J. M. (1992), *El cine español de la democracia. De la muerte de Franco al cambio socialista'(1975–1989)*, Barcelona, Anthropos, 121–347.

Evans, P. (1995), Cifesa: Cinema and Authoritarian Aesthetics, in Graham, H., and Labanyi, J. (eds), *Spanish Cultural Studies. An Introduction*, Oxford, Oxford University Press, 215–22.

Fernández, J.-A. (1995), Becoming Normal: Cultural Production and Cultural Policy in Catalonia, in Graham, H., and Labanyi, J. (eds), *Spanish Cultural Studies. An Introduction*, Oxford, Oxford University Press, 342–51.

Fotogramas (1997), Compromiso con el cine catalán, 1840, February, 129.

García-Fernández, E. C. (1985), *Historia ilustrada del cine español*, Barcelona, Planeta, 301.

Gubern, R., *et al.* (1994), *Historia del cine español*, Madrid, Cátedra, Signo e Imagen, 415–17.

Hopewell, J. (1986), *Out of the Past. Spanish Cinema after Franco*, London, BFI, 114–73.

Kinder, M. (1993), *Blood Cinema. The Reconstruction of National Identity in Spain*, Berkeley and Los Angeles, University of California Press. 183–430.

Labanyi, J. (1995a), Censorship or the fear of mass culture, in Graham, H., and Labanyi, J. (eds), *Spanish Cultural Studies. An Introduction*, Oxford, Oxford University Press, 207–14.

Labanyi, J. (1995b) Postmodernism and the problem of cultural identity, in Graham, H., and Labanyi, J. (eds), *Spanish Cultural Studies. An Introduction*, Oxford, Oxford University Press, 396–406.

Lasagabaster, J. M. (1995), The promotion of cultural production in Basque, in Graham, H., and Labanyi, J. (eds), *Spanish Cultural Studies. An Introduction*, Oxford, Oxford University Press, 351–55.

Molina-Foix, V. (1977), *New Cinema in Spain*, London, BFI, 22–7.

Monterde, J. E. (1989), El cine histórico durante la transición política, in Benet, V. J., *et al.*, *Escritos sobre Cine Español 1973–1987*, Valencia, Filmoteca de la Generalitat Valenciana, 45–63.

Monterde, J. E. (1993), *Veinte años de cine español. Un cine bajo la paradoja* (1973–92), Barcelona, Ediciones Paidós. 51–127.

Morgan, R. (1994), Realism and the Creative Process in Víctor Erice's *El sol del membrillo* (1992), in *Tesserae*, Journal of Iberian and Latin-American Studies, University of Wales, Cardiff, Vol. 1, 1 (Winter 1994), 35–45.

Smith, P. J. (1992), *Laws of Desire. Questions of homosexuality in Spanish Writing and Film 1960–1990*, Oxford, Clarendon Press. 129–62.

Smith, P. J. (1994), *Desire Unlimited. The Cinema of Pedro Almodóvar*, London, Verso, 138.

(Various authors) (1989), *La indústria del cinema a Catalunya*, Barcelona, Generalitat de Catalunya, Departament de Cultura.

Zunzunegui, S. (1985), *El cine en el País Vasco*, Bilbao, Diputación Foral de Vizcaya. 385–6.

Zunzunegui, S. (1989), De los cines de las nacionalidades a los cines de las autonomías: el caso del cine vasco, in Benet, V. J., *et al.*, *Escritos sobre Cine Español 1973–1987*, Valencia, Filmoteca de la Generalitat Valenciana, 65–78.

Conclusion

Throughout the 1980s and 1990s, Spanish cinema has enjoyed numerous instances of significant national and international success but against a background of industrial weakness and apparent long-term decline. For example, the astonishing international impact of Almodóvar's *Mujeres al borde de un ataque de nervios* (1988) undoubtedly opened a window for what Paul Julian Smith calls 'a mini-boom of Spanish art-house hits' (Smith 1994: 138), referring to films by Medem, Bigas Luna, Alex de la Iglesia, etc., which achieved foreign release and critical acclaim in the 1990s. Also, Fernando Trueba's Oscar success with *Belle Epoque* (1992) in 1993 provided a welcome boost for Spanish films in overseas markets and confirmed that Spanish directors and the Spanish industry could (occasionally) compete with Hollywood. However, other siren voices in the early 1990s could be heard, voices announcing Spanish cinema's imminent demise. In anticipation of the centenary of Spain's film industry in 1995, critic Romá Gubern wondered whether he would be attending a funeral rather than a celebration (Muñoz 1992: 30). In more alarmist tones, Ángel Fernández Santos, film critic of *El País*, talked of the savage curtailment of public film subsidies in terms of 'genocidio cultural' (cultural genocide) (1992: 30); and Pilar Miró, ex-head of the government's film-funding agency, argued that cinema in Spain had been disgraced by changes in government funding and was finished (Valenzuela 1992: 38).

The above voices were reacting to a situation in which, after the restrictive measures adopted in the 'Semprún decree' of 1988/89, Socialist policy had been to increasingly scale back the levels of public subsidy for the Spanish film industry. As noted in the Introduction, this process of curtailment and rationalisation was taken further by Carmen Alborch in 1994 and, after the PP victory of

March 1996, pursued even more vigorously by new Culture Minister Aguirre and her truculent Secretary of State, Miguel Ángel Cortés. On balance, and despite some notable exceptions, the subsidised, homogenised, ideologically centrist cinema made under the Socialist mandate, particularly in the 1980s, was to prove commercially inviable and according to Hopewell, dull and uninspiring (1989: 463). However, as Hopewell also indicates, from the late 1980s onwards, the cuts in state subsidies meant that producers had to cover their risks by seeking other means of amortising film projects, particularly through television contracts, vertical integration and more international co-operation (1989: 462–3).

As noted elsewhere, the period 1993–94 was perhaps one of the most difficult for the film industry in post-Franco Spain, particularly in relation to production totals and audience figures. Yet, it emerged from a commercial black hole and managed to survive the crisis. And, now, at the very moment in which Spain's Conservative Government is threatening to pull the plug on public support for the industry, the picture looks increasingly positive and there are clear signs that the business is strengthening (*Fotogramas* 1997: 169). Production figures virtually doubled in 1996 compared with 1995, gross box-office receipts for 1996 were up by 700 million pesetas compared to the previous year and since 1994, audiences have increased by nearly 5 million spectators. Indeed, global audience totals for 1996 have topped 100 millions, indicating a sustained rising trend in ticket sales (*Fotogramas* 1997: 172). The 'multiplex fever' seems set to continue with over 100 new screens planned for 1997. Moreover, as anticipated by Hopewell, vertical integration has begun to happen (witness the development of PRISA's tri-partite media operation: Sogetel (production), Sogepaq and Sogecable (Distribution/Exhibition), and television contracts have become the cornerstone of the film industry. Indeed, as much as 80 per cent of current Spanish film production depends on co-financing arrangements with television stations, public and private. PRISA alone, in conjunction with Canal + and Tele 5, has negotiated a series of deals which will produce fourteen features over the next two to three years, injecting 3,000 million pesetas into the industry (Alvarez 1997: 36). As if this were not enough, in a country in which classical literature in film form rarely, if ever, gained an audience, Pilar Miró's adaptation (spoken in verse) of Lope's *El perro del hortelano* (1996), was running at number six in the box-office returns for 1996 (Alvarez 1997: 34). The film's striking success represents just one example of the industry's current ability to generate audiences for a much wider variety of film types than hitherto, including the classics. Spanish films are also making greater inroads into foreign markets, as indicated by Amenábar's *Tesis*, which has been sold to thirty countries and Ventura Pons's *El porqué de las cosas*, currently among the top three grossing films in

El perro del hortelano, Pilar Miró, 1996   **28**

France (*Fotogramas* 1997: 169). In short, after decades of ideological and political manipulation, Spain's film industry reveals a remarkably healthy pluralism of output, accommodated within the broad spectrum of cinema, ranging from mainstream to arthouse, and all the while crossing and re-drawing its internal thematic and stylistic boundaries.

Reflecting the current upbeat mood, though inflected with a note of caution, Fernando Méndez-Leite, ex-head of ICAA and currently director of Spain's National Film School, recently remarked: 'Estamos en un momento interesante, movido, excesivamente eufórico' (We're in an interesting, changing, over-optimistic phase) (*El País Semanal* 1997: 36). Vicente Aranda also pointed out:

Estamos en un momento de expectativas, es de temer un catstrofe. Sin subvenciones, no podemos funcionar. Como las embajadas. A ellas no se les pide rentabilidad y el cine también representa a nuestro país, nuestra cultura'. (We're in a period of great expectation and there could be a catastrophe. With no subsidies, we cannot function. The cinema represents our country, our culture – like the embassies and we don't ask <u>them</u> to be profitable (Alvarez 1997: 36).

There is no doubt that public subsidies for filmmaking in Spain will disappear at some stage in the medium term (*Fotogramas* 1997: 172). Ideologically, the governing party is opposed to such public support and shows little commitment to treating film output as a national and cultural asset, crucially involved in projecting images of 'Spanishness' and Spanish culture at home and abroad. Indeed, in the run-up to the Single Currency and economic convergence

Conclusion

with Europe, PP will be far more concerned with Spain's public spending deficits and fiscal and monetary rectitude than with retaining costly state film subsidies. In the face of these changes, the industry is showing remarkable resilience and is experiencing a very rapid, perhaps over-heated, expansionary phase. As Méndez-Leite remarks: 'Se hacen muchas películas, pero pocas con un balance de sensatez. Se ha invertido mucho en proyectos que no eran necesarios' (A lot of films are being made, but very few in a sensible manner. A lot of money has been invested in unnecessary projects). What next? Hopewell is clearly right to argue that the future of Spain's film industry is intimately linked to the success of the television system, and its ability to produce film products acceptable to national and transnational entertainment systems and audiences (1989: 462). Whether this will lead to the production of bland 'Euro puddings', for an increasingly nondescript, homogeneous, transnational audience is a matter of conjecture. For the moment, what is remarkable is the sheer breadth and variety of Spanish film output, which is able to combine successfully the representation of cultural specificities and identities with an attractive appeal to the tastes and concerns of wider, international audiences.

References

Álvarez, C. (1997), El cine más cercano, El País Semanal, 19 January, 34–6.

Fernández Santos, A. (1992) ¿Ante un genocidio cultural?, El País, 4 June, 30.

Fotogramas (1997), Podium, 1842 (April), 169.

Fotogramas (1997), Se confirma el recorte de las ayudas, 1842 (April), 172.

Fotogramas (1997), 100 millones de espectadores, 1842 (April), 172.

Hopewell, J. (1989), El cine español después de Franco, Madrid, El Arquero, 462–3.

Muñoz, D. (1992), Los cineastas piden al Gobierno la creación de una ley del audiovisual, El País, 4 June, 30.

Valenzuela, R. (1992), El cine español humillado: Pilar Miró reunió a los profesionales descontentos, El País, 16 August, 38.

Index

Note: Page numbers in *italic* refer to illustrations.